A Selection of Travelers' Tales Books

Country and Regional Guides

30 Days in Italy, 30 Days in the South Pacific, America, Antarctica, Australia, Brazil, Central America, China, Cuba, France, Greece, India, Ireland, Italy, Japan, Mexico, Nepal, Spain, Thailand, Tibet, Turkey; Alaska, American Southwest, Grand Canyon, Hawai'i, Hong Kong, Middle East, Paris, Prague, Provence, San Francisco, Tuscany

Women's Travel

100 Places Every Woman Should Go, 100 Places in Italy Every Woman Should Go, 100 Places in France Every Woman Should Go, 100 Places in Greece Every Woman Should Go, 100 Places in Spain Every Woman Should Go, 100 Places in the USA Every Woman Should Go, 50 Places in Rome, Florence, & Venice Every Woman Should Go, Best Women's Travel Writing, Gutsy Women, Woman's Asia, Woman's Europe, Woman's Path, Woman's World, Woman's World Again, Women in the Wild

Body & Soul

Food, How to Eat Around the World, A Mile in Her Boots, Pilgrimage, Road Within,

Special Interest

Danger!, Gift of Birds, Gift of Rivers, Gift of Travel, How to Shit Around the World, Hyenas Laughed at Me, Leave the Lipstick, Take the Iguana, More Sand in My Bra, Mousejunkies!, Not So Funny When It Happened, Sand in My Bra, Testosterone Planet, There's No Toilet Paper on the Road Less Traveled, Thong Also Rises, What Color Is Your Jockstrap?, Wake Up and Smell the Shit, The World Is a Kitchen, Writing Away

Travel Literature

The Best Travel Writing, Coast to Coast, Deer Hunting in Paris, Fire Never Dies, Ghost Dance in Berlin, Guidebook Experiment, Kin to the Wind, Kite Strings of the Southern Cross, Last Trout in Venice, Marco Polo Didn't Go There, Rivers Ran East, Royal Road to Romance, A Sense of Place, Shopping for Buddhas, Soul of Place, Storm, Sword of Heaven, Take Me With You, Unbeaten Tracks in Japan, Way of Wanderlust, Wings

Fiction

Akhmed and the Atomic Matzo Balls
Billy Gogan, American

TRAVELERS' TALES

The SOUL OF A GREAT TRAVELER

10 YEARS OF SOLAS AWARD-WINNING TRAVEL STORIES

TRAVELERS' TALES

THE SOUL OF A GREAT TRAVELER

10 YEARS OF SOLAS AWARD-WINNING TRAVEL STORIES

Edited by
JAMES O'REILLY, LARRY HABEGGER,
AND SEAN O'REILLY

Travelers' Tales
An imprint of Solas House, Inc.
Palo Alto

Travelers' Tales and Solas House are trademarks of Solas House, Inc.,
Palo Alto, California. travelerstales.com I solashouse.com

Credits and copyright notices for the individual articles in this collection
are given starting on page 377.

Art Direction: Kimberly Nelson
Cover Photograph: © Galyna Andrushko, Bowman Lake
in Glacier National Park, Montana, USA
Interior Design and Page Layout: Scribe Inc.
Production Director: Susan Brady

Library of Congress Cataloging-in-Publication Data

Names: O'Reilly, James, 1953- editor. I Habegger, Larry, editor. I O'Reilly,
Sean, 1952- editor.
Title: The soul of a great traveler : 10 years of Solas award-winning travel
stories / edited by James O'Reilly, Larry Habegger, and Sean O'Reilly.
Description: First edition. I Palo Alto, California : Travelers' Tales, [2017]
Identifiers: LCCN 2017027117 (print) I LCCN 2017038662 (ebook) I
ISBN 9781609521240 (ebook) I ISBN 9781609521233 (pbk.) I
ISBN 9781609521240 (eISBN)
Subjects: LCSH: Travelers' writings.
Classification: LCC G465 (ebook) I LCC G465 .S664 2017 (print) I
DDC 910.4—dc23
LC record available at https://lccn.loc.gov/2017027117

ISBN: 978-1-60952-123-3
E-ISBN: 978-1-60952-124-0

First Edition
Printed in the United States
10 9 8 7 6 5 4 3 2 1

Table of Contents

Editors' Note

We launched the Solas Awards in 2006 because extraordinary stories about travel and the human spirit have been the cornerstones of Travelers' Tales books since 1993. Simply put, we wanted to honor writers whose work inspires others to explore. Each year we grant awards in 21 categories, and the stories in this book represent the Grand Prize Gold, Silver, and Bronze winners in the Solas Awards' first ten years. These stories are funny, illuminating, adventurous, uplifting, scary, inspiring, and poignant. They reflect the unique alchemy that occurs when the traveler—perhaps best called pilgrim—enters unfamiliar territory and begins to see and understand the world in a new way.

We hope you enjoy these stories as much as we do, and that you will head out as soon as you can on your own adventures of discovery.

For more about the Solas Awards, go to BestTravel Writing.com.

—JO'R, LH, SO'R

❧ ❧ ❧

Introduction

What Is a Great Traveler?

I have set foot in all fifty of the United States and have circled the world with my backpack four times. I am not unfamiliar with travel literature. And I like to think that I am not terminally naïve. But from the beginning pages of this collection of gemstone-quality travel tales, a subconscious notion began to gnaw at me, and when I was about a third of the way in, this notion broke free, snuck up from behind, fully formed now, and tapped the back of my skull forcefully enough so that my head involuntarily nodded and I heard an actual snort snap from my nostrils. I'd been had, suckered like a drunk in a Bangkok alley.

At first glance this book's six-word title had seemed perfectly innocent—even pure. "Ah, yes," I had thought, "*The Soul of a Great Traveler.* I know what that means, I know what to expect here . . ." But that tap on the head served notice that, once again, the joke was on me. Those six words are hardly innocent, and they do not so much constitute a title as they do a koan whose subversive nature is at first almost undetectable (a characteristic shared with the act of travel), but which sooner or later forces you to ask, "Exactly what *is* a Great Traveler?"

The Age of Exploration winked out long ago. Modern folks no longer sail the high seas in hopes of encountering unmapped islands or continents and unknown tribes. With notable exceptions—refugees, search-and-rescue teams, soldiers, suicide bombers—almost no one reading this book ever has taken or ever will take a trip on which the odds-of-death approach even one-half of one percent.

Few of us have a death wish, but most of us have a nearly unquenchable *change* wish. If we prefer not to be challenged or stretched we can always stay put, raid the fridge, switch the channel. But from our travels we ask for something different. When we leave home we want to see and hear and smell and ingest things that will leave us altered, dumbfounded, uncertain of our footing. Peering into a mirror in Paris or Kathmandu or Cape Town we do not want to see—and we *do not* see—the dullard from the bathroom mirror back home. When my brother, never a dullard, returned from a year in the old Rhodesia I spent half an hour unconvinced that it was actually him.

In my own youthful wanderings I passed hours in clichéd, intramural conversations with other backpackers, sorting out the once-popular riddle: "What distinguishes us righteous travelers from those swarming hordes of tourists?" But I abandoned that pastime thirty years ago, after an early morning poker game at a waterfront café on a roadless island off the coast of Kenya. As we went around the table, anteing up our shillings and congratulating each other on our righteous-traveler bona fides, a woman from Kentucky told of having recently survived a nervous and thirsty and reportedly quite stinky month trapped aboard a broken-down train in the middle of war-torn Sudan. She seemed astonishingly unimpressed with her newly acquired, conversation-stopping credential: "After a while," she told the awestruck rest of us, "you realize that, everyone on this planet, we're all tourists here."

The euro, the dollar, and the yuan have nudged aside the franc, lira, and pound sterling. The sea dragons have all been slain, the continents meticulously mapped, and even outer space is now open for business, visitors expected any day. On Earth, college students fly to Thailand for spring break. Taxi drivers wander the world. My haircutter, a Korean man in his seventies, amuses himself twice a year with three-week trips to any place that strikes his fancy: Italy, Vietnam, Peru, Tibet. "Oh, New Zealand!" he told me during my last trim. "You have to see New Zealand!" *Great Traveler*.

When a term loses its meaning we become free to redefine it for ourselves, and your rendition may differ wildly from mine. My Great Traveler is not boastful. She—and I say she only to try to tip the scales toward even—appreciates her place in the world, her privilege: not everyone is born into circumstances that afford the freedom and ability to travel. She sets forth alone, precisely because flying solo forces her to open up, be vulnerable, on the lookout for the unexpected and unusual. She listens. She engages fully with the moment-by-moment world that presents itself to her and with the locals who inhabit it, knowing all the while that her wanderings' deeper consequences will be internal and will result only from whatever interpretation she may bring to them.

A friend of mine maintains, "You can test the proof of this at any party: The game of life is won not by the guy with the most money or the coolest toys, but by the one with the best story to tell." His bon mot applies more fittingly to travel than to any other endeavor, does it not? We no longer expect, and we barely even appreciate, gift trinkets from our traveling friends, but we continue to treasure their stories. For me, a Great Traveler is one who has mastered the art of powerfully communicating an experience that touches the human soul.

The thirty writers who have lent their prize-winning tales to this book have obeyed the First and Last Commandment of yarn-spinning: *Thou shalt engage thine audience from the beginning even unto the ending.* Each has also followed the Travel Writing Caveat that I look for: *Thou shalt share thine essence in a way that calls forth the essence of thine audience.* And each of these thirty Great Travelers has accomplished these things while following his or her own unique travel and storytelling paths. To cite a few:

Lance Mason ("The Train to Harare") subtly infuses a remembrance of his first trip to Africa with the lulling, hypnotic cadence of a coach car gently rocking its way through the bush.

Matthew Crompton, on a journey through the Himalayan foothills ("Into the Hills"), recreates exactly the mental-emotional pitch of falling ill, while alone, thousands of miles from home.

In one of my personal favorites ("Remember This Night"), Katherine Jamieson proves that the close observation of a mundane domestic act (the ordering of a pizza) performed in a place where you do not belong (Guyana) can result in unforgettable art.

In Cold War Moscow, at the tender age of twenty-three, Marcia DeSanctis ("Masha") experiences complete empathy for another human being, a Russian woman with a (perhaps) less fortunate outcome in the birth lottery.

Carolyn Kraus's trip to Belarus ("The Memory Bird") to investigate the Holocaust murder of her grandmother demonstrates that Hell is nothing more than history brought present.

To read Peter Wortsman's account ("Protected") of a soldier's desperate mission—to spend what he knows will be his last night on Earth in the arms of his wife—is to know that all life, including your own, is a miracle.

And please forgive yourself if you feel just a little insane
after reading "The Bamenda Syndrome" by David
Torrey Peters. But please, tell me, how did he do that?

Welcome to *The Soul of a Great Traveler.* I trust that you will
enjoy it as enormously as I did.

Brad Newsham is the author of three books, including Take Me
With You: A Round-the-World Journey to Invite a Stranger
Home *(Travelers' Tales, 2000). He lives in Oakland, California,
and for 28 years, across the Bay in San Francisco, he was a taxi-
cab driver. He thinks of Paul Theroux as The Great Traveler of
modern times and believes Theroux deserves the Nobel Prize for
Literature. Learn more about Brad at www.bradnewsham.com.*

MATTHEW CROMPTON

❧ ❧ ❧

Into the Hills

A journey into remote monsoon hills of Sikkim yields
difficulty, insight, and transformation for a lone traveler.

The ball that we hurled into infinite space,
doesn't it fill our hand differently with its return:
heavier by the weight of where it has been?
— *Rilke*

THE CITY

The impression of Calcutta, arriving on a sweltering afternoon in early summer, is not of an ancient city existing, like
Benares, outside of time. Instead, it feels like a city built a
hundred years ago and then abandoned, left to moisture and
mold and dust while its builders crept off to sunnier pastures.
What makes the city strange, then, is that it feels populated,
not by its original inhabitants, but by scavengers, squatting in
the abandoned city in droves, peopling every decrepit inch,
like beings who have crawled up from the wild to inhabit its
lanes and shop fronts and markets, indifferent to the notion of
civilization that they are inhabiting.

The abstract shape of the city emerges as I travel into the center—traffic, noise, squalor, chaos, heat. My hotel room in a lane off Marquis Street is roasting, chemical with the camphor smell of mothballs resting in the bathroom sink. The pillows are lumpy sacks and the fan churns the baking air relentlessly. With the heat peaking into full force (an outdoor thermometer reads 36°C, or 97°F), I step out beneath my parasol and walk up RN Mukherjee Road, past the *poori* and chai vendors, the *nimbu pani* carts with their filthy glasses and handfuls of tainted ice.

When Hunter S. Thompson remarked on freaks at home in the freak kingdom, he could have meant this place. Calcutta—now Kolkata—is special in this respect. So far on the edges of the Indian universe that it's not on the way to anything, it attracts the real crusties and the genuinely strange. In the Eastern Railways tourist bureau near the Houghly River I meet a barefoot Korean man carrying a huge red wooden cross. I exchange a few pleasantries with him in Korean before he hobbles off, manic and sweating, his toes wrapped in a filthy bandage—"God Bless You!" he calls back after himself, "Jesus Christ! Jesus Christ! Jesus Christ!" And why not, I think? Here, everyone is welcome.

It is enough, I think, to be here in the streets, because the streets are always alive—in the morning people bathing and shaving and defecating and taking chai, in the afternoons hawking and pulling rickshaws and selling fruit and bearing burdens. In the evening, the heat and madness of Calcutta are barely diminished by the fall of night. As I walk the streets in the twilight I keep thinking, "There is no place on Earth that smells like this, no place that feels like this . . ." The night perfume is in the air, wafting in the scent of flower garlands and the bitumen stink of burning coal from cooking fires, the resinous ghost of sandalwood. In the vivisected bazaar of the twilight city, Muslim men are lit by bare bulbs hanging behind the ribs of butchered goats, and veiled women are chased across the street by screaming-yellow Ambassador taxis circa 1961 James Bond, and again, there are no borders anywhere.

My final morning in the city, before the nighttime sleeper train to Darjeeling, I take the metro south to Kalighat and the Kali temple there. "Kali is power," an old Brahmin in a dirt-stained shirt tells me amidst the goat shit and vivid hibiscus blossoms and stippled blood decorating the ground around the courtyard altar, where a goat has just been sacrificed to the devouring mother.

"What do people need power for?"

"For everything in life, friend, for everything you need power."

And I think: Do I not travel because I too am full of wishing? Have I not come here, to be apart, because I find that India is ruled by magic, still? Thinking better of goat sacrifice, I buy a lotus flower and a bundle of dried blossoms, and push with the small crowd into the dim interior of the temple, 400 years old and smelling of incense and human sweat. People are shouting prayers and mantras, incongruous for a quiet Thursday morning, but this intensity is what I love. A man presses a blood-red hibiscus into my palm, and as I move before the idol, I cast my blossoms with intent violence into the pile of offerings at its feet.

"What is your name?" the priest asks me as I stand amidst the crowd, shouting and screaming their prayers to be heard.

"My name is Matthew," I say, making sure my voice is strong and clear.

If there is a power to this moment, I want for it to hear me. All blessings are just echoes of our sincerest wishes, carried through the ether and emerging, real, on the farther side of time.

DARJEELING

Morning in Darjeeling is a monsoon hill town dawn, the clouds like a curtain around the city, thick as fog. In the diffuse gray light I walk downhill from my hotel high on the ridge, through the narrow, twisting lanes investing the hillside like an ant farm. In the main plaza at Chowrasta, dogs lie on the damp pavement, chewing at their flanks, porters with Sinic Nepali eyes carrying burdens up the fog-slick hills braced on forehead tump lines. I take a breakfast of milk tea and greasy fry bread wrapped in newsprint from a streetside stall, watching the gaggles of domestic Indian tourists transit through the square, enjoying joyrides on broken ponies, bundled in heavy woolens and skullcaps.

Darjeeling is the easy part of travel. For three days I live the life of some low-level colonial flunky of the kind who would once have escaped to this town from the violent heat of the summer plains, taking long breakfasts with tea in the cloudy bazaar and wandering the lanes with an umbrella beneath the sporadic rains.

Founded by the British East India Company in 1835, Darjeeling drew thousands of laborers from nearby Nepal, ensuring an identity at odds with the lowland state of West Bengal that eventually came to govern it, and in time, violent agitation for statehood as "Gorkhaland," resulting in limited (if to most unsatisfactory) autonomy in the form of the Darjeeling Gorkha Hill Council.

With the Chinese invasion of Tibet in 1959, thousands of Tibetan families fled over the eastern Himalayas, through Nepal, many to settle in Darjeeling, making it (along with Dharamsala) one of the primary centers for the Tibetan community in exile, undiluted by Han resettlement and Chinese government interference.

Talking to a Tibetan shopkeeper named Dorje on Hill Cart Road south of town one day, I ask him what he thought of the recent resignation of the Dalai Lama as the political leader of Tibet—curious about the views of a subject of one of the world's last great theocracies.

"He is still our religious leader, our spiritual leader, of course. But it is now 2011. We have so many young Tibetans who have studied at Oxford and Cambridge and Harvard—do they not also deserve a chance to lead Tibet?"

"And do you think that will happen with the Chinese still occupying?"

He shrugs. "We have autonomy, yes, but of course, autonomy is not independence. Independence is better."

He wraps up my Oreos in brown paper. "Anyway," he smiles, "anything is possible."

In the evenings I walk downhill through the bazaar to Joey's Pub—proper, British, wood paneled, Union Jack on the wall—and drink tall Kingfishers in the cozy, hazy space around low tables with other Anglophones, businessmen, and backpackers like some colonial social club, then stumble half-drunk up the hill in the darkness to my bed and sleep, thinking how easy it would be to remain in this congenial place living my small-town colonial fantasy, but feeling in my bones the emptiness of ease, knowing how reliably common actions lead to common results.

I began traveling, I think, as a way of seeking identity, or at least of embracing the estrangement I felt from my native conditions—an unchallenging university career that yielded few friends and no sense of belonging, short-time jobs temping or waiting tables, transplanted across the country to a home where in nearly five years I gained friends but never roots. Pico Iyer wrote in *The Global Soul* about the existential condition of elective statelessness, the vagrancy that carried long enough becomes an enduring facet of oneself, an unbelonging that, paradoxically, is itself homelike; and I find myself thinking of the sadhu back at the train station in Calcutta, just a week ago.

At nearly eleven P.M. at Sealdah Station that night, the platforms were still mobbed. The stationmaster would announce a train arriving at platform five and suddenly the mobs would bolt for it, shoving and contending in the Indian way, eager for a seat in the overcrowded unreserved second-class car in which they would be traveling overnight, to Varanasi or Lucknow or even Delhi, god forbid.

I was bone-tired and sticky with sweat, 34°C (93°F) outside even deep into the night, as I watched the scrum, the wolfish and pathetic packs of dark single men, the families with children, the immature soldiers with their mustaches and automatic carbines and sternly affected scowls, the women looking queenly and fiercely dignified in saris. It was through this maelstrom, the endless breaking cascade of people passing by, burdened with their baggage and identities, that I saw the lone sadhu. He was like a ghost, dreadlocked and shirtless, thin and ash-smeared, moving slowly, a wanderer without place or profession; in transit, perhaps, but unintent upon arriving. I felt a kinship there.

It's an unremarked-on fact that the regimen most associated with Eastern religions—the monk's way of structured meditation and work and prayer, the so-called monastic life—is in a very real sense a later addition to the project of enlightenment, an innovation of the civilized and bureaucratic consciousness. The Indian method, if it can even be called that, is simpler, wilder, improvisational— renounce your home, your possessions and attachments, and simply wander, intent on the knowledge that God, whatever that is, knows exactly where it wants to take you. I suppose this is how, two days later, I found myself in the hills of western Sikkim, squatting at nightfall beside a low earthen stove in the kitchen hut of a thirteen-year-old boy named Ronald Bhujel.

RONALD

Being enthusiastically received and, in time, feted by the very poor is one of the most beautiful and heartbreaking experiences in travel. Ronald, in his blue blazer and slacks, just let out from classes, had invited me to his home up a village footpath in the hills, late into a day of walking some fifteen kilometers west of Jorethang, where I had taken a jeep that morning from Darjeeling. I had climbed more than a thousand meters into the green hinterland of West Sikkim along the winding hill road, dehydrated and filthy and miserable, blinking into the sun and passed by blatting trucks. My feet were blistered and sore, and I was eager to rest.

High on the ridge amidst the terrace patches of maize and ginger where I could look down and see the thin gray-blue ribbon of the Raman Khola dividing the one-time Buddhist kingdom of Sikkim from the state of West Bengal to the south, I bathed in a low outhouse with cold water and borrowed soap, then changed into fresh clothes. Ronald was Christian, like most of his small community on the hill, and shared a single bare room with his grandmother, a poured-concrete box furnished with three narrow plank beds and a single cabinet, and decorated with lurid pictures of Jesus and the Sacred Heart. On the cabinet were sun-bleached photographs of an absent woman who I took to be his mother. I drank the sweet tea his grandmother had prepared for me and asked him where his parents were.

"This is my family, yes?" he said, smiling nervously at his grandmother and adult brother, his brother's six-year-old son Aryun, whom he also called his brother. "It is a small family," he babbled a little, "a good family . . ." and I knew then that his parents had died.

In time all the households of the village, some twenty people, stopped by to say hello and chat. I entertained the children by memorizing and then writing their names in Korean script and answered countless questions about my baldness and marital status. When darkness fell, I was ushered into the smoke-stained, biscuit-colored kitchen beneath the three-quarter moon and given warm beer and a bowl of fried organs, chicken heart and liver, the choicest pieces of a dish that was itself an extravagance.

I slept that night in a bed with both head- and footboard that was some nine inches shorter than my legs, necessitating a great deal of creative geometry and was woken stiff-necked at a quarter to seven by Ronald peering in the window at me, barking like an excited puppy: "It is time to wash your face!"

At the parting, Ronald and his family refused my money, eyes downcast, though my visit had doubtless cost them the equivalent of a week's worth of meals. As I walked down the hill with Ronald on his way to school, he mentioned again, as he had all night, that in three weeks he would have vacation, and that I should return, and we would travel Sikkim together, though I knew that this village was on the way to nowhere, and I would not be coming back.

On the main road, when I went to say goodbye, Ronald burst into tears. "If you can, you will come, O.K.?" he said, his lip trembling as he fought to maintain control. "Only if you can . . ." He was sobbing. I gave him a handshake and an awkward hug and then turned away down the road, knowing that my merely being here was the highlight of his whole year, that my having happened for a day into his life was a better thing for him than Christmas and feeling the sinking adult burden of having all of a child's hope projected onto you, knowing that you will break his heart.

I teared up as I walked away, thinking how happy I had been for that one night, a part of Ronald's little patchwork family high up on the ridge, squatted in the smoky kitchen with Aryun yawning and the lights of the villages faraway all glitter across the valley through the window. And the sense was with me as I cried, "I'm too far away from everything, too far from everyone I know, too far . . ."

Damn.

BARSEY TO PELLING

The paradoxical thing about trekking is that we spend much of our time while doing it simply wishing it would end. Few leisure activities offer, not just difficulty, but the passionate desire that the activity would cease, five minutes ago if possible. It is also unique in the level to which, having reached this point, you are committed to continue. Done reading a book? Just put it down. Through with snowboarding? It's only a few minutes to the lodge, and all downhill at that. But trekking usually finds us miles from anywhere, climbing an endless staircase of mud-slick stones through some bug-haunted jungle, and in this circumstance, the only thing less attractive than going on is turning back.

The trail from Ronald's village to the outpost at Barsey is hardly worth mentioning except in this regard, a deserted footpath through mossy rhododendrons and stands of bamboo, 15 kilometers and 1,500 vertical meters that only a hill person would describe (as they did to me) as "easy." When I reach the clearing at Barsey, three small buildings set on a hill at 10,000 feet and ringed by a low stone wall, it is both relief and anticlimax—the Kachenjunga massif hidden by the monsoon clouds and the buildings deserted except for a skeleton crew, much more living than working here, continuously scheming for money and openly contemptuous of my presence.

When night falls there is no power. I eat a dinner of *dal bhat* by the weak light of a single candle, feeling depressed, then retire to the huge empty attic dormitory where I slip into the twisting, feverish sleep of the ambiguously ill, my body achy and my belly full of gas.

When I awaken the next morning, I am far too sick to travel. In the attic on my mattress on the floor I sleep the entire day away, waking into the twilight of half-past five P.M., impossibly craving orange juice. Looking out the window, the clouds have cleared halfway to the horizon, and this little outpost feels like the end of the world, staring out at the waves of high green ridges without a single building to be seen. The most distant mountains are blue in the late-day light, and on those farthest peaks, beyond the green hills and the golden light on the rhododendrons, there are sharp fingers of snow. As I stand, shaky and feverish at the window, Kachenjunga swims for a moment out of the clouds above them, unbelievably high and white, lofty and imposing and impossible. Then just as quickly it is gone.

That moment of brightness here in my sickness at the end of the world only serves to underscore how empty and alone I am. It should feel liberating, I think, this being out in nature, miles from the nearest town, but instead it feels claustrophobic: the moment when you realize you've climbed up this far, and now you have to climb back down.

The next morning when I rise, the day itself bears all the native marks of a fever-dream—the same walled-in feeling, the same endlessness, the same inherent lack of meaning. My emotions are all mixed up, feeling ugly and loveless, keenly aware of my physical imperfections, so desperate for comfort that I curse the awful wilderness keeping me from the safety of the world.

In this abject mood I trek exhausted down the mountain, four hours of mud and leeches and stinging nettle, overgrown and jungly and airless. I find myself grown so tired of traveling that I want to quit and go home, trapped in this endless green maze in which everything seems out for blood. There are no vistas to be seen, and I would not care if there were, overtired and muddy and fed for two days on nothing but instant noodles and smoke-tainted water, gut-sick and diarrheal and so lonely it feels like I've never had any friends at all. And the horrible feeling is upon me that none of this, this traveling, this suffering, has any meaning to it at all.

I finally reach a road and walk six kilometers west along it to the tiny market town at Dentam, then take a jeep northeast along the high road toward Pelling. As I stare down at the sharp, unprotected drop to the valley floor hundreds of meters below, I find myself thinking about my relationships, realizing that I don't even know what love to feel sad for anymore, what love to regret, it all seems so distant.

At night in Pelling it rains, adding a voluptuousness to the darkness, the insects clicking all around like castanets, and I find myself reflecting, as I often do these days, upon Paul Theroux. "Travel," he wrote, "is a state of mind. It has nothing to do with existence or the exotic. It is almost entirely an inner experience."

Back in Calcutta, it was true, I had submitted my prayers to Kali. The devouring mother demanded sacrifice, and though it was often offered in blood, it was not in blood alone that it could be paid.

I thought: "Kali Ma, have I not sacrificed love? Have I not sacrificed comfort and sex and security and friends, to live this way, to bear these pressures, to be changed? Have I not offered up my fear, everything that is weak in me, to your teeth?"

I knew that I had come to the road alone only to travel it, to cast my fixed identity aside like a crab that has outgrown its shell. Oh, but how vulnerable, I thought, the rain drumming on the roof, my body as porous as a sieve; how fearful it is to go naked, into the vagrant wilderness, before a greater shell is found.

SEA OF FACES

Things come to fullness in time. A week later, I am in the lowlands again, on the platform of New Jalpaiguri Station, waiting, in the polluted haze and in the confusion of my memories, for a train. And in the *Times of India*, blown through the dust of the platform and past the trash and empty cups of chai, which I seize and read to pass the time, there is a story. It is a completely ordinary Indian story: eighteen infants, all terribly poor, dead in only thirty-six hours at a single Calcutta hospital; but it is the photograph that accompanies it that paralyzes me completely.

Poorly composed and snapped by some cub staff photog for this minor news piece, it shows a man, mid-thirties and mustached, his face a mixture of outrage and grief as he holds in both hands toward the camera the swaddled body of his dead child. Beside him, his wife, her head covered with a shawl, turns into her husband's shoulder, her features a mask of pure anguish, sobbing. Behind and all around is a sea of faces—dozens, a crowd, as there is always a crowd everywhere in India—but so wild with the symphony of powerful and conflicting human emotions that it arrests my attention completely, tears at the center of me, that I wonder at the meaning of myself at all.

God, I think, the smell of burning garbage filling my head on the sour breeze, how this place wounds me. This journey into the hills—Ronald and Aryun, the long walk, the leeches and the difficulty and the loneliness; the fear of death, loveless and alone—I know that these have taken a piece of my heart, as is the certain way of questions without answers. But there is a magic to living these questions here, lost in this most ancient of places, immersed in this most ancient of rites.

I stand on the platform in the center of myself, utterly broken and inadequate, but knowing that when I give my heart to India, India gives its heart right back, brighter than my own could ever be. And once again, as I have now for years—as the train draws up in the heavy air—as I meet the faces through the dusty windows peering into my own eyes—I thank the Universe that it has brought me through, and step, without expectations and without fear, into the waiting train alone.

A writer, photographer and educator (you have him to thank for those literacy tests where you read the text and answer the questions about it), Matthew Crompton is now proudly a citizen

of Australia as well as his native USA. Travel for him is partly about wonder and partly about fear, but mostly about transformation. He wonders very much about the person he would be today if he hadn't taken that impulsive trip to Guatemala in the wake of a bad breakup back in 2005. He's spending 2017 riding a mountain bike across the Tibetan Plateau and onward thru Central Asia (top tip: it isn't easy). Follow him at www.matthew crompton.com.

❧ ❧ ❧

Barren in the Andes

She asked herself what she really, truly wanted.

*B*reathless, I hurry along narrow trails between Quichua family farms, past barking dogs, squawking chickens, and curly-tailed piglets. My destination is a shaman who lives in this village on the outskirts of Otavalo, Ecuador. I'm going partly for book research, but mostly as a last-ditch hope that he can heal me. Back in Colorado, I tried everything—Eastern and Western medicine, herbs and tinctures, weird diets. And now I'm teetering on the edge of bitter despair.

I emerge from the foliage to a vista of 15,000-foot peaks rising above emerald fields, dotted with red-tiled roofs and grazing sheep. Two of these mountains are said to be ancient Incan gods: the male, Imbabura, and his lover, Cotacachi. When she's covered with light frost at dawn, locals claim it's semen from a night of passion. Their offspring—smaller, baby mountains—lie scattered between them.

The very earth beneath my feet is considered the fertile body of Pachamama, the World Mother, honored in agricultural rituals and indigenous festivities across the Andes. It's easy to imagine her generous curves filling this landscape, her skirts swirling into valleys and ridges, patchworks of velvet fields and silken pastures.

Fertility is a deep and ancient craving, at once visceral and mythical, elemental and universal. This, at least, is my impression as an anthropologist, or, more to the point, as a woman who cannot seem to have a baby.

At my side is my close friend, María, who was born in a nearby indigenous village. She easily navigates the path despite her Otavaleña clothes—ankle-length skirts, flimsy sandals, delicate lace blouse, strands of coral and gold beads. Her son, Yanni, skips and circles around us with exuberant five-year-old energy, a stick swinging in his hand, a braid swinging at his back. "Laurita!" he shouts, offering me a plucked flower. "For you!"

"*Gracias*," I say, blinking back tears.

I've played with Yanni since he was a baby. Over the years, a tender fact has throbbed beneath our laughter: if my first pregnancy hadn't ended in miscarriage, my child would be Yanni's age. And if any of the next five years of fertility treatments had worked, I'd have a preschooler, or toddler, or baby. I'd be holding his pudgy hand, or idly tousling his hair, or, what I crave most, kissing his tiny feet.

A few months ago, after years of heartbreaking negatives, a miracle of sorts occurred: I got pregnant again, naturally. But anxiety eclipsed the initial moments of joy; my body felt fragile and broken. Terrified I'd lose the baby, I refused to have sex with my husband, ate only hyper-hygienically prepared organic food, let no synthetic chemicals touch my skin. Despite my paranoid vigilance, after eleven weeks, I lost the baby. When the ultrasound showed no heartbeat, a D&C was scheduled for the next day, and my uterus was scraped raw.

Now, one month later, my heart still feels as raw and broken as my belly. If my body had functioned, a baby bump would just be showing. I place my hand over the plane of my abdomen, flat except for a smattering of recent bedbug bites.

After this second miscarriage, I mustered up my scant energy and planned a trip to Ecuador. My official reason was to do research on my book with María, whom I'd met years earlier in English classes I taught in Colorado. But at the heart of it, I needed to get out of my house, with its heavy, empty, childless silence.

The shaman's curing room is large and high ceilinged, yet cavelike, with soot-blackened adobe walls holding the scent of candle wax and wood smoke and incense. A bare bulb dangles above the packed dirt floor, illuminating the far wall, a riot of color—an Ecuadorean flag, a flowered oilcloth, strings of lights, images of saints and Virgins. A wooden bench lines one wall, and an altar in the corner holds candles, roses, stones, a lighter, cigarettes, scissors, and a golden, laughing Buddha covered with happy babies.

Behind the altar stands the shaman, a young man—early twenties at most—with a handsome, smooth face. After María explains my desire for a baby, she translates his confident response. "Yes, *cumarita,* I can help you." *Cumarita* is an affectionate Quichua term for *comadre*, or co-mother, a term meant to inspire trust. Something that I seriously lack. I have doubts about his ability to understand my situation—his life is probably all about *not* getting anyone pregnant—but María assures me he's been healing since he was fourteen. I smile politely as he puts on an enormous feathered headdress and arranges the stones and bottles on the altar.

María settles on the bench and pulls Yanni onto her lap, nuzzling him, breathing in his scent as he breathes in hers. She wraps her arms around him, whispers in his ear, kisses his hair, all in a way that makes it clear: she is his world, his own personal Pachamama.

I swallow hard and look away, back at the young shaman who is cutting rose petals into a small pile of red, pink, and white confetti beside the baby-covered Buddha. He then positions me smack in the center of the room and gives an instruction in Quichua, translated by María with a suppressed smile. "Strip to your underwear, *cumarita.*"

I stand, blinking, thinking of what hides beneath my clothing: a stretched-out, sweat-stained, grandma-style sports bra in an unflattering shade of beige. And covering my entire torso are angry, crimson bedbug bites, a downfall of traveling in rural Latin America with sensitive skin. And I don't even want to think about exposing my grubby, graying underwear. I shoot María a pleading look, and thankfully, she negotiates for me to at least keep my shorts on.

With a nervous shiver, I take stock of my body, which frankly, I've come to hate more with every month of infertility. Encased in the beige polyester are my ever-milkless breasts, six pounds of useless meat serving only to remind me of what I don't have. My gaze drops lower, to the faint surgical scar at my navel—a fruitless effort to reduce pain and restore fertility by scraping rogue endometrial cells from various reproductive organs. I take a wavered breath, trying to leave behind negativity and focus on this moment.

The young shaman is now opening a glass bottle, releasing the overpowering fragrance of cheap cologne. Feeling itchy at the mere smell of this stuff, I twitch my nose, scratch some welts on my waist. I know from anthropological research that the young shaman will probably spit this all over me. Which, of course, brings up a whole array of fertility-related anxieties like, *exposure to toxic synthetic estrogens!* These kinds of worries have transformed me into a fearful version of the woman I once was—only *slightly* anxious, but mostly carefree, traveling the world alone, leaping into adventures.

"*Lo siento,*" I say. "Sorry, but can you use something else? I just have, um allergies." I'm fairly certain there's no ancient Incan-derived term for synthetic estrogens.

The shaman glances at María with amused confusion. After she translates, a round of laughter ensues. His eyes lively, the young shaman puffs out his cheeks and does a fat guy impression. Yanni giggles so hard he practically falls off the bench. (Later I'll discover María claimed that cologne makes me swell up like a large balloon.)

Thankfully, the young shaman is willing to accommodate. "We'll just use liquor instead," he says, grinning, and picks up a green glass bottle shaped like a woman in large skirts—reminiscent of the old Aunt Jemima syrup bottles—filled, I presume, with alcohol. He chants and whistles a meandering tune as he circles the bottle in some type of blessing, then grabs a pinch of rose petal confetti, sticks it between his lips, takes a mouthful of liquor, and, as anticipated, spits it all over me.

I shut my eyes, try not to wince. But the blast, like a shock of sea spray, is surprisingly refreshing. As the young shaman spits wave after wave, I try to imagine myself as a goddess, solid and fertile as the semen-coated mountain Cotacachi. I envision Pachamama herself, rising through the earthen floor, filling me. I visualize the gusts blowing away the dark energy clinging to me.

It does require effort, however, to ignore the saliva of a strange man covering my body, and I'm relieved when he stops spitting and begins beating me instead. Gently, I should add, with a bundle of healing *chilca* leaves. It's actually a pleasant sensation, my body turned into a drum. He pounds the leaves on my chest, over my heart, as if giving it a new rhythm, a passionate, strong one. *O.K.,* I tell myself, *picture your womb as something lush, rich with potential, your breasts spilling over with milk, your body pulsing with the timeless rhythms of life and birth, a universal heartbeat.*

But no, I can't. It's too cold; I'm too shivery. My thoughts creep instead to the distinct *lack* of heartbeat on the ultrasound last month. That night, I'd lain in bed, staring at the overhead fan in the blue half-light, tear-soaked and sob-wracked. Near dawn, when I was cried out, I found myself repeating, *fuck, fuck, fuck,* a beating like a heart, a rhythm like a drum. It went on for a long, long time. Hours, maybe. By the time morning light came, I knew I couldn't bear another month of hope and heartbreak. A few days later, in my bathrobe, with damp tissues spilling from the pockets, I searched online for adoption information. Maybe, I thought, heavy with desperation and shame, if I adopt, then I'll get pregnant.

My gloomy ruminations continue as the young shaman taps me with shell-intact raw eggs (to absorb negative energy), and then (for reasons that remain unclear) blows cheap local cigarette smoke all over me, punctuated with a kind of smoky kiss on the top of my head. He then picks up the Aunt Jemima-style bottle, which he raises to his lips, presumably, to spit on me some more. Still half-lost in mournful memories, and vaguely aware that I already reek of a seedy, late-night bar, I take a deep breath and brace myself for the next round.

But this time is different. This time the young shaman, standing about six paces away, extends a lighter at arm's length before he spits the spray of liquor. A mist of alcohol blasts through the flame and catches fire. Catches fire!

And oh my God there's a fireball heading toward me, and holy crap I'm covered in flammable liquid.

Fear explodes through me. There is no time to dive out of the way. There is only time to squeeze my eyes shut and pray. A wave of heat rolls over me.

María and Yanni gasp on the sidelines.

I open my eyes, look down at my body. I am not on fire. Thank God, I'm not on fire! Chest pounding, I peer closer, at the light hairs on my arms. Unsinged. The fireball must have burned up just before reaching me. I let out a breath. *Oh, thank God, my bug-bitten flesh is intact. Thank God my broken body remains whole.*

The young shaman is already taking another mouthful. I steel myself, shut my eyes, and pray. Another wave of heat. A flash of fear. Afterward, a mental scan of my flesh. Still not on fire. *Thank you.* And on and on they go. There's nothing like fireballs blazing toward you to burn up pesky little anxieties like synthetic estrogens. By the time the flames stop, my body is quivering like a plucked string, but now thoroughly warmed. Pulse racing, sweat pouring from my armpits, I wonder what comes next.

The young shaman picks up a large, smooth, black stone from his altar. Andean shamans' stones have personalities, talents, lives of their own. He places his helper stone over my belly, and then, in a powerful voice, as if he's channeling the wind, shouts, "*Shunguuu!*" It's a *whoosh*, this word, and it *whooshes* right into me.

"*Shunguuu!*" he shouts again, with the force of a storm, and any silly thoughts that were not burned up by the fireballs are now blown away. *Shunguuu, shunguuu, shunguuu . . .* It is the perfect word for this focused power aimed straight into my center.

He then places two white stones in my palms and motions for me to rub them over my body, head to feet. I close my eyes and slide the stones across my bony elbows, my knobby knees, the curve of my hips, my breasts, my butt. And silently, I thank this body that has somehow not caught fire. This body that has actually, in most ways, served me quite well. This body that is my own familiar landscape. This body that is as sensitive as a cranky old lady. This body tied to this battered heart of mine.

The young shaman murmurs something to María, who translates, "Think about what you want, *cumarita*."

I am very practiced at wishing. For every birthday and shooting star sighting and heads-side-up penny over the past five years, I have wished for increasingly detailed versions of the same thing: *that I get pregnant with a baby in my own womb with my own egg and Ian's sperm and give birth to my healthy and beautiful and happy full-term baby.* There is no room for nasty surprises from the universe with that degree of specificity.

I now prepare to carefully whisper my wish, but then, I stop myself. I glance at Yanni, still curled on María's lap, watching me curiously, probably hoping for more fireballs. And then I surprise myself by asking, *Laura, what do you really, truly want?*

In response, something happens inside my chest. A kind of *whoosh* of sunlight into my heart. It's as if a doorway has opened, a passage I never knew existed. And on the other side, in the light, are tiny, tender feet, secret scents and whispers and kisses. There is a baby who nestles into my body, his world. A baby who is not inside my belly, but inside my heart, in this light-filled space that was here all along. This baby, these feet: This is what I want. This is the wish I whisper.

As the shaman wraps up his chanting, I finish rubbing the stones on my body, with a new gratitude now, a softness and lightness. Soon he gives me a final blessing and returns the stones to his altar, ending the ceremony. I stand, soaking wet in my shorts and sports bra, plastered with bits of rose petals, my heart still hurting, but stronger now, encased in this flawed but loved body. I bask inside my own hidden patch of light as the shaman explains that to complete the ceremony, I may not indulge in the following items for three days: chocolate, pork, fish, avocado, milk, chili, and showers.

For the next three days, I'll be living with a thin coating of alcohol and saliva and smoke and rose petal confetti on my skin and hair. But none of that matters because I'm not thinking so much about my body now, but my heart, and its surprise doorway, and the baby feet, and the glimpse of joy.

Glancing at me and nodding confidently, the young sha-man tells María one more thing. She beams as she translates, "This *mujercita*—this little woman—will have a baby very soon!"

Yes, I think, *this mujercita will.*

Back home, as my bedbug welts heal and fade and springtime blooms in Colorado, I embark on a nine-month-long adoption process, not as means to a pregnancy, but as a pathway to this baby inside my heart, *my* baby. My husband is supportive, but, as is typical in adoptions (and pregnancies), it's the woman who labors, the woman who, one way or another, delivers her child. My life quickly fills with reams of paperwork, endless trips to Kinko's, long waits in government buildings, social worker visits, background checks, huge money transfers, drives to parenting classes in Denver, obsessive email check-ing, anxious visits to the Department of State website, and multiple trips to Guatemala.

I deal with these tasks the way a pregnant woman deals with morning sickness and swollen feet and other annoy-ances that pale beside the monumental and sparkling antici-pation of *the baby coming.* At the three-month mark, instead of an ultrasound, I'm rewarded with photos of the newborn whose spirit is growing inside me. As his arrival nears, some-thing inside me thrums. Something stronger than kicks or hiccups—something inside my chest, the beating of ten thou-sand shimmering wings.

Just before Christmas, my nine-month-old son and I cuddle in blue afternoon light filtered through his bedroom curtains. We gaze into each other's eyes for long stretches, breathing in each other's scents, lost in our secret spaces between skin. And

as his eyelids close and his breathing grows rhythmic and he
drifts to sleep, I cup his little hobbit feet in my hands, raise
them to my lips, and kiss the soles.

*Laura Resau is the award-winning author of eight novels for
young people, all set in places where she's lived or traveled, including Mexico, France, Guatemala, and Ecuador. Resau's travel
essays have appeared in anthologies by* Travelers' Tales, Lonely
Planet, *and others. This piece won the Grand Prize Silver in the
Seventh Annual Solas Awards. She lives in Colorado with her
husband and young son and donates a portion of her royalties
to indigenous rights organizations in Latin America. For more
about her writing, please visit www.Lauraresau.com.*

PETER WORTSMAN

෴ ෴ ෴

Protected

The fates take strange twists indeed.

$\mathcal{I}$t was my last night in the lavish villa on the lake in Berlin-Wannsee where I had holed up for the winter. A noted Indian economist was scheduled to lecture on the underlying causes of the global financial crisis and its effects on the developing world. Call me an escapist, but I was not inclined to listen to the sad statistics. The world's affairs would muddle on without me, I thought, intending to grab a quick bite and slip off unnoticed to attend to my packing.

Such dinners were always a festive affair, the guest list sprinkled with Berlin society. My tablemate to the left, the wife of the German theologian seated beside the Indian economist, was a tall, stately woman of late middle age with prominent cheekbones, Prussian blue eyes, and tightly braided, blond hair, who wore her years like a string of pearls. Straight-backed, head held high, as if she were not seated at table, but rather astride a saddle, ears pricked for the sound of a hunting horn, she had what in former times would have been called an aristocratic bearing.

Socially maladroit and constitutionally incapable of making small talk, a tendency further aggravated by chronic insomnia, I either clam up on such occasions or put my foot in my mouth.

Prodding myself to say something before taking up knife and fork to dispatch the appetizer, two luscious-looking, seared sea scallops on a bed of wilted seaweed, I wished her, "*Bon appétit!*"

"*Gesegnete Mahlzeit!* (Blessed meal)," she replied.

"Bless the chef!" I countered, immediately regretting the flippancy of my ill-considered response. "Please forgive me, but I'm not a believer."

She smiled to make clear that she took no offense. "Religion is a personal matter. My faith," she affirmed, "makes me feel *beschützt* (protected)."

A striking choice of words, I thought, while savoring the flavor and firmness of the first scallop. "I myself altogether lack the foundation of faith," I confessed, "Given my family history, feeling protected is simply not in the cards."

She seemed concerned, sympathetic, as though suddenly fathoming that I was missing a middle finger.

"I'm the child of refugees," I said to set the record straight.

"Oh?"

I might have changed the subject but I chose not to. With me it's a compulsion, a need to lay my cards on the table.

"My father's departure from his native Vienna was . . ." I searched for the appropriate adjective, "precipitous."

"Precipitous?"

"Involuntary," I clarified.

"I see."

Decorum should have compelled me to change the subject. But impatiently lapping up the second scallop whole, my tongue rattled on.

"Huddled, to hide his prominent nose, in the sidecar of a motorcycle with a swastika flapping in the wind, he was driven by an accommodating member of a motorcycle gang, who agreed, for a fee, to drop him off at sundown at a wooded stretch of the border with Czechoslovakia. And when, at the sound of what he took for a gunshot—but was, in fact, an engine backfire—they suddenly stopped, convinced his time was up, my father held his breath as the motorcyclist dismounted, only to return moments later with a bleeding hare he'd run over, knocked its head against the fender, and asked my father to be so kind as to hold it for him. Fresh meat being scarce, he meant to have it for his dinner."

The arrival of the entrée, one of the chef's signature dishes, rack of venison prepared "von Himmel und Erde" (Heaven and Earth) style, i.e. stuffed with a puree of mashed apples and potatoes, came as a welcome point of punctuation.

She eyed me in between bites with an intense, but not unfriendly, gaze, as if, I thought, considering a rare wild flower, which aggravated my malaise.

To smooth the way for my escape, I let slip that I was leaving early the next morning for a trip to Poznań, Poland, and so, unfortunately, would have to skip dessert and miss the lecture, to pack.

"To Posen?!" she burst out, employing the old German name of the region and city ceded to Prussia following the Congress of Vienna and reclaimed by the Polish in the wake of World War II; promptly correcting herself: "*Poznań!*" to make clear that she harbored no secret dream of re-annexation.

I nodded to indicate that I understood.

"*Ich bin auch* . . . I too am"—she hesitated a moment—"*das Kind von Flüchtlinge* . . . the child of refugees."

It was the way she said *Kind* . . . child that made the years fall away from her face and gave her voice the candor of innocence.

"I come," she blinked, embarrassed and proud, "from a long line of Prussian aristocrats, the landed gentry of Poznań, Posen, as it was called back then.

"The War was practically over. The Russians were advancing from the East. It was a winter so bitter and cold the children broke the icicles from the windowsills and sucked them like candy. A decorated tank commander in the Wehrmacht who'd been away a long time, and whom the family thought dead, miraculously broke through enemy lines, and came rolling up in his Panzer in the dark of night to the family estate."

She described what followed in vivid detail, like an eyewitness, yet with a certain distance in the telling, like she couldn't decide whether to embrace it or hold it at arm's length.

"The officer leapt out in his neatly pressed uniform, in which the War hadn't made a wrinkle, tipped his cap, worn at a jaunty tilt, hugged his two sons and his trembling wife, who took him for a ghost."

She paused to mimic the hollow look in his eyes.

"That night the officer told his wife he wanted to make a blond-haired, blue-eyed daughter.

"'Are you mad?' his wife protested in a whisper, not wanting to wake the children. 'The War is lost, we already have two sons to raise. Why bring another child into this world?'

"But the officer insisted, and his wife dared not refuse a decorated hero of the Reich."

Turning away, the theologian's wife bowed her head to mark a private moment, shut her eyes tight and seemed to be peering inward, straining, as I suddenly fathomed, to remember the moment of her own conception.

"Bright and early the next day," she continued, her voice now taking on a strange solemnity, "Father put on his perfectly pressed uniform, set the cap on his head at just the right angle, pausing briefly in front of Mother's vanity mirror to approve his appearance, said he'd only be a minute, and as Mother watched from the bedroom window, he smiled, patted the protruding cannon, lifted the hatch, climbed in, set the great metal elephant in motion, and poking his head out, waving to her at the window one last time, leapt out and hurled himself under the rolling tread."

They cleared the table and brought in the dessert, a wild berry parfait that neither of us touched.

"Did she mourn for him?" I inquired.

"There was no time for mourning," my tablemate shook her head. "With the Russian artillery thundering ever closer all through the day and into the night, Mother pulled herself together, took a pick axe, buried Father's remains, and fled with the clothes on her back and a small bundle, with my brothers in tow, and the seed of a child planted in her womb, walking all the way to Berlin.

"Father posthumously had his wish, a blond-haired, blue-eyed daughter," she shrugged, with a look that wavered between disapproval and a proud affirmation of self. "The four of us lived together in a cramped attic room with a ceiling through which it rained and snowed. In that leaky attic I grew up with barely enough space to stretch my arms and legs, but there," she smiled, "I felt protected.

"When I grew up I met and married my husband"—she nodded at the theologian, who cast increasingly concerned looks to see his wife so stirred up with a stranger, to which she replied with reassuring nods. "I became a kindergarten teacher, had a long career, and just retired last year."

She was horrified, she said, at the number of broken families her pupils came from, one in three in Germany. She hoped to devote her "golden years"—the hackneyed expression took on a freshness framed by her radiant, tightly braided blond head—volunteering to help children in need.

I had stuck around too long to escape the economist's lecture, but I was preoccupied and don't remember a word of what he said about the present crisis or his prognosis for the future.

I kept glancing at the theologian's wife, now seated beside her husband, her hand in his. Born of conflicting legends, we were bound in braided tragedies. And though I still can't fathom what it means to feel protected, and doubt I ever will, as disparate as our destinies are, there is an undeniable parallel between the motorcycle that carried my father to one kind of freedom and the tank that took her father to another, on both of which history hitched a ride.

Peter Wortsman's restless musings have been included in six volumes of The Best Travel Writing. *This story won the Grand Prize Gold Award in the Sixth Annual Solas Awards and comprises a chapter in the author's travel memoir,* Ghost Dance in Berlin: A Rhapsody in Gray, *recipient of a 2014 Independent Publishers Book Award (IPPY). The book was inspired by his time spent as a Holtzbrinch Fellow at The American Academy in Berlin in 2010.*

KATHERINE JAMIESON

ॐ ॐ ॐ

Remember This Night

The neighbors might talk—but it will be worth it.

The teenage girl you live with, the younger one with the jutting chin who rarely smiles, is laughing at *America's Funniest Home Videos*. She giggles as a kitten falls off a window ledge onto the back of a large dog, as a small dog runs so fast it trips and flips over itself, and as a parakeet recites words that have to be bleeped out for the viewing audience. Your legs are so sweaty that it's painful to pull them from the stuffed chairs you have swung them over. With your hands you try to separate your skin, swollen with heat and sun, from the vinyl, but after a few inches you wince, fall back in the chair, and decide there's really no need to move again tonight.

Just as you are settling into the home videos marathon with its echoing canned laughter, the TV begins to flip through channels. A denture commercial with lush bubbles surfacing over pearly teeth . . . a group of young, happy people wearing McDonald's t-shirts and dancing in line . . . an old episode of *Sanford and Son*. The changing continues, as if a higher power is trying to decide what's best for you to watch this evening. Finally, the pixels coalesce into a staticky image of two uncommonly attractive young people—male and female—and after one glance at the nonchalant grins of those faraway actors you've already divined the ending.

You and the girl are unmoving. Since neither of you comment on the fact that the television has changed its own channels, it's as if nothing has happened at all. Though you have only been in Guyana a little over a month, you've become accustomed to the shortage of options represented by just two television stations, one public, one private, both of which play mainly pirated shows from the United States. One evening you may be apprised of the weather in Tampa, and another you could see a live gospel concert from Dallas. The only things you can count on, really, are the local news broadcasts and a 4:00 P.M. daily showing of *Days of Our Lives,* the nation's favorite soap opera, which has spawned a generation of Guyanese children named Ashley and Alison. What you will watch tonight, however, is largely beyond your control, and this is a fact that you find strangely pleasing.

Sweat stipples your arms and legs, and for a moment you mourn the lack of air conditioning. You remember summer nights in Maryland and the whirring, icy breath on your forehead when you rested your face against the rumbling machine. The little plastic edge of the vent you bit against, causing the cold air to rush directly down your throat. Looking out the window at the dark, quiet streets as you sucked in the chill; these are some of your first memories of being alone as a child.

You allow yourself only a few minutes of self-pity tonight. It is true that you have never been hotter. That the relentless heat has inhabited and possessed your body in a way you could not have imagined before you arrived in this country. That your brain is fatigued by the heat, and your thoughts have frayed and gone soggy in the equally unmerciful humidity. But this is not the point. You look at the girl guiltily. She has probably never felt air-conditioning. There is no life for her without this heat.

Your legs and ankles are festooned with little pink-red dots, marks of fresh mosquito penetration. Languidly you imagine an *America's Funniest Home Videos* about mosquitoes. Guyanese lore has it that if you pinch the skin around the mosquito stinger as it is biting you, it will be forced to keep sucking your blood and explode. That might make for a good episode. The mosquitoes are staying away tonight because the girl has lit several "coils," flat, dark-green solid chemicals that create a force field of noxious smoke around which the mosquitoes dance. Ash dropping from the smoldering ember slowly recreates the spiral shapes on the ground in gray, druidic markings. The odor permeates your skin and clothes. Tonight, in bed, you will smell it in your hair.

There's a knock on the door. No one is home except you and the girl, the appointed guards of the house. You pause and listen. Shirley, the girl's stepmother and your host for the next few months, has warned you about opening the door for anyone. "Teefmen come anytime," she has said. Another knock on the door and you emerge from the protective smoke into a swarm of eager black specks that, despite your swatting hands, fill with your blood and fly away. Your blood, flying all over the room, perching on the doilies and crawling back into the dark places under the sofa.

Between the metal bar and frilly curtains, you catch a glimpse of white skin. Todd. Flushed cheeks, slightly upturned, freckled nose, a pink Oxford shirt, khaki pants. Your neighbor, another young volunteer who has, like you, just graduated from college. Every day you walk together through the pitted roads of Georgetown to the training center to sit with the twelve other volunteers and listen to lectures on sustainable development, cultural sensitivity, and all the diseases you might contract while living in the tropics. You undo the many locks.

Todd looks wild-eyed, agitated. "Enid's Christian music is driving me crazy. What are you doing?"

You slap your leg, flick off a carcass, rub the red spot. "Nothing. You know, watching TV."

He comes into the house, and you lock the door immediately behind him. The girl had twisted in her chair briefly when Todd first appeared, but now she is chuckling again at the movie.

"Hey, Regina."

"Hello, Todd," from the back of her head.

He is rubbing his hands together nervously as he enters the house, which is crowded with furniture, rugs, stacks of telephone books, and piles of letters. He pushes the sweaty hair away from his head, surveying the room as if he's surveying the whole country, uncertain how he ended up here. Enid is an elderly widow, a born-again, Pentecostal Christian who really wants Todd to become one too.

Regina is laughing out loud now, and her laugh is thin and high-pitched. She has a voice that sounds like it's going to complain even when it isn't. Shirley told me from the beginning that she's "Uncle Reggie's daughter," born to another lighter-skinned, Portuguese woman during their marriage. Regina sometimes visits her birth mother on weekends, and returns saying nothing. While Shirley and Reggie have darker skin and call themselves "Afro-Guyanese," Regina has a long face more reminiscent of Madeira than Nigeria, and a tangle of wild eyebrows.

You feel the tension coming off Todd in waves. You see him assessing the mold that creeps from the windows down the baby blue walls, the cracked figurines in the alcoves, the crush of furniture and heat and smoke in the room. You can almost feel his loneliness too, with its pungent whiff of despair.

"It's not the loneliness," he'll tell you later, "it's the aloneness." Though you don't quite get the distinction, you begin to get the sense that he wants you to help him solve this problem.

"Are y'all hungry?" he asks us after a few minutes of watching the gorgeous, grainy movie characters flirt. A few hours ago, Shirley had served you rice and curried chicken from a dented pot. You and the girl both nod.

"O.K., I'm going to call for a pizza," he announces, as if this were a fine and honorable accomplishment. And, as if performing some kind of amazing circus trick, he adds, "and I think we should rent a movie, too. Anything."

You begin to protest. You are volunteers here; you are guests. You are supposed to be "living at the level of the people," you are supposed to be respectful of the resources of the country, you are supposed to be a model for sustainable development. You are supposed to take what you get, and be happy with less.

But Regina has already turned her head around. Her face, below her unkempt eyebrows, has changed. Her eyes are bright, and there is something like a faint smile on her face. Shirley is at a church meeting. Reggie is down the road playing dominoes. Nikki, the eighteen-year-old, is on a date with her forty-year old boyfriend, and Frankie, the older brother who comes and goes getting thinner and thinner, is out. The Americans are desperate, and now she's going to be the only one around to eat their pizza.

Todd is moving toward the phone. Curried rice and chicken, *America's Funniest Home Videos*. No options. To live with no options makes you feel noble, humbled to the situation. But Todd is not so settled with this arrangement. He's tired of pretending that he has no money, that his parents back in rural Virginia aren't well off, that he doesn't own a Jeep Cherokee across an ocean and won't be a lawyer in a few years anyway. This whole thing you're doing depends on

your ability to feign you don't have access to luxuries—like
air-conditioning—that Regina will never know. To endure
the heat and mosquitoes when you know that not so very far
away your college friends are sipping Cosmos and gyrating
under strobe lights in Manhattan nightspots.

Regina watches you.

"O.K.," you say, "go ahead."

Todd picks up the little plastic phone and dials the five
digits he's memorized. Five numbers, you have realized, are
much easier to remember than seven. The pizza place is new
and brightly lit, located on the same circle where the city's
most famous church, the tallest wooden building in the world,
stands. But it's a tough market here on the tip of South America because the Guyanese do not eat pizza. This restaurant,
like another Italian place where you will eat Thanksgiving
dinner a few months later, is for people like you, people who
are trickling in from Europe and the U.S. as the country opens
up after decades of colonialism and dictatorship. But there are
not enough of you, or you go home too quickly. Both places
will be closed within the year.

"Yes, with pepperoni," Todd is saying. "Yes, and extra
tomatoes. Thirty minutes, O.K. Directions? Let me put someone else on."

Regina comes to the phone and begins speaking with the
most excitement you've ever heard in her voice. Her Creolese
is so thick you only catch "up de back road," "Cuffy monument," "front house with cracked window." They hang up.
You are officially waiting for your pizza to be delivered.

Todd is on a roll now. "I'll head down to the rum shop for
sodas—why don't you two get the movie?"

You have no desire to peel yourself from your sticky chair
again, but he is insistent. Todd's eyes are glistening with a
kind of wild desperation you've never seen before. Then
again you've only known him a month. Time has telescoped

since you arrived here, and you often forget that your new friends—Todd—and your family—Regina—are essentially strangers.

You know Todd to be sheepish, reserved, making everyone laugh with his deadpan humor. He's polite, Southern, and he often looks down when he speaks. But tonight, tonight he is staring at you with manic hazel eyes, his thin hair plastered to his forehead like one possessed. *This night is going to be different,* he seems to be saying. *We are going to remember this night.*

Regina is happily along for the ride. She slides her feet into her plastic sandals and goes to wait by the door. Todd has already departed on his quest for sodas, thrusting a $500 Guyanese bill into your hand as he rushes out. As you leave, you will lock the door tightly and pray that the "teefmen" don't decide to show up in your absence. Shirley has had this house for fifty years and it's crammed with possessions from brightly painted cement wall to cement wall. To your jaundiced eye, much of it looks old and broken, but still you would feel terrible if any of it disappeared forever into the Guyana night. You leave the television on as a precaution, as if intruders might be kept at bay by scripted American wisecracks and meaningful sidelong glances.

It's a short walk around the corner to the small video store. The night is starry and loud, men slamming dominoes down at the rum shop, babies crying, packs of dogs roaming the street, barking at nothing and each other. You can see Regina's face silhouetted in the moonlight, placid, unspeaking. You talk to fill the silence, asking her about her school, about Nikki's boyfriend George, about Shirley's church. She nods, or answers in a few words. You don't know if she's just shy or if she dislikes you, or if she is so excited by the pizza and movie she can't speak. You worry that you are too talkative and too foreign, and that you will never be accepted by this girl and, by association, her country where you are to live for the next two years. Then, suddenly, she slips her small warm hand into yours. You walk the rest of the way to the movie store afraid to breathe too hard because maybe the hand will fly back. But she does not move it.

There are a few hundred videos packed into the tiny store lit by a dangling bare bulb. The girl behind the counter is twirling her hair extensions and watching the same romantic comedy playing on your TV back at Shirley's. Dub music superstars are plastered on the walls: Petra, with bati-rider jeans perched on the top of her thighs, leers at you over her shoulder, while Beenie Man seems to thrust his pelvis right out of the poster. You think how unlike the characters in the American movie these Caribbean stars are, how bland and goofily uncertain the Americans seem compared with these brazen performers. You hope that by the time you leave this country, you will have absorbed some of this confidence and sheen.

It turns out Regina loves horror movies. She picks up several boxes showing people with axes jammed in their skulls, but you shake your head. Your suggestions of dramas and romances, even adventures, are greeted with solemn, silent disapproval. Finally, you compromise on *The Shining*, which both you and certainly Todd have seen before. You pay the equivalent of a two-week average Guyanese salary to become a member of the store, the girl writing your name in careful script on a little hand-printed cardboard card.

At home, Todd is prostrate on the stoop with the cold sodas pressed against his head and neck, an open one tipped precariously against his stomach. Back inside, you light more mosquito coils and turn up the fan so that smoke billows and gusts through the room. It has been half an hour, maybe more, since the call and you realize that you did not leave your number with the man who took the order. George-town is a city with few street signs, lit only by occasional guttering bulbs, and it's easy to imagine your driver—and your pizza—lost on the winding, unpaved roads.

Even though you were not that interested in the pizza to begin with, even though pizza sounded like a foreign and unwelcome intrusion to your night, the thought of it never arriving strikes panic in your heart. Not for you, you tell yourself—you'll be fine. But Todd. You look at him, swatting obsessively at his ankles, trying to focus on the television Americans. He is not all right. He's on the edge, talking more and more about going home to the States and to his dog Faulkner, a black lab puppy who just broke his leg. Talking about not knowing why he's here, not knowing how he'll make it. He is depressed and he is confused. He needs pizza.

Finally, you hear a car on the dirt road. It rumbles past the bonfires of trash wafting sweet smoke, past the cemetery with its gravestones sinking into the waterlogged ground, past where the neighbors' many roosters wander in the road all day. Halting in front of the house in front of yours, its lights shine brighter than anything else on the street. Walking over the planks to the road, you appreciate the fact that the delivery car is unmarked, that it looks like hundreds of other white Toyota Camrys that cruise the streets of Georgetown, white being the color used cars are painted when they are imported, refurbished and resold. It could be a taxi, or a friend coming to visit. When the telltale flat white box is delivered through the window, however, you know the neighbors will begin talking.

But you forget: it is telltale only to you. The neighbors have never seen pizza delivered before; they have never tasted it. This delivery may as well be from another solar system, an alien handing over its mouthwatering intergalactic offering. When you give the driver the exorbitant amount of cash owed for the transaction, you cup it in your palm, concealing the colors of the high bills: the green-orange thousand, the pink-blue five hundred. This the neighbors will understand, and they would talk, though never to your face: *Look how de white gyal does trow money about!* They would think you wasteful, show-offish.

In the house, rejoicing has already begun. Regina and Todd have prepared the enamel plates. The box does not disappoint, its rich smell cutting right through the mosquito coil air. Pizza, the all-in-one food that requires no utensils, that completes itself in a perfect cycle of sauce, cheese, and bread. You and Todd are enraptured by the convenient, extravagant food of your country, and you dive into its comforting textures and tastes.

But you've forgotten Regina. She puts her fingers in the box gingerly, lifts a slice to her mouth. She has seen the commercials and so she knows how it should be eaten, tip first, raised up as if the entire piece could be descended to the gut in one gooey, delicious mess. Like all Guyanese, she does not waste food, crunching chicken bones between her teeth to suck out the marrow. She is a girl who knows how to eat. But this is a new delicacy, and you watch her face as she struggles to discern the strange spices on her tongue. It's as if you have taken her back home to feast in the kitchens, camps, and dorm rooms of your past. She is feeding on the food of your memories.

The box is empty soon enough, the soda bottles drained of their brilliant sugar water, and you feel satiated and guilty at the same time. The box holds only grease stains now, and little strands of cheese which Regina pries off with her fingernails. When she goes to throw it away it's far bigger than the barrel will allow, and it sits, balanced over the top, sharp angles jutting up to the ceiling. Shirley will wonder when she sees it, unaccustomed to finding trash like this in her house. She has already dug your strange rubbish out of the bin several times and transformed it into entirely new implements: empty metal tubes of toothpaste have become soap dishes, glass bottles now hold candlesticks, a wire hanger is used to clear the drain.

It's movie time. Even with the bright lights of the house, even in the thick nighttime heat, the scenes of mental breakdown and perilous snowstorms seem terrifying. The VCR clicks loudly and makes buzzing noises, and a message at the bottom of the screen "Bubba's Video Store—Not for resale" flashes at random, but still you find yourself quaking and jumping. The spectral twins appear and you release a small scream. Regina and Todd stare at you.

"Haven't you seen this before?" Todd asks.

Regina says nothing but seems to be communicating that the slasher films would have been much better.

Hours pass and the thrill of the evening begins to wear on you. Nothing has happened and everything has happened. By the time Jack appears with his long knife, Todd has fallen into a stupor of nostalgia, lethargy, and grease from which you wake him on the sofa. As his eyes flutter open, you meet them and see desire for many things, near and far, including you. You have also craved the long length of his body next to yours, but the raw need in his eyes still takes you by surprise. For now, you have no privacy, nowhere to go without Regina coming along. Looking back at the characters fighting their way through the blizzard in the labyrinth, you regain yourselves. Pizza will have to be enough, tonight.

"You need to go back to Enid's," you remind him, and he nods, shaking it off.

Calling goodnight to Regina, he shuffles toward the door. You hug him, and his rumpled shirt releases a familiar detergent smell because it is one of the ones that hasn't yet been washed here.

"I'll see you tomorrow," you say, and he nods silently.

He walks toward the dirt road, glancing back at you once. His expression is lost in the darkness.

The next morning you will wake up with a slight hangover from the chemical smoke. Nikki will be pulling dead frogs out of the shower. The TV will be blasting *The Price Is Right.* Shirley will have used your pizza box to patch a hole in the roof. And Regina will be quiet and sullen again. But as you pass by her on your way to the kitchen, where you'll reach for a glass of passion fruit juice, she will flash you a quick and startling smile.

Katherine Jamieson is a graduate of the Iowa Nonfiction Writer's Program, where she was an Iowa Arts Fellow. Her essays and articles have been published in The New York Times, Narrative, Meridian, The Common, Alimentum, Brevity, *and numerous editions of* The Best Women's Travel Writing *and* The Best Travel Writing. *This story won the Grand Prize Silver in the Ninth Annual Solas Awards. Based in the woods of Western Massachusetts, Katherine leads a dual life as a reclusive writer and performer with a Latin GRAMMY-winning musician (her husband). You can read more of her writing at katherinejamieson.com.*

DAVID TORREY PETERS

ॐ ॐ ॐ

The Bamenda Syndrome

Insanity is very much a point of view.

*I*n mid-June of 2003, Raymond Mbe awoke on the floor of his dirt hut. A white moth had landed on his upper lip. In a half-sleep, he crushed it and the wings left traces of powder across his lips and under his nose. The powder smelled of burnt rubber and when he licked his lips, he tasted copper. Outside the hut, his eyes constricted in the sunlight. A steady dull thud, like a faraway drum, filtered through the trees. "I hate that noise," Raymond told me later. "The sound of pounding herbs with a big pestle. Every time I hear it, I know that a short time later they will stuff those herbs up my nose."

Two hours later, Raymond's nose burned as the green dust coated the inside of his nostrils. A muscular man in a white t-shirt cut off at the sleeves held Raymond's arms twisted behind his back. Across a table from Raymond, a loose-jowled old man in a worn-out fedora had measured out three piles of crushed herbs.

"Inhale the rest of it," said the old man.

"Please," Raymond pleaded, "I have cooperated today. You don't have to force me."

Deftly, the man in the sleeveless tee twisted Raymond's elbows upward, leveraging Raymond's face level with the tabletop. Raymond considered blowing away the herbs. He found satisfaction in defying them, but already his arms burned with pain. He snorted up the remaining piles of green dust. Herbs mixed with loose snot ran from his nostrils. The piles gone, Raymond's arms were given a final yank and released.

"Oaf," Raymond muttered and wiped his face with his shirt. No one paid attention; already the old man had motioned to an androgynous creature in rags to approach him. Four other patients stood in line waiting for their turn.

In the bush that ringed the compound Raymond pretended to relieve himself. Glancing around him to make sure no one watched, he fell into a crouch and crept into the foliage. The scabs on his ankles split anew at the sudden effort. Glancing at the pus seeping across his bare feet, he remembered that he had once had a pair of basketball shoes. They had been white, with blue laces.

One hundred yards or so into the bush, he emerged onto a small path that ran in a tunnel through the foliage. Raymond stood up and began walking, brushing aside the large over-hanging leaves as he went. In places, the sun shone through the leaves shaping a delicate lacework on the path. The tunnel dilated out onto the bright road. It had been three months since Raymond had seen the road. Under the mid-morning sun, heat shimmered off the pavement and mirages pooled in the distance. The road appeared empty.

"So, I did it. I placed a foot on the road. Very close to where I had last seen my mother. Then I walked across."

"Oh it was terrible," said the tailor who works alongside the road, "We heard him screaming and laughing down on the road. He was like an animal or something possessed. I was scared."

In June, I traveled to a village named Bawum, outside the city of Bamenda in the Anglophone Northwest Province of

Cameroon, to interview a priest named Father Berndind. Bawum consisted of a single road, high in the cool grasslands, lined for a mile or so with cinderblock dwellings and the occasional open-front store. Behind the houses ran a network of dirt footpaths connecting poorer thatch-work houses built of sun-dried brick or *poto-poto*.

Berndind had launched a campaign to eradicate the practice of witchcraft from his parish. Plenty of priests wanted to do away with witchcraft; Berndind was unique because he waged his campaign from a seminary that bordered the compound of a witchdoctor. His neighbor was Pa Ayamah, a healer renowned for his ability to cure cases of insanity caused by witchcraft.

I went to Bawum with a post-graduate student named Emmanuel, a thoughtful, good-natured guy who grew up in one of the sun-dried brick houses across the road from both Ayamah and the seminary. We agreed that he would introduce me to both Berndind and Ayamah, as a friend rather than a foreign research student, as long as I paid for food and transportation. He had written a Master's thesis on F. Scott Fitzgerald's *The Great Gatsby*. "It's funny," he said, "You come from America to study Cameroonians, and all I want to do is study Americans."

We arrived on a Saturday night. Emmanuel took me to Mass the following morning to meet Berndind. The church was bright and airy, but struck me as weirdly out of place among the green underbrush and dirt paths. It was built in a pre-fab style; the type of church that I remember having seen in lower-middle-class areas of Iowa and Nebraska. On closer inspection, I saw that parts of the church had been hand-built to look prefabricated. Inside, I felt underdressed. I was the only man not wearing a sport coat. In Yaounde, fashion tended toward the sort of suits worn by comic-book super-villains; lots of bright color, wide pinstripes, and shimmery ties. From the somber colors assembled in that church, I gathered that the trend did not extend out into the provinces.

I felt better when a young man who wore a ratty blue t-shirt and taped-together flip-flops wandered in. He was short and strangely proportioned, a squat upper body rested on thin legs, like a widow's walk on Greek-revival columns. He plunked himself down in the pew in front of me. Seated, his feet barely brushed the ground, but his upper body took up almost two spaces. Halfway through the Mass, he craned his head around and stared at me. He pointed at my chest and whispered loudly, "Hey! I like your tie! Very shiny!"

A wave of heads spun around to appraise my clothing choice. "Um. Thank you." A few older men glowered at me and I blushed.

After the Mass, while I waited outside the church to meet with Berndind, I saw the boy walk by and slip into a thin trail that led into the bush. "What's the story with that guy?" I asked.

"Oh, that's Raymond." Emmanuel said, "Nobody pays any attention to him. He's a patient at Pa Ayamah's."

"I wasn't there," said Emmanuel's sister, "But I heard about it. They had to take him back bound at the wrists and ankles."

"Your teeth have worms in them." George Fanka told Emmanuel. We had stopped to visit Emmannuel's Aunt Eliza, before going to Bawum. "That's why they hurt. They are filled to bursting with worms."

"Worms?" Emmanuel asked.

"I am good with worms," George Fanka assured him. "I can pull worms out of pile also."

George Fanka did not fit my idea of a native doctor. He was my age and sported a Nike track suit. He styled his hair like a mid-'90s American rapper and had a cell phone hung from a cord around his neck.

A few years prior, Emmanuel's Aunt Eliza had come down with a mysterious illness. She spent a good chunk of her life savings on doctors unable to give her a diagnosis before she hired George Fanka to come live with her and treat her. She was a bulky, ashen-faced woman whose frequent smiles were followed by equally frequent winces. Once too ill to stand, under Fanka's care, she had recovered enough to walk into the town center.

The night I met George and Aunt Eliza, we sat in her cinderblock living room drinking orange soda. For more than two hours George talked about his abilities as a healer. "Well, Sir," he said when conversation turned to successful treatments, "I come from a long line of doctors. It's in my blood. My uncle is a famous doctor."

"That's why he came here," Emmanuel said, nodding at his aunt. "She needed someone who could live here and George's uncle recommended him."

"Everyone in my family has the ability. There are contests you know. Yes, Contests. Contests." George repeated certain words, as though his audience were intermittently hard of hearing. "All the doctors get together and we compete to see who is the best. I won a contest, you know." He talked quickly and eagerly.

He took a swig of orange soda, smacked his lips, and hurried on. "I won a contest and that's how I lost my toes. Well, only on one foot but that's how I lost them. I'm a diviner; that's what I do best."

"Wait, you lost your toes?"

"On my right foot," George replied. Abruptly, he dropped his soda bottle on the table. Emmanuel lunged forward to keep it from spilling. George didn't notice; he was already bent over in his chair, tugging off his Nikes. He gripped his sock by the toe and pulled it off with a flourish, like a waiter revealing a prized entrée.

He was right. His right foot had no toes. There was a line of angry, puckered scars where his toes had been. They looked disturbingly like anuses. Aunt Eliza said something in flustered Pidgin to George, who was proudly inching his foot toward my face. Emmanuel moved as though he were going to intercept George's foot, but when he saw me lean in for a better look, he leaned back and asked, "Are you scared?"

"No," I said. "Just caught me by surprise."

"Yes, sir!" said George, ignoring the interruption, "My toes were burned off by lightning. After I won the contest, I was too proud—I had been playing with my abilities too much. So someone threw lightning to hit me, but it just got my foot."

George was still holding his foot high in the air, speaking from between his legs. I peered closely at his foot. "Take a good look!" George said gleefully.

A number of people in Cameroon claimed the ability to throw lightning. I had asked about the phenomenon repeatedly, but while everyone said it was possible—and some had even promised to introduce me to people who could do it—tracking down lightning-throwers seemed to be a wild goose chase. An English anthropologist named Nigel Barley had spent a year with the Dowayo tribe in Northern Cameroon asking about lightning rituals, only to find that their method of directing lightning was to place marbles imported from Taiwan in little bowls set on the mountainside. My own investigations into the phenomenon were inconclusive. My best lead, a professor at the University of Yaoundé, had suggested that lightning could be thrown by coaxing a chameleon to walk up a stick.

Nonetheless, there have been some very strange lightning strikes across Africa, many of them having to do with soccer. On October 25, 1998, eleven professional soccer players were struck by lightning in a crucial game in South Africa. Two days later, eleven Congolese soccer players were killed by a second lightning strike, this time a ground steamer. The worst lightning strike ever recorded occurred at a third soccer game in Malawi, when lightning struck a metal fence, killing five people and injuring a hundred more. The official response of African Soccer officials to the lightning strikes speaks to the common interpretation of these events: they banned witch-doctors from the African Nations Cup.

I had no idea what toes burnt off by lightning might look like, but if I had to imagine, they would have looked something like the scarred puckers lined up on George's foot. I wondered if he had maybe cut his toes off himself, or lost them in an accident, but the wounds looked cauterized, like they had drawn up into themselves.

"Yes, sir," George continued from between his legs. "It might have been another jealous healer, or maybe the spirits thought I was too bold."

I asked George if he could throw lightning. He dropped his leg and cried, "Certainly not! I am a healer and a Christian." He fixed me with an offended expression and wagged his finger back and forth, "That sort of thing is not what I do. What I do is, see, hold on . . ." He grabbed an empty glass from in front of him. "I make soapy water and I tell it what a person's illness is. Then I look into the water and I can see which kind of herbs I need to find. The next day I go out into the forest and get them."

"I get headaches," I said. "Do you have something for that?"

"And my teeth hurt," Emmanuel said. George looked up my nose and at Emmanuel's teeth. I needed to sneeze more, he told me. Emmanuel, he diagnosed, had teeth full of worms. We made an appointment to return the next day for treatment.

Pa Ayamah's compound looked similar to all the other com-pounds that dotted the green hills of Bawum: a few huts of sun-dried brick in a clearing surrounded by dense bush. In places, the sun sparkled through the tall trees and sent shadows flitting across soil padded smooth by human feet. Even in rural Cameroon, I had expected an insane asylum to look somewhat clinical—whether or not it was run by a witch-doctor. I saw none of the usual tip-offs: no nurses, no white buildings, no corridors or wards. Only the weathered, hand-painted sign, "Pa Ayamah—Native Doctor," marked that I had found the right place.

In front of a smattering of brown huts, dusty men in chains shuffled about an open yard. Others not chained had their feet encased into makeshift stocks of rough wood. Everyone smiled at me, as if I were a regular stopping in for an evening beer at the neighborhood bar. A man with his hands tied to his belt tried to wave in greeting and nearly pulled himself over. He grinned ingratiatingly, obviously wanting me to share the joke. I managed a disoriented smile and realized that I had never before seen anybody tied up. A very old man with sunken eyes approached me and held out his hand. Without thinking, I reached to shake it, but recoiled when I saw that it was purple with infection.

"Antibiotics?" the man said hopefully.

Behind me, Raymond burst out from one of the huts, bare-foot, and pulling on a t-shirt as he ran. "Hey! I saw you at church!" he cried

I turned with relief away from the old man. "Oh yeah," I said, my voice more eager than I intended, "I remember!"

"You do?" Raymond came to a stop in front of me.

"Yes. I do."

"And I remember you!"

We beamed at each other.

"What's your name?" Raymond asked.

"Dave."

"Antibiotics?" the old man said again, thrusting his purple hand towards me.

"No, no!" Raymond said loudly, leaning in toward the old man, "He's a missionary."

"What? No, I'm not."

"But you're white. And I saw you at church."

"I'm a student. I came to talk to Pa Ayamah"

"Never seen a student here," Raymond commented. "But, oh, come, I'll show you where Ayamah stays." He grabbed me by the arm and pulled me away from the old man, whose parched voice faded as I walked off, "Antibiotics?"

Raymond led me on an impromptu tour of the compound, tugging me along by my sleeve. A good portion of Ayamah's land was devoted to raising corn, planted in rows of raised dirt. Beyond the cornfields were small houses, where women related to the patients lived and prepared food. Raymond confessed that he had no relations among the women, but many of the patient's families couldn't afford both the treatment and food, so a female relative was sent to care for the patient. The few women I saw did not give me the same welcoming smiles as their relatives. I tried to say hello to a pretty girl beating laundry in a soapy bucket. She returned my greeting with a sneer, as if she had caught me attempting to watch her bathe.

Beyond the women's huts were the patients' quarters. The huts were small and dirty with a fire pit in front of each one. An aging man with a barrel chest and wooly hair chased chickens with a broom. He was laughing and shrieking. When he cornered a chicken, he spit on it and clapped his hands delightedly. "That's where Pa Ayamah is," Raymond said. I followed his finger to a long building with a tin roof. "You can just go in."

"Thanks for showing me around," I said extending my hand, "It was nice of you."

Raymond shrugged and clapped me on the shoulder. He was significantly shorter than me and had to reach up to do so. "Oh, I know how it is. I used to be a student myself."

Clouds hung low in a leaden sky the morning Emmaunel and I presented ourselves at George Fanka's door for treatment. He had exchanged his Nike track suit for a red Adidas shirt and assumed a businesslike air, though his cell-phone medallion still hung from his neck. He led Emmanuel and me to a small wooden shack, consisting of two rooms, padlocked shut. The first had a bed, a small stereo, and was decorated with magazine cutouts of American pop stars. A large stuffed baboon guarded the second room. "I'll sell you the monkey," George said to me.

"I couldn't get it through Customs."

George shrugged and led us inside the second room. Most of the room was taken up by a large table, filled with old water bottles that contained many colored liquids. Red, brown, and green tree barks lay ground up in newspaper. I sat with Emmanuel on a bench and sniffed at the air, which smelled stale, like the corridors of a natural history museum. George perused a few bottles and handed me a little bit of brown powder twisted up in cigarette cellophane. "For your headaches. It is a type of tree bark, O.K.? You snort a bit of that and then you will sneeze for a while and your head will clear."

I nodded. George pulled out a dirty flat-head screwdriver. "Let's get rid of those worms," he said to Emmanuel. "They are in your gums." George poured a white suspension over a cotton ball and directed me to hold a piece of paper below Emmanuel's chin; from my position I had a clear view into his open mouth. I hesitated when I saw the screwdriver poised above Emmanuel's teeth, suddenly worried about tetanus. But, I reasoned, when performing oral surgery with a screwdriver, is the status of one's tetanus shot really the primary concern?

"Hold the paper steady," George chided.

Emmanuel's gums looked inflamed, the inside of his mouth very pink. George rubbed the cotton ball across Emmanuel's gums. Little white spots appeared against the pink, then what looked like whiteheads began to form in the gums between the teeth. George reached in Emmanuel's mouth. He pinched one of the whiteheads between the screwdriver and his thumbnail and began to pull. The whitehead stretched and began to pop out in segments. George grunted and forced another finger into Emmanuel's mouth. The last segment of the whitehead thing popped out with a little spurt of blood. George held it up for my inspection. It was a small, white, segmented worm, squirming, and covered in blood. It was about a four or five millimeters long, and fat like a maggot.

"They die fast in the open air," he said, and dropped it onto the piece of paper I held. The worm curled up slowly and was still.

"Fuck," I said. I had watched carefully for any sleight of hand, and saw none. The worm had just appeared, a fat zit growing in stop-motion capture. I wanted to be skeptical, but the disconnect between my eyes and brain created a dead spot in my thoughts. I felt seasick. "Fuck," I said again.

"You say that a lot," said George, dropping another worm on the paper, "Uh oh, I only got half of that one. If they die in there, they rot." Emmanuel winced. His gums bled profusely by the time George got the other half out and still the whiteheads seemed to swell of their own accord. By the time he was done, George had pulled four more worms out of Emmanuel's mouth.

A few days later, I asked Emmanuel if his teeth felt better. "I think so," he said, "but I also went to a dentist who told me the pain was from an infection. He gave me medicine for it.

So I don't know if I feel better because of George or the medicine. I'm glad I covered all the options."

A prominent American biologist who visited the University of Yaounde was skeptical of my story. He had not heard of such a worm. When I returned to the United States, I went to my University library and looked up parasitic worms. To the best collective knowledge of Western biologists, there are no segmented parasitic worms that live in human mouths anywhere in West Africa. Apparently, the worms I'd seen did not exist.

Pa Ayamah was a tall man with folds of skin hanging off his face. His eyes looked coated with oil and slipped around, as if the sockets were too big for them. He spoke no English; Emmanuel translated for us. The three of us sat in a line of rickety chairs, pushed against the far wall of a dark dirt-floored room. Ayamah sat very still, but his stillness seemed to come more from a force of energy held back, like a coiled spring waiting to be released, rather than any sense of relaxation or ease.

Ayamah began by announcing that he was the sixth generation of healers to specialize in the mentally ill. He was the sole heir to 200 years of practice. Ayamah spoke to Emmanuel, not me, and Emmanuel waited until Ayamah finished before he translated the words.

"He says that the knowledge will die with him," Emmanuel said. "His sons have left him to try to become businessmen in the cities."

Ayamah spoke again, sharply, and stared at the empty space in front of him when Emmanuel translated. "They will end up as market boys. He says that they have forsaken their heritage to be market boys. He finds it shameful." Ayamah wore an old fedora with a snakeskin band. He took it off after he began to speak in earnest. According to him, there were three causes of mental illness. The first was God, by which

Emmanuel explained he meant fate and I understood to mean natural causes. The second reason people went crazy was because they neglected their ancestors. Finally, Ayamah said, people might go crazy because one of their enemies placed a curse upon them.

"What happens after people go crazy?" I asked. Ayamah puckered his lips and blew in exasperation. He gave a response that lasted over a minute. Emmanuel cleared his throat and gave a one-word translation, "Encopresis."

"That means shit-smearing, right?"

"Yes, and they fight with it. Many things having to do with shit."

"What does he do about it?" I gave up any pretense of trying to phrase my questions in the second person. Like Ayamah, I began to speak to Emmanuel directly.

"He has someone clean it up. They can make a real mess."

"No, I meant for the treatment." Emmanuel relayed the question. Ayamah said that he didn't spend too much time trying to determine what type of insanity a patient suffered from, since he used the same method to treat all of them: he and his assistants tied them up and beat them. Eventually they became docile, and he then stuffed a special blend of herbs up their nose mornings and evenings. "He also maintains a small shrine to commune with his ancestors in the spirit world," Emmanuel explained. "And he might consult the Bible for wisdom."

"The Christian Bible?"

"Well, they translated it into the Bawum dialect," Emmanuel said.

"Yeah, but isn't it sort of a contradiction to commune with one's ancestors and then consult the Bible? You know, one God, above all others?"

Emmanuel translated the question and laughed at Ayamah's response. "He says 'What's the difference?' Jesus is just a really old ancestor of yours. If he wants really old knowledge he talks to Jesus. When he wants to talk to someone more up-to-date he consults his own ancestors."

Emmanuel waited a moment to see if I had any more objections and went on. The only modifications Ayamah made to his treatments were for those who threw their shit. He chained shit-throwers hand and foot. For everyone else, he simply took a log, drilled a hole in it, and after sticking the patient's leg through the hole, nailed in place a second length of wood to close off the hole. Ayamah assured me that it was difficult to get very far dragging a log on one foot.

"Doesn't that bother you?" I asked Emmanuel.

Emmanuel scratched at a five o'clock shadow contemplatively. "I guess it might have, but I grew up in this village. You might say that the sight of madmen in logs was part of my childhood."

Ayamah picked his nose and blew snot on the floor.

"What about Raymond?" I asked, "How come he doesn't have a log on his leg?"

Ayamah chuckled slightly when Emmanuel translated the question. His response had a lot of sound effects. At one point Ayamah acted out hitting something with his walking stick and cried, "*Bam—Whacka—Bam!*"

Emmanuel turned to me when Ayamah was finished. Again the translation was noticeably shorter than the story. "He said Raymond was a hard case. He never threw his shit, but he made trouble in other ways. He thought he wasn't crazy. They had to beat him to make him understand he was unwell. Once he understood, he was docile."

Joseph, the cook agreed with all the others, "I was one of the people who brought him back. Some other men had gathered and asked me to help them. I like him. He likes the food I make. I wasn't happy to see him like that."

Whenever I try to explain the worms I saw in Emmanuel's mouth, I get stuck on that exact fact. I saw them. I saw them

come out of his gums. After a while, I came to the conclusion that I had three ways to explain what I'd seen: I could
decide that I had been deceived, I could decide that my eyes
had deceived me, or, finally, I could alter my entire world
view to encompass the possibility of non-existent worms
residing in people's gums.

Unconsciously, I think I explored the first and third
options, but consciously, I chose the second. Though the
first option was probably preferable, the second option
seemed more plausible. My disorientation in Cameroon felt
like more than simply the result of culture shock, I had the
nagging suspicion that I was experiencing things I wasn't
equipped to understand. Which was more probable, I asked
myself, that the world was out of whack, or that I was?

I had my erratic behavior as evidence. I acted aggressively. I fought with strangers. I went to the unrestricted
pharmacies and invented pill cocktails. I felt unafraid of
garrulous and dangerous men. For someone who prided
himself on having lived alone in foreign countries since he
was young—who worked to approach other cultures on
their own terms—I was suddenly, disturbingly, patriotic.
Cameroon may be a rough and difficult place, but millions
of people have no problem catching its rhythm and logic.
My experiences elsewhere, or maybe my youth, had made
me arrogant. Rather than admit to myself that I had arrived
unprepared for certain experiences, I narrated my own
explanations to myself. But much like a lie built upon a lie, I
found myself unable to revise my stories to fit events without
admitting that I knew nothing, and so instead my stories,
and therefore understanding of the events around me, grew
more and more fantastic.

By the time I met George, I was frequently making up the
world as I went along. More to the point, I didn't know when
I was doing it, and when I wasn't. Given all this, I was willing
to believe that I saw worms come out of Emmanuel's teeth,

and I was also willing to believe that worms did not come out
of his teeth at all.

On my way home from my interview with Pa Ayamah, I
came upon Raymond crouched on a log, reading a pamphlet
that outlined how to set up a library in accordance with the
Dewey decimal system. "Hey, the missionary!" he called out,
grinning, "How's the church work?"

I took a seat next to him. He held the pamphlet up for my
inspection. "I'd like to go to a library again. Now I just read
about them."

"Did you used to go to libraries?"

Raymond laughed. "I wasn't always like this. I used to
study economics at university. I was good at it too."

Like what? I wanted to ask. In my few encounters with
him, he struck me as odd, but living in Ayamah's compound
would give anyone a few quirks.

"Why did you quit?" I asked.

Raymond waved his hand airily. His wrists were too
thick to make the gesture look natural; it came off as studied or affected. "My uncle. He put a curse on me." Once he
started talking, the story rolled out of him. I got the sense
that no one had ever asked him before, he kept skipping
back and forth through his story, trying to construct it in
words.

Raymond was the son of a polygamist father who died
when he was six or seven. As tradition dictated, Raymond's
father's brother took Raymond and his widowed mother to
live with him. Raymond's uncle and his jealous wife beat and
underfed him. While we talked, Raymond pulled back his
lips to show me how hunger had ruined his teeth. "Worst of
all," Raymond confided to me, "My uncle was an evil man. He
was a member of a secret society. The only thing he was good
at was witchcraft."

After finishing lycée, both Raymond and his uncle's son were awarded opportunities to study at the University of Buea. "My uncle was furious that I should go to the same university as his son. He kept asking me who I thought I was. But he couldn't stop me and my mother secretly gave me some money." During the school year there was not enough money for Raymond and his cousin to come home, so Raymond stayed at the university studying economics, while his cousin came home during breaks.

"What type of economics did you study?" I asked when he paused to breathe.

He furrowed his brow. "How do you mean?" he replied.

"I mean what exactly did you study economics for?"

Raymond inhaled sharply and shifted his seat next to mine so he could grasp my knee. His face was mottled with little scars, but beneath them the skin was unlined. The whites of his eyes were completely clear, remarkable, given the dust and dirt on the path. "Oh you, know," he said in an off-hand tone. "Lots of different things."

Abruptly, Raymond lifted his head and looked off toward the tops of the trees. "Do you smell something burning?" he asked.

I sniffed the air. "No. I don't smell anything."

Raymond shrugged and continued his story. After months without seeing his family, Raymond's uncle called him home just before exam period. When Raymond left, his uncle gave him 10,000 francs. His uncle had never done anything like that before. Raymond later found significance in the action, "The money was cursed." At this point in his story, Raymond stood and began to wave his hands, acting out his words. His crisp accent contrasted remarkably with his torn blue t-shirt and the caked dirt on his legs and pants.

Raymond returned to school in time to begin cramming for exams. Although he felt he had much work to do, his thoughts kept on focusing on the 10,000-franc note he had stashed away in his economics textbook. "It was calling to me. Like a beautiful prostitute. Something you know is wrong, but attracts you so much." Twenty or thirty times in a day he would stop what he was doing and check to see if the money was still there.

"It got very bad," Raymond said, his voice almost pleading, "This obsession with the money. I was studying all day for the exams, but I was thinking about the money. The night before the exams, I got sick. It was like a fever, and my chest was tight. I was sweating and moaning and I put the textbook with the money in it in my bed."

"The experience you describe kind of sounds like an anxiety attack," I interjected, "Maybe you were stressed over exams."

Raymond rolled his eyes, as though a child had interrupted him. "This," he said slowly, "was not an anxiety attack. I was afraid to trust anyone. It was terrible. I locked myself in my room and held the book with the money in it to my chest. I was like that for twenty-four hours; I missed my exams. Finally it was too much. I took the 10,000 francs and went to the market to buy medicine. But instead of medicine, I asked for poison."

"They sell poison in the markets?" I had never seen any, but then, I hadn't looked.

"For animals. But they wouldn't sell me poison, so I tried to buy Valium to take an overdose, but I was wild and out of control, so they wouldn't sell me any."

"If you could spend the money on Valium, why didn't you just buy a shirt or a radio or something to get rid of it?"

Raymond shook his head impatiently, his wide-set eyes bulging. "Don't you see? They controlled me! I couldn't spend the money on anything but poison! Why of all the ways to kill myself did I try to use the money to buy poison? The money made me do it!"

Raymond noticed he was shouting, lowered his arms slightly, and gave me a weak smile. "Sorry, I forget myself sometimes. Not exactly a smart thing for a madman to do." I shrugged. "Go on."

"I went home in a rage and pulled down the light from the ceiling of my room and tore it open." He forgot his fear of yelling and began to act out tearing apart a light with flailing arm gestures. "And I took it so there were two wires, full of electricity, and I grabbed one with each hand so the electricity could flow through me and cure me of the fever." It was quiet on the path; I could hear the whir of grasshoppers and the gurgle of a nearby stream. Against those noises Raymond's long toenails scraped the bare dirt while he stood in front of me. His arms grasped imaginary wires and his body writhed while muted screams escaped through clenched teeth as he pantomimed his suicide attempt. It lasted long enough for me to grow frightened. Just as I was about to say something, his body dropped motionless on the dirt.

"He was shouting about being on the road." The sunblackened man whose job seemed to be to remain ever seated on the lawn chair in front of the tailor's shop agreed with everyone else. "So what? I'm down on the road everyday. It's nothing to get so excited about." He took a pull on his cigarette and nodded sagely at his own words.

By American standards, most foreigners I met who were living in Cameroon behaved bizarrely. Every ex-pat I met had his or her quirks; some of the Peace Corps volunteers were downright zany. A volunteer named John, who had lived in the desert for a year an a half without running water, electricity, or a telephone, had, after a few beers at bar in the Hilton hotel, repeatedly called room service demanding to know why they kept calling him.

In Yaounde, I had met a group of wealthy expatriates who had set up something of a European infrastructure and society nestled subtly within the world of Cameroonians. That wealthy, European bubble was not one that was particularly easy to find, and I was happy to have gained their acceptance. They were the twenty-something offspring of diplomats and exporters and they lived a lifestyle that struck me as quite glamorous at the time. Plus, they seemed taken by me; I was new, strange, and for short periods, I had enough money to keep up with them.

It ended when I forgot which person to be with them. One night they took me to a club, some fancy club, where I was ripped off on the entrance fee. Inside, I went to the bar and ordered myself a beer. I asked the barman if he had change for a 5,000. He said he did. He took my money and brought me a tiny beer.

"And my change?" I asked.

"There is none."

I decided to be friendly, "Look man, you can keep 2,000 of it as a tip if you want, but there is no way a beer is 5,000 francs. I pay 200 at the bar by my house."

"This isn't the bar by your house."

"Just give me the money."

The barman didn't say anything more. He simply nodded to a large Frenchman who had a whore hanging off of each arm. He shrugged off one of the whores and grabbed me by the chin. He yelled something in my ear in slurred French. I told him I didn't understand what he said. I understood him the second time, when he told me to fuck off and slapped my cheek Godfather-style.

I got angry then, and forgot where I was. I forgot that I was a twenty-one-year-old middle-class American boy, who was very far from home. I forgot that a flashy nightclub in an expatriate inner city was not my turf. I forgot that I have not been in a real fight since fourth grade, and I forgot that any large Frenchman who has two whores and slaps my cheek like the Godfather is someone not to be fucked with. Instead, I swelled with the sort of self-righteous pride that you find among students at small liberal-arts schools in the United States. Places where things are fair, prices are marked, and some cheesy-looking French Mafioso-wannabe is an abstraction of the movies.

Who the fuck does this mustachioed and obvious low-life exploiter of the African people think he is?

I bitch-slapped him.

The music was loud enough that only a few people heard it. There was a moment where no one moved, not me, not the whores, not the French guy. Then I remembered where I was. With as much dignity as possible I turned my back and walked out of the club. Behind me, the Frenchman was organizing a group of large men. Once outside, I got in the first taxi I saw.

My girlfriend was at the club. She was very confused by my disappearance. I called her on her cell phone and told her what I had done.

She paused a moment, then said, "But a beer here is 5,000 francs."

Raymond awoke in a hospital, his burned hands fastened to the side of the bed. He had been examined while unconscious. A foreign doctor, an Arab, Raymond thought, had found evidence of possible brain anomalies and ordered a few basic tests to be conducted at the provincial hospital. The doctor concluded, though, that Raymond was most likely suffering from something like anxiety or depression. Raymond felt otherwise. The pieces fit together easily in his mind. His illness was caused by witchcraft on the part of his uncle, most likely with the help of a secret society and most likely with the help of other members of his family. Why else was he suddenly called home? Why else the sudden gift of 10,000 francs, from a man who had never before given him anything? His uncle had given him a gift of bewitched money.

Raymond's conjecture wasn't implausible. Although I found it hard to draw the same initial conclusion as he did, the description of his relationship with his uncle and his uncle's actions follows an almost classic model of bewitchment. Accusations of witchcraft most often occur within families, or at least along some form of kinship lines. Witches and the bewitched nearly always know each other. If Raymond suspected his illness was caused by witchcraft, he would look to the person who hated him most: his uncle.

With a little knowledge of witchcraft, the seemingly innocuous gift of money becomes more suspicious as well. While traveling around Cameroon, I found that while I could not leave any of my belongings lying around because they inevitably would be stolen, loose cash left in plain sight was never touched. In the town of Kribi, a group of children went into hysterics when I picked a 100-franc coin off the beach. The instant I touched the coin, the children screamed "No! Drop it! Drop it! Mami Water, she'll get you! Mami Water! Mami Water!" The youngest of them were nearly in tears. In Kribi, no one touched lost money because of the belief that Mami Water—a mutation of the mermaid myth—used money to entice men into the ocean to drown.

The story varied place to place, but the theme was the same: don't take money from strangers. Cash was the perfect medium for sorcery.

Although Raymond remained distrustful of his uncle, he nonetheless left the hospital with him. His uncle remained silent, while his mother pressed his hand and told him that they had borrowed a car and arranged to bring him to Yaoundé where he could be given modern medical treatment. Instead, they drove west into the grassland regions along the

Ring Road. In the village of Bawum, they parked the car on the path that led to Pa Ayamah's compound.

"My uncle got out of the car and walked away. He came back with two men, who opened my car door and pulled me out. I was so shocked I didn't do anything. I fell out of the car and they began to beat me while my uncle and my mother watched. I cried out for my mother to help me, but she kept repeating, 'These men are going to help you.' Then my uncle stood between us. I cried her name many times as they beat me and I began to bleed." Raymond inhaled audibly and pulled at his ear. "My mother began to ask if it wasn't enough, but my uncle pushed her into the car and they drove away."

Almost an hour had passed since I had sat down next to Raymond on the path. We were both sweating in the sun. He lifted the bottom of his t-shirt to wipe his sweat away, leaving trails of dark blue in the light blue fabric.

"They had me chained to a post the first two months," Raymond said, and picked at a stray thread on his shirt. "At first I tried to reason with them. I yelled for days about the rights of man and how it was not right to treat me as they did."

"Were you speaking in English?" I asked.

"Yes, some Pidgin, but mostly English. I don't speak quite the same dialect as they speak here. It's really kind of funny, because I was trying so hard to reason with them, but I was talking about the rights of man, you know, *liberte*, *egalite*, and *fraternite*, which must have sounded like complete nonsense. It's no wonder everyone thought I was crazy. A total madman!" Raymond laughed at the memory, but the sound came out dry and mirthless.

By midway through my stay, I had so convinced myself that I was unbalanced, that it took me a while to notice when other people were acting more absurd than I. In a crowded market, I had been pulled out of a taxi by a gendarme with the disgruntled, bovine face of a cop who once had a desk job. He demanded my passport and vaccination records. I produced them and he scowled at the vaccination card. "Your records are not in order," he declared. He blew his whistle and told the taxi driver to move along. The taxi man said he would wait for his fare.

"What is the problem with my records?"

"Are you contradicting me?"

I reviewed what I had just said in my mind, wondering if I had accidentally misused the French words. "No," I said. "I am not contradicting you."

"Good." He squared his shoulders and adjusted his gun belt. Three other gendarmes, brandishing automatic rifles, appeared behind him. They couldn't resist a white kid in a taxi. Tourists hemorrhaged cash at the sight of a couple of Uzis. I sighed and asked what could be done to "remedy" the problem.

"You're missing a vaccination," he said.

"Which one?" I asked.

"You don't have an AIDS vaccine."

"What?"

"You need to have an AIDS vaccine. You don't have an AIDS vaccine."

"There is no AIDS vaccine."

"What?"

"I said, there is no AIDS vaccine."

He blinked and turned to one of the other gendarmes. "This guy, where does he come from? He says there is no AIDS vaccine." He guffawed loudly, the other gendarmes coughed out half-hearted laughs.

I stepped toward him. "Look, I'm telling you there is no AIDS vaccine."

He laughed, "Oh yeah, then how come so many people are sick?"

My words came out soaked in condescension, despite myself, "Well, vaccines cure sicknesses. If there was an AIDS vaccine those people wouldn't be sick. What you have here in Cameroon is an epidemic, something that happens when there is no vaccine."

A small crowd had gathered around as soon as I was pulled out of the taxi. It must have been an interesting scene: an angry white boy who sneered out broken French at four gendarmes who patted their guns like puppies.

The cop tried a new tact. "You think just because there isn't an AIDS vaccine I can't arrest you for not having one?"

I was mad then, and didn't bother to control myself. "What's it going to take for you to leave me alone?"

"You're under arrest."

"For what? Not having an imaginary vaccine?"

The growing crowd cackled with pleasure. A young man cried, "Careful, they almost arrested me for killing my imaginary friend! But I swear, I wasn't anywhere near that imaginary car crash!"

One of the other gendarmes told him to shut up, but couldn't totally repress a smile.

The bovine-faced cop was less amused. He put my passport in his pocket and reached for his handcuffs. "You're under arrest."

I pulled out my cell phone and told him I was dialing the embassy. The cop hesitated. The crowd hooted in surprise. It was a new trick for them; they didn't have an embassy to call.

"You lack respect!" the cop screamed.

"On the contrary, I have only used the *vouz* form, where you call me *tu*."

An Anglophone who corrected his French was the final straw. Exasperated, he threw my papers back in my face and told me I was too clever for my own good. This was apparently an insult powerful enough to redeem him. With renewed swagger he turned to berate the assembled crowd.

The taxi-man clapped me on the shoulder as we drove away, "Hey, you argue like a Cameroonian," he said, "I planned to overcharge you, but forget it now."

After months of striving to fit in, I had only to mock a half-witted policeman in order to be accepted.

Raymond squinted at the sun. "I think I will go get a snack."

"What are you having?"

"It's mango season. Mangos."

I walked with Raymond to the center of the compound, where he had left a plastic bag of mangos. The fruit was everywhere; at night the falling fruit thumped in the forest like giant raindrops. We sat against a plank across from a schoolroom chalkboard posted under an overhang.

Rules
1. Take medicine at 9:00 and 5:00.
2. Clean personal space.
3. No fighting.
4. Bathe twice a week.
5. Attend nightly prayers
6. No crossing the stream.
7. No crossing the road.

The letters were written in a shaky hand, and it looked like there had once been nine rules, but the last two, too low to be shielded from rain by the overhang, had washed away. "Can I take a picture of that?" I asked, pulling a little point-and-click from my pocket.

Raymond looked eagerly at the camera. "I've never taken a picture before."

I gave the camera to him and showed him how to zoom in and out. "Can you take a picture of those rules?" He stood up and carefully lined up the shot, trying different angles.

Behind him, a large man carrying a load of wood walked around the corner. His hair was cut in a flat top, and his t-shirt sleeves had been torn off to reveal arms that looked like they had been drawn by a comic book artist. In a single fluid motion, he dropped the firewood, caught one of the falling sticks and flung it at Raymond. The stick flashed past Raymond's ear as the shutter clicked. With a roar the man was upon us, towering over me and dwarfing Raymond. Raymond smiled benignly and lowered the camera. There was a quick exchange in Pidgin and Raymond handed me back the camera. The man fixed me in a hard squint, and I, in an attempt to look away, ended up reading his t-shirt, which advertised a music festival. "That is a madman!" he growled. "You don't give him your things." I didn't say anything. He backed away with a menacing finger pointed at Raymond and I stayed quiet while he gathered his firewood and stalked past us.

Raymond switched back to English and said in a steady voice. "He is one of the men whose task is to beat and control us. He doesn't want me talking to you."

"Why not?"

"Because I am a madman, of course. Just as he said." Raymond picked at the gaps between his teeth during the silence that followed. I couldn't tell if he was serious. He may have been a bit odd, and perhaps he talked in church and wouldn't explain what he knew of economics—but in the time I knew him, he was always lucid. In fact, he was the most friendly, forthcoming, and sensible person I had met in days.

"O.K," I said finally, "But you don't really seem like a madman. Forgive me for saying so, but mostly you just seem unlucky."

Raymond held out an empty hand and a sour look crossed his face. "As I told you, I am a simple man. It was my uncle's witchcraft that drove me insane. The madness is there, even if it doesn't show. Not to you. Not to me. But it is there."

I put the camera back in my pocket. "People write books about that, you know. The insane are insane because they don't know that they are insane. By that logic, I would say your belief in your own madness proves you are fine."

Raymond sighed and spat on the ground. In the sunlight, his scalp shone through his hair. "That's a fun word game," he said at last. "But some of us in places like this require more than that. We must prove our insanity to ourselves."

"How could you possibly have done that?" I cut in.

Raymond pointed at the chalkboard. "Do you see rule number 7?"

"Yeah. Don't cross the road."

Raymond turned and pointed in the direction of the road. "You might think that Pa Ayamah has that rule to keep us from wandering through town. That's not it. Pa Ayamah says that this area is protected. Out on the road, we are exposed once more to the demons that cause our madness. If we cross the road, we go mad again."

Raymond tapped his head. "A few days before you arrived, I went and tested his rules. I'm a madman all right."

After the AIDS vaccine incident, I wrote an e-mail that described the event to my professors in the United States. It was meant to be humorous, but apparently taunting armed police just doesn't strike the same funny chord in the States. I got a call from my Journalism professor shortly afterwards. Rather than saying outright that he felt worried, he told me about two psychological syndromes.

The first was the Florence Syndrome. It's a condition that affects young people—usually artists—when they travel to Florence, Italy. Suddenly they find themselves inside a world that they had only seen in books. All their lives, they studied art printed on a page or projected from a slide. But in Florence, there is no book to close, no switch to kill the projector. They overdose on art. Their brains overload and they lose perspective. The art becomes an obsession, an addiction, as crippling as any drug, and the importance of their lives before Florence slowly fades.

The Jerusalem Syndrome is more serious, and religious, rather than artistic, in nature. People from a culture like America's—only 200 years old—go to Jerusalem and find themselves inside of history. Scraps of the Bible, or the Torah, or the Koran, are made tangible before their eyes. They have no chance to close the Bible and decompress, instead the Bible is all around them, they are inside the Bible. A man with the Jerusalem Syndrome finds himself at the wide road of religious history, the course of which traces its path all the way to him. And what must it mean that all that is holy and recorded leads to the moment of his arrival in Jerusalem? Simple, he is the Messiah.

While my professor talked, I thought of the spring leaves outside his office in Massachusetts and contrasted it with the bare dirt and open sewers I saw from the balcony. Was he really paying five dollars a minute to tell me these stories?

"Let's talk about this other pattern I've noticed," he continued. "Lots of young people go to Africa. But they all go through programs and organizations. They have a safety net, Peace Corps, NGOs . . . but when they cut themselves loose, they change. They become disillusioned, they get mad, they take on Africa single-handedly." My professor paused. I heard static. "They pick fights with men carrying guns. Any of this sound familiar?"

"I see what you're getting at," I said into the mouthpiece, "but tell me, does this particular syndrome have a name?"

His laugh sounded dry across the line. "Not that I know of. But in your honor, we'll just call it the Yaoundé Syndrome. Take care."

"A moth that tastes like copper?" The eminent biologist frowned.

"That's what he told me."

"I really don't know about that. But hey, maybe he was having a seizure when he ate it. Epileptics taste copper and smell burning rubber before seizures. The 'Epileptic Aura.'" The eminent biologist's belly shook with a chuckle.

Raymond stood on the far side of the road and waited to go insane. Nothing happened, and it wasn't long before it was clear that nothing was going to happen. It was all bullshit, the rules weren't worth anything. He was fine.

"Please," Raymond shouted to the empty road, "I have crossed the road and nothing happened. What's more, I will cross it again!" He was almost hysterical with laughter as he sprinted back across the road. Three months of beatings had almost convinced him. He remembered how seriously he had begun to take Ayamah's mumbo jumbo and hooted at the thought.

"I felt like celebrating. It felt wonderful to be so free," he told me later. "It was a wonderful celebration. I knew at that moment that I was cured. Probably there was nothing wrong with me in the first place."

Four times he crossed the road. Each time he proclaimed his accomplishment to the uncaring trees and dusty rocks. Then it was ten times. His voice was hoarse with laughter and he barely had enough breath to keep it coming. Standing in the middle of the road, he raised his hands heavenwards and shouted, "I am free to cross the road. Free to cross the road!"

Just beyond the far side of the road, a stream ran fast and clear over brown pebbles. A young girl had been wading in the water, her red dress turned dark at the hem. Frightened by the shouting, she ran to the nearby cooking shack where her mother was pounding huckleberries. The mother wiped her hands on a rag blackened by kitchen smoke and told her daughter to go inside. Outside the sound of shouting carried across treetops. On top of a bridge made of split logs, a group of villagers all faced the same direction. The mother followed their gaze. A young man skipped and laughed as he crossed and re-crossed the road, proclaiming his accomplishment each time. The women clucked their tongues in dismay, while the men discussed how to subdue him. How sad that so promising a youth could be so hopelessly and so obviously insane.

David Torrey Peters is a writer living in Brooklyn. "The Bamenda Syndrome" won the Grand Prize Gold in the Third Annual Solas Awards and was published in The Best Travel Writing 2009.

AMY BUTCHER

෯ ෯ ෯

Flight Behavior

The annual sandhill crane migration
helps explain why and how we leave.

Ecstatic is not a word I would use to immediately describe Hal, though on a predawn morning in central Nebraska, standing together in an unheated viewing blind along the Platte River, it is precisely this word he provokes. He stands rapt before his camera, his fingers flitting over buttons he'll soon use to focus and zoom and shoot, in clear possession of an enthusiasm I have seen only in the very young, and in this way, he defies expectation. Hal is seventy-six, for one, with hair the consistency of a child's—peach fuzz, fading out—and a hunched demeanor that suggests, regardless of whatever might've come before, a life now lived stuck in stagnation. He is slow to speak, he tells me, and slower still to move. The skin on his hands is translucent, nearly blue, and covered in the minutiae of burst blood vessels and liver spots that conjure a certain sense of pointillism, as if he is a man made of many things—colors and experiences alike—though up close, as he is now, he looks remarkably ordinary.

Ordinary in a sense, although today Hal and I are one with the Earth. This is what was advertised to us on posters—in the lobby, at the front desk, adhered with blue putty to bathroom stalls—and what our tour guide, Bill, reminded us as he led us first through prairie grass and then winding through mulch into these woods where we now stand. It was cold then, unfathomably dark, and carried with it the silence of 4:15 A.M., and so it was with some apprehension that we moved, sluggishly, via a small red laser attached by carabineer to Bill's denimed hip, its beam so subtle in shape and shade that I worried aloud that I might trip.

Hold steady, Hal told me, simply, as if intent alone could do the trick.

We stand now in a place unassuming but miraculous: a small, thatched viewing blind not more than thirty feet from the winding bank of a particularly shallow stretch of the Platte. This is south-central Nebraska, the middle of America, the middle of absolutely nothing, a place that appears, in many ways, apathetic to either coast, thousands of acres of empty farmland giving rise to a Burger King and a Taco Bell, a few blinking traffic lights, and "Grandpa's Steakhouse." But every spring without exception, this town of Gibbon, Nebraska—or, more specifically, the famed Rowe Sanctuary, owned and operated by the National Audubon Society—manages to draw in several thousand people, all of them out-of-towners from the Florida Keys or Cincinnati, Dubuque, Iowa or the Carolinas. They come from Canada or they come from Texas, Washington state or Washington, D.C., flocking by minivan—almost always blue—to see what has been hailed as "one of the world's greatest natural wonders" by *National Geographic* and "one of fifteen of nature's most spectacular shows" by CNN.

Gibbon, Nebraska is right up there with the aurora borealis, with South Korea's Cherry Blossom Festival, with the Great Migration crossing, in which half a million wildebeests traverse the Masai Mara River, which separates Kenya from Tanzania. Just last week, in fact, the *CBS Evening News* aired a special segment on this very place, with anchorman Scott

Pelley offering that it is, frankly, "awe-inspiring." Despite the world's often terrible or grizzly news, here, he said, was a blip of footage "of nature [going] along as planned," complete with its own "rhythm, sound and beauty," dazzling unique and indifferent to humans.

That beauty that Pelley speaks of—the thing that everyone has come to see—appears at first as a swatch of gray, uniform and blurred. There is a prehistoric cooing, a rising noise as the sky fills with light. And then, in one smooth gesture, an estimated six hundred thousand sandhill cranes lift their wings and then their legs to rise in unison above the river, the prairie, and bulbous trees. It is like this every year: for reasons we cannot know, Bill tells us, they select this particular stretch of river, this exact same swatch of trees and yellowed land, as their only prolonged stop in what will prove a several thousand-mile migration, a custom so engrained it is as if a part of bone, or beak, or feather.

I am not from this part of the country, though perhaps this goes without saying. I am from New England, a town thirty miles from a grocery store, a place whose economy thrives from felling timber, a little farming, some welding, some forestry. The woods there are dense and dark; there is no vastness like Nebraska's vastness. There is no kindness like you find here.

Like the birds and nearly everyone, really, my time here in Nebraska is temporary. Unlike the birds, however, I have no final destination—no place I feel my body drawn to. I am young and often feel younger, explorative in the way I think the young cannot help but be. Upon arriving in this state two weeks ago, in fact, I had never even heard of the sandhill cranes, but since then, they are all I hear: they purr in every cornfield, every pasture, every plain. They purr, yes, absolutely; there is no other verb to describe their constant noise. The first time I heard it, it was like a choir—echoing, without barrier, across the infinite and vast nothingness. I rolled my window down, stopped my car along the shoulder.

Nebraska, is what I thought, simply.

And yet while my knowledge of their existence remains relatively new, I take great comfort in their migration. It is one of the largest in the world, Bill tells us, certainly the largest bird migration in North America, and in Nebraska at this time of year, it is all anyone can talk about.

Have I been out to the Rowe?

Have I made my appointment to see the birds?

An appointment, as it were, consists of twenty-three dollars paid in advance for a man like Bill, his carabineer, and expertise.

"Do not talk," he advised us earlier. "Do not cough. Try not to sneeze."

Any movement, however subtle, threatens startling the birds and, beyond disrupting their natural schedule, risks a premature departure before the sun is up for us all to see it.

"How disappointing," Bill reminds us, "how sad to have all of this be in vain."

Our viewing blind, then—and our careful concealment within its hay-stack walls—is of particular significance: we must take on the appearance of the land, because it is precisely the land the birds know and trust.

"Keep in mind," Bill told us earlier, "these birds are far smarter than we even know. We can't even begin to mine that depth."

That depth, he advised us all, is what has brought the sandhill cranes to Gibbon, Nebraska every year for at least the last several thousand. Likely more, he says, even if we can't prove it. According to a poster hanging in the sanctuary's gift shop, the oldest known sandhill crane fossil is an estimated two and a half million years old, or double the oldest remains of the majority of birds still alive today.

"Let's put it this way," he said, "these birds predate us all."

Their antiquity, then, makes them valuable, their permanence a symbol of significance. The land here has been built up, the highway now an ashy stroke connecting eight hotels to another eight. And yet the birds continue coming, and with them, many thousands of tourists who pay great money and drive great distances to stand in a frigid viewing blind and watch them, to bear witness in this way, to take photographs and shape memories and buy postcards they'll soon mail home.

And in this time, the birds gain back over 20 percent of their body weight, just enough to sustain them for the coming months as they travel farther north. It is here, in Nebraska, for these four weeks that span mid-March to early April, that the birds feast and rest, feast and rest. They eat bugs, Bill tells us, rodents, frogs, snakes. They eat seeds and corn and berries and, on occasion, the smallest of mammals. They spend their nights roosting in the river, so recognizant are they that they know that to remain alive is to hear predators coming: coyotes, foxes, bobcats, even the occasional raccoon. When they once again take flight, it is with the sustenance of Nebraska, the sustenance of America, this place that proves the only thing connecting the places they have been—namely, California and Mexico—and the places they will go: northern Michigan and Canada, Alaska, even Siberia.

"Siberia?" I'd asked earlier, standing in the lobby, as we waited for the last of us to pee. That traced geography—to my mind—required a level of concentration I felt unaccustomed to at 4 A.M.

"Yes," Bill said. "Yes. Many will go on to travel as far as Siberia."

Siberia, indeed.

So I have paid fifty-six dollars to see them twice—once at dawn and once at dusk—and I've driven many hours and bought a guidebook and booked a hotel room beside a pool, because I trust, the way humans are wont to, that this payment will translate into experience: into the birds, unfathomably significant, and my place—there, beside them—as they rise.

As a tourist, I learned quickly, it is not possible to lodge within nineteen miles of the roosting birds or even Gibbon—proximity to this portion of the Platte is reserved for Nebraskans who've long owned homes along the river: families, mostly, it seems to me. Tourists are required to stay in the neighboring Kearney, pronounced *carnie,* in their Holiday Inn or Howard Johnson, Wingate, Best Western, or Ramada. There are, in fact, twenty-one hotels in Kearney, all of them seemingly apropos of nothing at most any other time of the year. But in spring, for these four weeks, they create a cluster of illumination— a modern-day Northern Star, instructing tourists where to go.

Kearney makes me think of a man with missing teeth, his denim overalls, his aluminum doublewide. I think broken lawn chairs in the front yard, a Chihuahua that barks until someone yells.

A woman in pink hair rollers, predictable stereotypes, predictable people.

But last night, pulling into town as late as I did at the suggestion of a bird enthusiast I'd met at a rest stop, I found first a Thai restaurant and then a Mexican grocery, an Italian buffet, and half a dozen big-box stores: Target and Best Buy and Wal-Mart, plus a CVS, Rite-Aid, and Home Depot. Here, it seems, is what this part of Nebraska can offer visitors when it cannot offer the sandhill cranes: a good meal and a choice of rooms and your friendly neighborhood pharmacy, all conveniently located just off the highway.

And, when in season, of course, the sandhill cranes.

But it was precisely Kearney's distance that made us nervous—what if we overslept? What if there was highway construction? Which is why, upon arriving a full hour early, I found myself in good company in the sanctuary's lobby. And while one might argue that it is not terrifically easy to make a friend at this hour of the morning, I found I befriended Hal nearly immediately. We were the only two there alone, and we took notice of this immediately.

"Isn't it a little early for someone like you?" Hal joked, implying my young age. Around us, older couples shared single Styrofoam cups of free coffee and embraced for warmth, and Bill began to take roll.

Indeed, our group of twenty or so bird enthusiasts had a median age, I'd guess, of sixty—mostly women in mauve windbreakers and men wearing navy sweatpants with bed-fussed hair. The women's coifs were permed, or going gray, or nearly absent, trimmed so short along their scalp that they reminded me of my brother's buzz cuts—how, when he was small, he'd sit at the backyard picnic table as our father ran an electric razor over his sun-soaked skin, blond hair falling in patches to the hot cement.

These women thought of children, too—they spoke at length about "grandbabies." Their recitals, their vocabularies. Their voices peaked when they found a parallel: Susan's granddaughter in Missouri was enrolled in a jazz and hip-hop class, just like Mildred's granddaughter in southern New Jersey. And *how about that,* they clucked with joy.

These couples were lifelong bird lovers, watchers, amateurs, some, maybe, experts. I was, of course, no bird enthusiast, and in fact, remained rather indifferent about most things. I was the only one of us under forty, having turned twenty-seven the previous month. Hal guessed twenty-five and I felt a swell of pride that when I corrected him, as if those years could really matter. I spent them mostly fumbling, spending money I barely had.

How invigorating, then, to spend the past two weeks seeing what felt like everything: wind turbines churning in silent violence, wind turbines that rest, stagnant, against the sky. I've seen lobster crates roped down to eighteen-wheelers and lighthouses, erect and red against green earth. I am in search of ecstasy, though of course I do not call it that. And yet it is precisely that very term that implies what I am after: a concrete sense of experience, to feel outside myself. The town where I come from expects that all will choose to stay. It is a quiet but crushing confine, meant, I think, to provide comfort, though its comfort does not speak to me. In fact, the idea of lifelong stagnation is so great a fear, I fear it could crush me.

So there is solace in these birds; in their constant, annual movement.

And it is precisely this sense of movement that I have begun to actively seek. These two weeks, I have traveled 1,572 miles, some twenty-four highway hours, and spent the evenings in dimly lit bars at quiet exits just off the highway, and while not ecstaticism, necessarily, I've found the pleasure inherent to these experiences unparalleled to all else I've known. There is a quiet beauty in being lost, in being but one body flitting between two transitory spaces, and Hal champions me for this—how, despite my age and the early hour, I have shown up here regardless.

He says, "Birds aren't normally of interest to someone your age."

A real trooper is what he calls me.

But I am not the only one. At his last count, Bill informs us, the Rowe Sanctuary estimated a hundred and seventy thousand cranes sleeping beside us in the darkness. Two weeks ago, it was half a million, and by this time next week, only a few thousand will remain. It is a predictable occurrence—their departure from these Plains—and it is hard not to envy them for that freedom, how it is *expected* that they will go

Standing shivering against the viewing's plywood, the window covers open, the sound near tangible, Hal tells me he was an army brat—a truth he shares with nearly everyone, he tells me, because it implies a certain sense of impermanence.

"We always lived all over. Every land you could think to live: China and Vietnam, very briefly in Korea."

Texas, too, he says. And he spent a little time in western Florida.

"I didn't much enjoy the heat," he says, "which is why I live now in Kansas."

I think about Kansas and imagine it an arid place, prairie-like and hot. Not tumbleweeds, exactly, but lizards flat like pancakes on the roads, foxes and prickly wildflowers, certainly. Hal tells me that in Kansas, there are no lizards, and that the heat is only cumbersome in summer—the winters, he says, are cold.

"And anyway, it's the change I like," he says. "So I take the few months of heat like I take everything."

This is not Hal's first time viewing the cranes, though it is the first time he has come alone. Next month, he says, will mark the one-year anniversary of her death—his wife of forty-seven years. This springtime viewing of the birds in flight was something they did with regularity; last year, his wife was here to stand beside him, just like all the many years before, and they watched the birds take off together—their wings extended in perfect angles, their bodies gleaning, alit with light.

It was still so smooth in the quiet dawn, he said, that the water mirrored their departure.

"Birds everywhere," he said. "On the ground, horizon, sky."

He explained that during their most recent visit, Hal and his wife learned that the sandhill cranes are believed to pair for life, though their guide conceded it was nearly impossible to trace each partnership from year to year. Still, Hal tells me, enthusiasts take comfort in the birds' likeness: their elegance so much like our own, we flatter, their shared inclination for monogamy. Very few roam alone, and there's a lesson, Hal tells me, in that. His eyes narrow when he looks at me. He stacks his sneakers one on top of the other for warmth.

They are a creature, he reflects, open to love, to company lifelong and migratory, and I, too, prefer this idea of pairing, how the birds can be nomadic and, yet, not alone.

"I met my wife," he says, "and everything about the world I knew changed."

He meant, among other things, his world of impermanence. Unlike Hal, who saw in travel a certain freedom, his wife feared the dangers of mobility—she would not fly, would not board a boat, and once famously called the ranger's station outside of Yosemite to inquire about the road's stability.

"Are they steep or winding?" she wanted to know.

Hal tells me this and laughs; it is a part of her, he says, he learned to love. And it was worth it, all those years, to give up the open road, the atlas stained with grease and coffee, the paper-wrapped hamburger with its softened pickles and grated onions. It was enough to be beside her. But in the eleven months since her death, he has seized his own vitality—visiting first their daughter in San Diego, then their youngest son in Baltimore, and most recently, he took part in an eight-hour, elaborate bird-watching tour along the California coast, a package that promised viewings of more than a hundred and fifty birds. Hal counted a hundred and forty-four, but he says he wasn't about to complain. When I ask him which was his favorite, he pauses.

"Hard to say," he says. Then, "The pelicans."

In June he'll fly to Anchorage to spend four weeks in remote Alaska, camping outside of Denali with his two sons and both their wives. He did the same trip as a young man, he tells me, long before the government thought to expand Denali. It was smaller then; you could sleep beside the mountains.

By fall, he'll be in Maine—more specifically, Kennebunkport—where he'll watch the leaves catch fire, the most impressive display of foliage the nation has to offer. They are colors I know well, and when I offer this to him, he says, *Soon I'll know them, too.*

"The things I never saw," he said. "All these things I never did."

However far from her I am now, I am reminded of a woman I met many months ago on a plane. We sat, stalled, on the tarmac of Charlotte Douglas International; she was but bone beneath her blanket. When finally I inquired where she was headed, her face lit, jubilant.

"Maine," she said. She was ninety-eight, visiting—for one last time—each of her five adult children in their respective homes across the country. Her itinerary freighted her down the West Coast and to southern Texas, to Minnesota and Lynchburg, Virginia. It spanned well over a month, and at its culmination: a nursing home.

But when I expressed condolences, she said there was no need.

"This is just the way it goes," she said, "if you are lucky."

If you are lucky. If you get to live before the living stops.

It seems to me a matter of perspective: the way we choose to think about a life, about a landscape or loved one or circumstance. After all, even from the farthest edge of our viewing blind, Hal and I see only darkness: there are no birds or beaks or wings. We know and trust that they are there—we have a rising sense of their frenetic noise—but without the glint of sun cannot see their multitude, those birds, all several hundred thousand, converging and veering across the Platte.

As we approach our third hour within the warming viewing blind, Bill tells us to, at last, "hush up." Prepare our cameras, he ushers softly. Their prehistoric noise, he notes, has built. Hal pushes his elbow into my stomach, ecstatic. "Get ready," he says—as if I am his child, as if I stand on tiptoes at his feet. As if the very years that have brought him here with regularity have altogether faded away, have rendered him open, once again, to an altogether new experience. Hal is not old or without love; he is, above all, held captive by its renewal, by these birds preparing to rise from murky darkness, however traveled, however weary.

I raise my binoculars to my face and unexpectedly lower my camera. It is not, I know, what matters. I have come to see the birds, and when at last they finally rise, they do so in unison, their wings extended at an enormous length, their density above the river like a churning turbine, roiling quickly, rising up.

A single blade of gray, interrupting this empty landscape.

"Amazing," Hal says to me, and *amazing,* I repeat. There's no way for me to know it now, but three months from this quiet morning, I'll find myself in a parking lot in Fairbanks, Alaska—a place I've chosen to see because of Hal. Nothing about it will seem out of the ordinary: it is simple yellow grass that gives way to birch. But it's here, in Creamer Field, I'll read that the sandhill cranes land, having at last reached Alaska.

And have I heard of them, a stranger will ask? Have I ever heard of sandhill cranes?

"Yes," I'll say, and will think of Hal: there in Denali, many miles south, beside his daughters, beside his sons. Beside the comfort that he seeks—that he knowingly extracts—from the art of movement. I remember the origin of *ecstatic:* that it means, quite literally, "to be or stand outside"—of oneself, one's environment, one's consciousness, I suppose, or in a viewing blind along the Platte, many hundred miles from one's origin.

That day in Nebraska, Hal said to me, "The world requires no audience." And while I could admit that that seemed true, that it would indeed go on without our presence, it seems nothing if not miraculous when our lives align so that we might bear witness.

When we begin to notice, for the first time, that we are not altogether different, or alone.

Amy Butcher is an essayist and author of Visiting Hours, *a 2015 memoir that earned starred reviews and praise from* The New York Times Sunday Review of Books, NPR, The Star Tribune, Kirkus Reviews, Glamour, Cosmopolitan, *and others. Most recently, her work won Grand Prize Gold in the Tenth Annual Solas Awards, earned a notable distinction in* Best American Essays 2015, *and was awarded grand prize in the 2014 Iowa Review Award in nonfiction as judged by David Shields. Her 2016 op-ed, "Emoji Feminism," published in* The New York Times Sunday Review, *inspired Google to create thirteen new female-empowered emojis, due out later this year. Additional work has appeared in* The New York Times, The Iowa Review, Guernica, Gulf Coast, Fourth Genre, The Rumpus, The Paris Review *online,* Tin House *online, and* Brevity, *among others, and has been anthologized in* Tell It True: The Art and Craft of Creative Nonfiction *and* The Best Of Vela. *She is a recent recipient of Colgate University's Olive B. O'Connor Creative Writing fellowship as well as grants and awards from the Kimmel Harding Nelson Center for the Arts, the Academy of American Poets, Word Riot Inc., and the Stanley Foundation for International Research. She currently teaches a range of courses on the essay and literary journalism at Ohio Wesleyan University and annually at the Sitka Fine Arts Camp in Sitka, Alaska.*

LANCE MASON

☙ ☙ ☙

The Train to Harare

A lesson in Africa, circa 1988.

*I*n Africa, we are all children. Everything is new, and
everything is old. The sapling sprouting among the
creepers is new; the forest, old. Though the baby in the *kaross*
sling is new, his tribe is old. The dawn's breeze swirls the
dust over the Magadigadi Pans and is gone, but the ancient dust
remains, the scorched powder of a continent's bones.

The heat of the Kalahari, thick and mighty across this
sweep of gasping desert, has a life force of its own. Like an
animal, it waits, resting, through the African night. But with
the day it stirs, and grows with the sun, gathering power like
a sky-borne fist. It stalks you as you move, watches for weak-
ness. If you stumble, it will thrash you. Show frailty, and it
will murder you. Still, this is Africa, and there are many ways
to die. This is known, but no one knows Africa.

From the Gabarone railway station, Sunday morning,
late October, the sky grades from ink to plum to, in the east,
vermillion. Botswana is well into the dry season. Hundreds
of miles north, in the Okavango Delta, the hippo drags the
smooth barrel of his belly through the mud-strewn grass,
along the swampy troughs that lead from pool to pool, stream
to stream, all of them shrinking. He, like the elephant and the

antelope, follows the receding water, still taking life from the rains that came but now have fled.

But that is north, up where the rivers spilling out of Angola form that broad, fecund, swampy paradise on the skirts of the Kalahari. Here in the south, across the border from Johannesburg, all is parched. The heat grips its human victims, threatens to grind their strength to sand against the desert's stones. Threatens to, but doesn't. For the Africans are at one with the heat, as though with that animal that could kill you and eat you but doesn't because you are one with it. As strong as the heat is, the Africans are stronger.

It was 1988, and I was in Botswana absorbing the hospitality of friends who worked there. It was one of many such trips I would take—and still take—moving, exploring, untangling the twisted shoelaces of my life. I had been up with Dan to the Delta, seen the hippos and the marabou storks and the *tsessebe*, the malachite kingfisher and the bat-eared fox and the mud-encrusted, blunt-brained Cape buffalo, black-eyed and brutish.

Dan had taken a break from his duties with the State Department, and we'd gone from Maun by bush plane into the center of "the Swamp." We bought provisions at the trading post of a mad Australian who lived full-time in this back-of-beyond, and belonged there. At the post we'd found a guide, and the three of us set off—Dan, Kamanga, and I— covering the hilly grasslands by foot and the waterways by *mokoro*, Kamanga's dugout canoe. We'd tramped and camped in the open, swam in ponds that the crocodiles had surrendered, and followed elephant spoor within sight of a lion's kill. Three boys in the wild woods, pure and without purpose. On the best of nights, the horizon danced around us under the blue-white branches of a forest of lightning.

Now it was over. I was back in the bake room of Gabarone, on the platform with my pack, waiting for a train. I was leaving Botswana. The train would take me north-northeast along the border, up to Francistown on the Bulawayo line, then on to Harare. From there I would fly to Sydney, and on to my new job back in New Zealand.

But, for now, I stood in the rising, ticking heat. Dan had dropped me off on his way to the embassy—even on Sunday morning, he had work to do. Our trip to the Delta had cost him some valuable desk time, and now he had to make it up. So I waited in the station's shadows and tried to comprehend Africa.

The wild Africa of storybook, the vibrant, frightening terra incognita on whose verge Burton, Speke, and Stanley stood, staring and trembling with excitement, has long since passed into history. That Africa, the biologic, ecologic, uncategorizable cosmic diversity of forms and species has died, in its skin as well as its heart. The Africa we think we know, or at least recognize today, began much later.

In the 1930s and 1940s, confrontation blossomed around the world between geographic sovereignty and imperialist politics. European powers adjusted to new political equations, and Britain surrendered its jewel, India. The culture of Empire was dying. But the stakes were high here, conflicting interests not so easily moralized or recalculated. Opposing wheels of change churned against each other through the 1940s and 1950s, and ideologies, greed, lust for power, old scores, and the myriad promises of what the end of colonialism would bring all combined to set Africa at large—and African countries individually—on a violent path to self-determination. To this dream called *independence*.

The now-terrible irony is that the exploitation and suppression of Africa, honed by European and Arab interests over centuries, found, in the surge to independence, willing collaborators among black African opportunists and outside con-men and -women. As freedom-hungry Africans threw themselves headlong into their passion for self rule, they too often acquiesced to the charisma of leaders and movements with agendas geared toward tribal and/or individual supremacy. Amin, Obote, Mobutu, Arap Moi, Kabila, Mugabe—the litany of abusers and consequent abuse reads long and sorrowful. Assassination, coups, backdoor deals, cults, civil war, ethnic cleansing, genocide. If Conrad was right, and there is darkness here, it was and is in the hearts of those who led Africa to its current state of decline.

The old black-and-brass steam locomotive snarls and squeals into the station, setting loose in the enervating heat a score of Botswana Railways personnel to scamper or drag themselves from desk to door, from baggage to cart, from cargo storage to track-side dock. Passenger carriages roll in behind the engine, conductors step down, and with no special ceremony, I hump my pack onboard and find compartment C-10.

Botswana Railways wears its livery with pride, only a year into its own independence from National Railways of Zimbabwe. The tan-and-green paint is holding up, as is the serviceable gray leather-and-fabric upholstery on the seats in my compartment. It isn't my compartment, but one I share with two others, both black Africans. He is a minister, in clerical dress, on his way from Johannesburg to Selebi Phikwe. She is traveling to Francistown "on family business." They are both solicitous of my welfare, and we speak of the heat.

Botswana is one of the success stories of independence in Africa. It has no coast, landlocked between South Africa to the south, Namibia and the Caprivi Strip to the west and north, and Zimbabwe and other countries to the east. It has vast expanses of desert, mineral wealth that escaped early detection, and a small native people. The Bushmen of the Kalahari are short and sinewy, not designed by their God for the heavy manual labor that slave-traders to Arabia and the New World were dealing in. So, Botswana was never the exploitation target for outsiders and corrupt Africans that its neighbors were, and it has moved into the current century with a reasonable promise of survival and success.

The train rolls along its narrow-gauge tracks, headed north-northeast, due in Francistown that afternoon. For a century, Francistown had been an outpost for frontier survival, gold mining, and the cross-border trade with Rhodesia. It saw, over that time, uncounted tons of legal, if blood-stained, elephant ivory pass through the hands of the merchants and agents in this sun-seared, tin-roofed settlement. Now, 1988, ivory export is illegal, but rumor claims that hasn't extinguished the trade. Poachers and smugglers move the contraband by other means—bribes, mislabeled goods, trucks by night. But the sins of Francistown aren't my concern. I am a vagabond.

I have traveled by rail in many countries prior to this, through Europe, Great Britain, the Americas, and New Zealand. But, as Botswana's wilderness rolls past the carriage window, I can make only one comparison to these scenes of the great Kalahari. Only once have I seen so inviting a stretch of uninviting country. Twelve years ago, I crossed Australia by train. West of Adelaide, spanning thousands of square miles of sand, saltbush, and desiccation, is the Nullarbor Plain, flat as a page and hot as a griddle. You get a hero's welcome in Perth just for traversing that God-forsaken desolation. Yet, as in Botswana, a certain comfort can be found in its near-emptiness. Knowing that life is actually being sustained, albeit tenuously, by some few hardy species in such waterless terrain makes the place seem less unkind than it appears. And it appears very unkind indeed. For in these deserts, life seems a stranger to the day. At dawn, the disc of the sun slices through the seam between sky and land, and, until it sets on the other side of Earth, your views are of sweeping, barren tracts that appear unmarked by man. The sandscape's reaches are so vast, yet within range of one's eye, that, as a mere human speck, you feel like a grain of soil on Nature's ground. And blessed to be so.

Evidence from anthropology and archeology shows that Africa, before the white man's maps, was a galaxy of clans, tribes, and native nations. It is now beyond modern conception to grasp how diverse and generally functional it was, and today it is too complex to list the factors of change that have brought much of Africa to its knees. If a single statistic could show what is squeezing the continent's breath from its body, it would be one given to me by a fifth-generation Anglo-African. He was a farmer from Kenya with a graduate degree in rangeland management from Cornell University. As near as he could estimate from available research, the black population of Kenya circa 1900 was 350,000; in 1998, it was 35 million. Are these figures true? The first one may be unreliable, but the second one is close. And then consider Rwanda: 2 million people in the 1950s; forty years later, 9 million. These facts alone paint a broad-brush sketch of what faces Africa. Kenya, as it stands, cannot possibly provide the work and food needed for 35 million people. Add to these at least another dozen African countries in similar or worse condition, and the scope of the calamity takes shape in one's mind.

With bursts of steam and whistle, we arrive in Francistown. Around and through the station pulses the street bazaar. Food vendors, trays and baskets on their heads, sashay along the tracks and carriage-sides, selling fruits of all colors, sausage sandwiches, corn snacks, and fizzy drinks. Sweet and spicy food aromas mix with the oil smells of the train. Hawkers sell handicrafts and trinkets—bangles and beads, fabrics and hats, buffalo horn napkin rings. It's momentary commerce, and the traders will survive the day, if not much richer for it.

The black-garbed minister left us at Selebi Phikwe. Now the African lady, tightly wrapped in her banana-flower prints, and with business in Francistown, also disembarks. As do I, changing to a NRZ train, bound for Harare on the line through Bulawayo.

Some socio-economic process about which I can only guess has given National Railway of Zimbabwe very different rolling stock from Botswana Railways. Or, at least, this stock is different. The BR wagons were of painted steel and "sensible" upholstery, evidently designed, assembled, and finished as utilitarian conveyances for people used to the serviceable basics as a way of life. But the NRZ carriage I enter is a traveling Edwardian parlor—walnut wainscoting, carpeted floors, purple mohair and velour upholstery, burgundy velvet curtains, copper washbasins. It is generations old, pre-WWII, perhaps pre-WWI, and was built and outfitted, probably in Britain, for well-to-do African travelers. Then it served exclusively white families; the men, women, and children who had followed on from Cecil Rhodes in the colonization and wealth-gathering of British East Africa. They and their successors had turned Rhodesia, later Zimbabwe, into a farming economy unsurpassed in Africa. Hence the luxury trains, though they were no longer white only, and no longer luxurious.

From Francistown to Bulawayo, I share my compartment with a new passenger, a Zimbabwean man. A large man. A black man. A large, well-dressed (except for his shoes, which were tatty), black man on his way home to Bulawayo. These attributes, as I list them, may seem obvious, irrelevant, or pedantic. If so, consider this, as well: He is carrying twenty kilograms of rice in a burlap sack.

What does all this mean, all this description? I say these things about this man because, in Africa, nothing is superfluous. I tell you he is black and a Zimbabwean so you know that he comes from the historical majority in that country, and has historical reasons to support the current (and still current) dictator of their republic ("leader" would be a poor choice of words, though that black president and his party, only eight years before, wrested Rhodesia-Zimbabwe from its legacy of white rule and white control).

I tell you our man is well dressed because this shows he isn't part of the poor majority of his country. I tell you he is large, because that means well-fed and powerful, things that tend to go hand-in-hand in Africa. The shoes are a different thing. Good Western-style shoes are not for sale in the bazaars and shops here, and good ones get old and show their age and may not be easily repaired or replaced, despite one's station in life. So if his shoes are broken, it means that Botswana, and certainly Africa, is possibly as far afield as this man, this well-fed, well-placed, native African man, has been.

Why is all this relevant? And what about the rice? I'll let him tell you, remembering this was 1988: "While on business in Botswana, I bought this rice. It is becoming difficult to find in our country now, and very dear. It is a disgrace. The farms in Zimbabwe were once the finest in Africa. Everything was here"—he gestures at the expanses of arable land rocking past the carriage windows—"and it was cheap for us. Now we must go to Botswana to buy rice. *Botswana!*" He uses the voice of disgust and derision to refer to his neighbor to the west. It is unimaginable to him that poor, desert-filled, humble Botswana could sell him rice cheaper than his own proud country, that it makes some kind of economic sense for him to haul twenty kilos of uncooked rice back from Botswana to his home in Bulawayo.

I have heard rumors of this embarrassment. From living, working, and traveling in its former colonies and Great Britain itself, I have tried to keep current with the affairs of the Commonwealth. Though it is my first time in the country, indeed in Africa, I have heard that Zimbabwe is gradually slipping away from its once prosperous, well-fed position in the agriculture and economics of East Africa, indeed of all of Africa.

"And not only rice. Corn, too, and cornmeal. Melons. Meat. All of it is becoming scarce and expensive."

What can I say to this man? This is Africa and he is an African. This is Zimbabwe and he is a Zimbabwean. I am a foreigner, a stranger with no more advice or comfort to give this patriot and his bag of rice and his marketplace anxiety than a surprised landlubber, watching and listening to the report of a sinking ship, could give to one of the sailors onboard. So, I ask the fool's question.

"Is the government doing anything about it?"

"Oh, yes," he says, "our government will face this. Our government will take us out of this crisis." He has been watching his country slide past the window in the setting sun. Now he looks at me with conviction on his face, but fear in his eyes. "Robert Mugabe and his people—we can trust them. He will fix this. Mr. Mugabe will save us."

A decade passes before I return to Africa. Now it is 1998, again October, and Michael, another friend with the State Department, is running the reconstruction and rehabilitation of our embassy in Nairobi. In August, more than two hundred people were murdered by Al Qaeda fanatics in the suicide bombing of a bank and the American Embassy. Twelve of the dead were Americans; the rest were Kenyans going about their daily business.

Michael has taken me to the site of the bombing. Nairobi's Ground Zero. The embassy building, now a perforated block of scorched concrete, squats windowless on a busy corner of the city. Plans to relocate it, or at least redevelop its security, had been delayed and delayed in Washington. Beside it, an eight-story commercial building, the location of the bank, is caved in like a dollhouse that's been dropped from a great height. Nearly all the deaths were there. The bombers, blocked from entering the embassy compound, but on a mission for their cause, detonated the weapon anyway and orphaned hundreds of children in a few seconds. Once again, zealotry triumphed over human reason and compassion. Once again, Africa was chosen as a battleground for ideologies, and innocents paid the price in blood and lives.

From Nairobi, I travel south trough Zambia and, once again, into Zimbabwe, where Robert Mugabe is in his eighteenth year of uninterrupted power. Lounging on a hotel patio, I pick up a copy of the *Sunday Mail*. Like most of the country's newspapers, it is government-controlled because, after twenty-five years of "independence" and "self-determination," the Zimbabwean on the street, according to national policy, is not yet ready for free access to the news. The headline story is of a manhunt: a local shaman and his client are on the run from police for having removed and eaten the heart of a twelve-year-old virgin in an effort to cure the client of AIDS.

The traveler, the Zimbabwean man on the train, with the small cargo of rice for his family, comes back to my thoughts. I recall his unshakable faith in Mugabe to lead his country into the light, and I ask myself if there is an ungovernable terrain between Africa and its future.

Lance Mason was raised by working parents, products of the Great Depression. His first job was in his brother-in-law's gas station in Oxnard, California. During school vacations, he picked lemons, packed lima beans, laid fiberglass, sold hotdogs, and spliced cable

for the local phone company where his mother worked. Mason studied at UCSB and Loyola University, where he earned a BS, and then at UCLA for his graduate degree. He has taught at UCLA, the National University in Natal, Brazil, and Otago University, Dunedin, New Zealand. In addition to overseas teaching, Mason has lived, worked, or traveled in more than sixty countries during a dozen trips around the world. His first publication was a piece in Voices of Survival *(appearing alongside writers as diverse as William. F. Buckley, Jr., Joan Baez, Indira Ghandi, Arthur C. Clarke, and Carl Sagan). His work has appeared in* upstreet, City Works, Sea Spray, The Packing House Review, New Borders, Askew, The Santa Barbara Independent, *and* Solo Novo, *as well as several professional journals. Mason's collection of award-winning travel memoirs,* A Proficiency in Billiards, *was published in 2016. This story shared the Grand Prize Bronze in the Tenth Annual Solas Awards.*

⌘ ⌘ ⌘

Ashes of San Miguel

There's bones on the beach. There's ashes in the jar.
Ghosts in the air laughing at fools in the bar.
But somewhere inside, this river don't run to the sea no more.
Give me a sign, amigo, can you tell me,
Did you go down laughing when you finally fell?
— "Ashes of San Miguel" by Roger Clyne

*L*et us begin with death. That is the place that, for me,
everything seems to begin in Mexico, or at least the
place where everything eventually winds up. In San Miguel
de Allende, behind every elaborately carved wooden door,
the specter of death lurks in one of its guises, which are many.
Sometimes death menaces. Sometimes it mourns. Mostly, in
Mexico, it laughs.

To understand why this matters, it is necessary to rewind,
lets say two years, to the onset of my mid-life crisis, which is
not, it turns out, the variety that induces one to acquire German sports cars and sculpted twenty-five-year-old Adonis
husbands, but is instead, the true-blue, perhaps distinctly
American, variety that induces a crippling fear of death.
There I was, sequestered in my sanitized home, diligently

fondling my breasts for ominous lumps, making friends with
my freckles and moles, watching them for oozing or weeping
or creeping, jolting awake in the middle of the night certain
the pain in my right arm was a sign of a heart attack even
though I could distinctly remember slamming it against a
rock during a volleyball game, eating my veggies, riding my
bike, slathering on sunscreen like a mad woman, when the
universe, that mother with an elegant appreciation for beauty
but a sense of humor that can only be described as sadistic,
decided to plop me in the middle of Death-Ville for a month
long writers workshop.

I first dubbed San Miguel Death-Ville when I dropped my
suitcases in my hotel room, which was strangely elongated
and sparsely decorated, but made up for these defects by
boasting a gorgeously tiled bathtub. Also, it featured a heater
that resembled an archaic toaster, with an article posted beside
it titled, "Carbon Monoxide: Secret Killer That Takes Sleep-
ers Before They Awake."

In addition to this melodramatically worded literature
(though I'd be damned if I dared try to turn on the heater,
even if artic winter hit), I saw a painting. I say "saw a painting" as if I had the option of missing it. I didn't. It was an
oil original the size of, let's say, a sofa, hung over my narrow
bed, painted by some authentic Mexican named Smith in
1994, according to the signature. It boasted five figures, four
disturbingly happy clowns and a cackling skeleton (at least I
think she cackled—she seemed to do so mostly at night) wearing a crown of flagrant orange flowers. If you want to get your
blood going, try waking up in a bitterly cold room, shivering
in a narrow bed, to the sound of church bells clanging and
strange birds squawking and the sight of four clowns and a
hippie Grim Reaper leering down at you in the moonlight. It's
a page right out of Stephen King.

Which brings me back to death (not that we ever left).
Death has a long and honored tradition in San Miguel. Well,
death has a long and honored tradition in all places, whether
we like it or not, but in San Miguel, they like it. They celebrate
it. Little laughing skeletons are everywhere, dressed up like
whores and window washers and Elvis, reading and dancing
and laughing. Mostly laughing. Why are Mexico's dead so
happy? It could be because they are never forgotten.

Over margaritas, a Mexican painter told me that death, for
the Mexican, is not an ushering out of the land of the living.
Rather, it is a change in form, the way a river, say, might turn
into steam on a hot summer day. The Mexican dead are still
citizens of their communities. On Dia de los Muertos, the living wander up into the hills where the dead are buried. There,
they offer them gifts, sing with them, laugh with them, dance
with them.

In the next town over, Guanojato, they celebrate Dia de Los
Muertos as well. But there, every day is death day, for every
day, their museums display gape-mouthed mummies and their
churches flaunt the yellowed bones of saints. In Diego Rivera's
house, the guides will tell you that Diego ate human flesh for
inspiration, that he went to cemeteries at night and filched
meat from corpses. He did this because he wanted to get in
touch with his Aztec history, which is featured a few hours
away in Teotihuacán, in the form of crumbling pyramids.

There, you can climb the narrow stairs to sit in the place
where priests cut out the hearts of human sacrifices, offering the still beating organs to the gods in hopes of warding
off apocalypse. Macabre, yes, undeniably so, but history tells
us that many of these sacrifices were volunteers. According
to Aztec religion, the honored dead—warriors who died in
battle, women who died in childbirth, and those who died as
sacrifices—became gods and goddesses. These honored dead
visited the living again and again, in the forms of butterflies,

hummingbirds, bright things with wings. The dead still visit the living in Mexico. In fact, it seems they never left. Mexicans maintain an intimate relationship with death.

I am old enough now to have acquired a mid-life crisis, which means I am also old enough to have made a certain personal acquaintance with death. I wouldn't say that I know it exactly. It mystifies me, haunts me, the way that men did when my skin was smoother, my limbs leaner, my body making an ascent into full bloom instead of gradual descent to dust. I saw death first when I was twelve. I think, perhaps that acquaintance with death was the most positive I have had, for I was not afraid, only fascinated, as I stood over my grandmother's embalmed body, poking her skin, entranced by the waxiness of her skin, the way her face had morphed in death into that of a stranger.

Later, at the age of twenty-one, I stood over another body, my beloved father's this time, minutes after his heart attack, horrified at the bolts of purple that had crept along his skin, at the stillness of his cold chest pressed against my cheek, at the cuts on his fingers that would never heal. We had planned a trip to the zoo that day.

Five years later, I encountered death again as I stood beside the tiny grave of my favorite kindergarten student, two days after a horse's wayward hoof stopped his heart. I was enraged as I watched his mother scream, "My baby, my baby," while they lowered his pint-sized casket into the ground. I wanted to kill death.

I have met death, and though our first acquaintance was cordial, I have come to view him as a thief, a plunderer of lives, in short, a killer. Never have I stood at the bedside of an ailing loved one, watching him suffer, begging for the mercy of death. For me, death has shown no mercy. He has always crept in on jaguar's feet and stolen suddenly what, in my mind, was not his to take. And I have hated him for his work.

If I could, I would pull that leering skeleton from the painting over my bed and slap him.

"Who do you think you are?" I would ask.

And I suppose, he would laugh, maybe adjusting his flowery crown with knobby, skeletal fingers. "I am death," he would say, offering no more explanation than that. He would only laugh, the way he does in the little figurines that stare out at from the carts of street vendors in San Miguel. In a fit of peevishness, I yanked the painting off my wall and thrust it behind my dresser.

But death is persistent. He appeared to me again and again in many forms, in the face of the Aztec god Quexocoatl, whose macabre visage was carved on the walls of the pyramids in Teotihuacán. In the skulls of sacrificed humans displayed in Teotihuacán's museum. In the final tortured works of Frida Kahlo displayed at the Heart of Frida Museum in San Miguel.

The site of this museum is lovely, holding at its core a peaceful courtyard in which one can sit and peruse one of the many featured Frida texts. Around this courtyard, various rooms flaunt a collection of Frida's letters and a handful of her drawings, scrawled on the backs of losing lottery tickets. As a self-proclaimed Frida enthusiast, I had placed a visit to this exhibit at the top of my "San Miguel To-Do List."

My first exposure to Frida was in my mid-twenties, when I was more than open to being impressed by wanton displays of fetuses and feminine sacrifice. As a college sophomore, my teacher, an avid feminist, showed slides of Frida's paintings, and I wept quietly at my desk as vision after gory vision flashed in front of my eyes, each painting doused in blood and buckled with pain. Later that semester, I gave Frida a mental standing ovation and wrote a fiery paper dedicated to the power of her work, the rhetorical equivalent of a resounding, "You go girl."

So years later, when I, now a tenured Frida acolyte, wandered the halls of the Heart of Frida exhibit, I was surprised by my reaction to her childish love/hate letters and scrawled Crayola protests. I was surprised, most of all, however, by the fact that I would label anything created by St. Frida as such. And yet, the only thing with which I walked away from The Heart of Frida exhibit was a resounding sense of pity. No. Pity is too kind. Disgust. I am ashamed to say, I was disgusted with Frida Kahlo, that celebrated painter of indelible images, for her abominable lack of vision, her crippling lack of imagination, her ignoble inability to see anything in life but pain.

And as I walked down the narrow cobblestone streets that led back to my hotel room, with its resident manifestation of oil paint death, I wondered if death had not, in fact, already shown me some small mercy. Breathing the gardenia-perfumed air, listening to the laughter of children dressed in red, watching the slow progress of a mongrel dog contentedly sniffing its way past Kool Aid-colored buildings, I wondered if my current obsession with death had, in fact, endowed me with an unprecedented ability to appreciate life.

Of all of Frida's paintings, the one that is most applicable to my current state of mind is the oil painting entitled *Thinking about Death*. I have been thinking about death incessantly, whether I like it or not. And yet. And yet. Something about the way Frida thought about death, the way that she exulted in the macabre and doused her metaphorical body in pools of blood while her physical body was still working, more or less, made me want to slap her.

"Frida," I want to say to the painting, "you are still alive. Why all the death talk?"

She only stares, frozen in agonized thought, with a little skeletal manifestation of death sneering from the center of her skull.

"Frida, your eyes still see. There are butterflies and bananas and blazingly blue beetles to be admired, and all you do is ruminate on the sewage in the street. Your ears still hear, and yet, you drown out the sounds of the wind flutes, craning for echoing screams. Your skin still feels, and you ignore the cool rain trickling over your shoulders, the wind licking your throat, the sun slipping its fingers up under the hem of your gorgeously colored skirt. I know what you think. Life is pain. Life is ultimately pointless, ending, as it inevitably does, in death. And I know what you mean. I get you, Frida. I am almost as old as you were when you wrote those tortured letters. I am old enough to have made an acquaintance with death. I am old enough to know that life is not all butterflies and wind flutes and cool rain. And yet. And yet. Along with the sewage and the screaming, those things are here too."

My most recent acquaintance with death came only two years ago. It was, perhaps, the most brutal encounter I have had thus far. I could argue, probably accurately, that it induced my aforementioned mid-life crisis. My last encounter with death began with a phone call.

"Hello," I said, and the on the other end, "Tawni, Dea is dead."

Just like that.

Dea was dead, you see, and I threw the phone. Dea, the beautiful one I remember best hip-hop dancing during a lightning storm, wearing a gauzy yellow dress and flowers in her hair. My Dea, the one with the Grumpy Dwarf tattooed on her calf, the Dea who sang like Macy Gray and did a dead-on pterodactyl impression. Laughing Dea, the girl stood beside me in blue at my wedding, the girl who gave me the honor or standing beside her while she gave birth to her son. That Dea. She was dead.

I had seen her the day before, and she had laughed, like always. I had seen her the day before, and hours later, she had hung herself from a porch, at night, watching, I imagine, as she died, the dancing of van Gogh stars. Thirty years of life reduced to a can of ashes, and at the funeral, I saw my own bewildered rage mirrored in the eyes of her nine-year-old son, who found her hanging. Dea was dead. Dead from impetuousness and impulsiveness and unadulterated self-pity. Dead from exactly the kind of self-indulgence Frida Kahlo displayed in those letters at the Heart of Frida exhibit. Dead from a lack, perhaps, of ever having bothered to live

The day after Dea's death, I awoke to see a jade-colored hummingbird flitting outside my window, and I wept, because it occurred to me how lucky I was to be there to see it. A hummingbird, the Aztec symbol of everlasting life hovered outside my window, and I knew that because Dea had never bothered to live, I would live for both of us, sucking up, along the way, enough color and song and sun and love for two.

It turns out that Dea's death has given me, along with a fear of death, an irrepressible love for life. Every breath is a miracle. Every morning I wake to hear the whir of hummingbird wings, I am keenly aware that this day could be my last. And I am thankful all day, for the blazing of the morning sun, for the banging of the lunchtime boom boxes, for the meandering of the evening traffic jams. Yes, even for the traffic jams, I am grateful.

And yet. And yet. During my last week in San Miguel, I woke up in the middle of a black night ripped by gashes of moonlight. I woke up, and my liver hurt. I woke up, and even though death no longer stared down at me from that painting over my bed, I felt him in the room. I felt him, and I worried about the way I had been drinking while in San Miguel, about night after wild night of margarita after margarita after tequila shot after margarita. I wondered if one could acquire cirrhosis in a month.

Staring into the darkness, spinning and dizzy, I held on to my pillow like a drowning woman clutching a floating bit of wood. I held on and wondered if one could fall off the edge of the world. And I knew one could. I knew Dea had.

What scares me most about death is this. Some nights, I am standing on the edge of that dizzy ledge where Dea stood that one night when all of this—the pain and the pretty—became too much. I am standing, looking down, into an abyss that goes on and on into forever, and I am remembering the Sunday school stories about hell, and even now, even after all of these years, I am still that little girl kneeling by her bed, praying to a god that never hears, begging him not to throw his little girl into hell.

I wonder about my Dea. I wonder where she is now, if that night, when she was standing on the edge, and her foot slipped, if she just kept falling and falling, with no one to catch her. I wonder what will happen to me if my foot slips. I wonder if the god that judges after we die was even more cruel, to Dea, to Frida, than I have been, if he judged them more mercilessly, if he cared less about their pain.

I wonder if Frida is in hell. I pray that she is not, because for all of my pretty words, on those nights, after I wake up and research cirrhosis on the internet, after I wake up and stand, hands against the tile, crying in the shower of my little San Miguel cubicle, letting the hot water shatter my skin, after I stand there like that, the pain of my life, the pain of my impending death, washing over me like the water—in that moment, I am Frida. And I pray there is a god who is kinder than I.

The Aztecs, for all of their bloody sacrifices, believed, a tour guide told me, in a kind afterlife. There was no concept of punishment after death. Only heaven. Heaven for everyone, regardless of the lengths to which they were driven when the pain became too much. That kind of death is a death I want to believe.

The week before she died, Frida painted a different kind of picture, a lush montage of watermelons too beautiful to eat, and she called her final masterpiece *Viva la Vida*. And I wonder if Frida, in those last moments, looking back over her pain, knew something I didn't know. Did death, standing there, staring over her shoulder as she painted those last strokes, whisper something in her ear, something sweet and warm that erased those years of agony and made her life, in retrospect, beautiful?

I wonder if Dea, while dangling and looking out over those Van Gogh stars, saw things that I had never seen, beauty unimaginable. I wonder if in that moment, life became bigger for her, if it was like all the stories say, if a tunnel of light stretched out in front of her, out and into forever, and she danced away, through that tunnel, into something too big and beautiful for words. That is the way I want to see it.

Those laughing skeletons, a museum curator said to me, do not represent death. They represent the life of one who has lived. On Dia de los Muertos, people build altars for their dead, altars laden with gifts that symbolize the lives of the dead ones.

For Dea, I would build an altar, an altar decorated with Grumpy Dwarfs and pterodactyls, an altar with a silver *milagro* of a nine-year-old child's hand, an altar to hold that yellow dress she wore that night she danced, laughing, flowers in her hair, under a night sliced by jagged lightning. I would build that altar, and I would sit by and wait for her to fly over, the way the Mexicans say she would, fly over and sweep down, maybe to touch me, maybe to sweep my face with a gentle kiss, a breeze or a raindrop. I would ask her questions.

I would say, "Dea, beautiful laughing Dea, broken bleeding Dea, how did you go down? Did you go down laughing? Are you laughing now? Was that laughing skeleton hanging over my bed a picture of your face?"

❧ ❧ ❧

Tawni Waters's debut novel, Beauty of the Broken, *was released by Simon & Schuster in 2014. In addition to winning the prestigious International Literacy Association's Award for Young Adult Literature, it won the Housatonic Book Award, was named an Exceptional Book of 2015 by the Children's Book Council, was shortlisted for the Reading the West Book Award, and was included on the Kansas State Reading Circle List. It was adapted for the stage by Sacramento's Now Hear This and is being adapted for the screen by Jeff Arch, award-winning screenwriter of* Sleepless in Seattle. *Her poetry book,* Siren Song, *was released by Burlesque Press in 2014. Her novel,* The Long Ride Home, *was published by Sourcebooks Fire in September 2017. Her work has appeared in* The Best Travel Writing 2010, *and myriad anthologies, magazines, and journals. She teaches workshops and retreats at various universities and conferences throughout the U.S and Mexico. In her spare time she talks to angels, humanely evicts spiders from her floorboards, and plays Magdalene to a minor rock god. This story won the Grand Prize Gold Award in the Fourth Annual Solas Awards.*

ॐ ॐ ॐ

The Memory Bird

Bearing witness never ends.

O n a warm and windy July morning, we were headed south on the Partisan Highway out of Minsk, Belarus. Marina, the friend of a Jewish Belarusian expatriate I knew back home in Detroit, was nervous at the wheel of the little twenty-year-old Soviet-built Moskveech she'd just learned to drive, its doors wired shut and a red fire extinguisher skittering around on the dashboard. The car was coughing out smoke as we passed a six-foot-high wooden obelisk topped with a red star that marked the Minsk city limit. Farther on, the road bisected a factory district, then passed blocks of gray apartment complexes that had sprung up after the war on the outskirts of every Soviet city. Up ahead, a goatherd urged his flock along the highway beneath a sign proclaiming: "Pay your taxes. You'll feel great!" Atop many of the telephone poles lining the road, storks' nests were perched like giant straw hats.

Packed into the narrow back seat of the Moskveech were Lev, a sixty-year-old self-taught Belarusian filmmaker with intense black eyes and tufts of white hair ringing his shiny bald head, and Ina, a Belarus State University history teacher who was also curator of the one-room museum of Jewish

History that occupied the corner of a basement near the center of Minsk. Jews now made up only three percent of the city's population, but given that Minsk had been nearly half Jewish before the war, the collection Ina had shown me the day before was alarmingly skimpy: a few dozen artifacts of Jewish life in Minsk that had survived—a treadle sewing machine, a matzo press resembling the wringer on an old washing machine, a lone prayer book rescued in 1944 from the smoldering ruins of the Minsk Ghetto, and a scattering of photographs including one of skulls spilling out from an upended gunny sack discovered at the site of a Holocaust slaughter.

Lev and Ina made an odd pair: the professor in her prim black skirt and bobbed gray hair; the filmmaker with his rumpled slacks and t-shirt, his solid row of gold-capped bottom teeth, and those two clownish puffs of white hair. Neither Ina nor Lev spoke any English, so for the most part, we spoke Russian, which I'd studied as a college exchange student in Moscow back in the Seventies. Marina translated what I couldn't express or failed to understand.

These three would be my guides as I neared the end of a long, winding journey that had led me from my home in Detroit, where I'd raised two sons and worked as a teacher and journalist, to today's destination, Blagovschina Forest on the outskirts of Minsk, in search of my father's, my grandmother's—and ultimately my own—history. The impetus for this journey was my discovery, a decade after my father's death, of documents in a box of his papers and letters, my first solid clues to the fate of his Austrian Jewish family.

But in truth, my journey to wrest my father's history from the shadows had commenced long before I discovered the box of his papers. Growing up with a single mother scarcely out of her teens, I'd known my father only through his letters that arrived, sometimes daily, throughout my childhood. These letters revealed nothing personal about my father.

Instead, they were entreaties that I renounce the materialism of my childhood world and pursue what he called "the Spiritual life." My father's letters were bitter diatribes against that slough of evil that comprised my young world—the schools, the churches, books; my mother, teachers, friends.

My father, Otto Kraus, had escaped to America in the 1930s, a few years before his widowed mother and most of his Viennese family were exterminated. He'd given his first name at Customs as Proteus, the Greek god of prophecy and sea change. As Proteus, my father had earned a doctorate in German literature and had taken a teaching job at a college in Florida. After the war, in what I imagine to have been a tumult of guilt and sorrow, my father tucked Proteus the Shape-Shifter away behind an initial and, as Otto P. Kraus, embraced the rigid, ascetic personal brand of Christianity that he would preach for the remainder of his life. Denouncing this earthly swamp of mortal error that seethes below a plane of pure ideas became his obsession, ultimately replacing even his class curricula and leading to dismissals from first one university, then another.

Defrocked as an academic, my father, by then past forty, had lit out for California with the fifteen-year-old girl who would become my mother. The younger sister of one of his students, the teenager had sat in on one of his classroom sermons and had listened intently. A few years later, I was born—the second of the couple's two children—but before my second birthday, my father had wandered off to begin a new life, taking his message to the streets. I'd been in his presence only twice since I was a toddler.

Both times I'd gone looking for him in the Los Angeles neighborhood where he rented a room in someone else's apartment, I'd come upon my father scavenging through the alley dumpsters and piling into his shopping cart the old sweaters, dog-eared magazines, and broken toasters that he would later haul to the Salvation Army. During each of these visits, my father had insisted that, despite the barrage of letters he'd sent me throughout my childhood, given my mother's worldly ways, he likely wasn't even my father.

When I'd tried to engage my father in conversation, he drifted off to that higher plane, and soon—launching into the same lecture I'd received as a child in his countless letters—he was speaking of the life of the Spirit, "This is your true father," he'd concluded during my last visit, wagging a crooked index finger that, I noticed, matched my own. Soon, he was trundling his shopping cart back down the alley. With a hollowness in my heart, I watched him disappear—a small, dark figure in a cracked leather jacket and his head in a book.

Soon after my second visit to Los Angeles, my father died. "I want my body burned," he'd stipulated in a will discovered after his death. "I want my ashes taken out with the trash."

For years my father's instructions had haunted me, and I'd sought in vain to uncover the source of his all-encompassing bitterness. My first real clue was a yellow cable I found in the box of his papers, informing my father that the money he'd sent for a visa to enable his mother's escape from Nazi-occupied Vienna on a boat to Cuba was forfeit, since Cuba had just then declared war on Germany. The cable, dated December 22, 1941, might as well have been my grandmother's death warrant. The Nazis were already rounding up Vienna's Jews. Before finding his papers, I'd known almost nothing about my father's life in Vienna and nothing whatever about my grandmother, not even her name.

Armed with the yellow cable and my grandparents' marriage certificate, the fruit of patient research by an Austrian specialist at the Mormon archives in Salt Lake City, I'd set off in for Vienna, where I unearthed my grandmother's property documents and, eventually, her 1942 deportation record. As I held the thick ledger in my hands, I stared at the one-line notation: "Berta Kraus, destination: Maly Trostinets." I'd never heard of the place. Returning home, I could locate only a scant paragraph here and there in Holocaust histories describing events that had taken place at Maly Trostinets, named for a village outside Minsk in Belarus, then a Nazi-occupied state in the Soviet Union. Between 1941 and 1943, the surrounding woods had been the site of a slaughter that claimed more than two hundred thousand souls, including Partisans, Soviet soldiers, at least sixty thousand Belorussian Jewish prisoners from the Minsk Ghetto and—according to wildly varying estimates, between forty and eighty thousand foreign Jews transported east from the ghettos and concentrations camps of Germany, Austria, Poland, and Czechoslovakia. Only a handful survived to tell fragments of the story.

The war ended, the Cold War froze, thawed, then froze again; the Soviet Union disintegrated; the Soviet state of Belorussia became the nation of Belarus. But the evil of Maly Trostinets has remained obscure, shrouded. Six decades later, the largest, most efficient Nazi extermination camp on former Soviet territory appears as little more than a footnote, though it ranks fourth among death camps in Europe in the number of Jewish lives it ended.

Later that summer, I returned to Vienna with a Belarusian visa, purchased a ticket to Minsk, and boarded a train, setting out on the same railroad tracks that more than sixty years earlier had carried my grandmother on an odyssey that ended in a forest trench near Minsk. Armed with my halting college Russian, I retraced my grandmother's final journey, determined to confront that tragedy from which—in sorrow, guilt, helplessness or bitterness—my father had turned away. Doing so, I hoped to reclaim a shard of my own buried history.

"Why do you want to go there?" the round-faced young man sitting opposite me in the train compartment inquired in English when I told him I was headed for Belarus. He smiled, adding matter-of-factly, "In that place is only poverty and dirt."

I shrugged. "I have friends," I told him.

That was true in a way. Through my Russian neighbors back home, I'd contacted a local community of Belarusian Jews, several of them survivors of the Minsk Ghetto. These ex-patriots, in turn, had put me in touch with Marina, a forty-year-old Minsk resident who'd invited me to stay in her apartment. As a Jew in an anti-Semitic country, Marina had hoped to emigrate from Minsk to America after the breakup of the Soviet Union when emigration laws had relaxed. But when both of her parents had fallen ill, Marina postponed her trip in order to care for them. Meanwhile, the window of opportunity slammed shut. Emigration laws tightened. Immigration to America became next to impossible. Belarusians could enter the U.S. only by winning permission in a national lottery. Now Marina was likely stuck in Belarus for good.

My young compartment-mate stretched his hand out to me and introduced himself as Tomás. An affable Czech with blue eyes and straw-colored hair who worked for the Subway sandwich chain, Tomás was bound for Warsaw to break ground for a new franchise, after opening forty-two new Subways in Prague that summer.

I inquired whether Subways and Golden Arches had sprung up in Belarus, reportedly the most backward country in Eastern Europe.

"One under construction in the center of Minsk," Tomás replied. "Already they have a McDonald's."

He pulled out his wallet, extracted a folded paper and waved it in the air. "This work permit. It takes me years." He frowned. "I go four times, but I always fly out the same day. If I can catch a flight." The small fleet of Belarusian-operated planes was substandard, he said. They weren't permitted to land in many European airports.

"Too loud," the Czech said. Besides, "Nothing happens in Minsk. Nothing. Economy—worst in Europe." He shook an index finger in the air. "Money—worthless." The red and blue rubles traded by the fistful were virtually play money. "No matter—it's nothing to buy," Tomás added. "They have a horrible dictator too, this Lukashenko. It's like the worst days of Soviet Communism."

A middle-aged man wearing a plaid tie and shiny brown shoes seated next to Tomás had been listening, shaking his head and smacking his lips noisily while using a jackknife to saw off hunks of a pungent salami wrapped in newspaper.

"They brought it all on themselves," he broke in between mouthfuls. In flawless English, he introduced himself as a history professor from Warsaw.

"Wasn't it a democratic election?" I asked the professor.

Brushing bits of salami from his moustache, he laughed. "Yes. Lukashenko won in a landslide. Belarus is a nation of followers. They're too scared to be without Communism, so they elect this guy, Lukashenko—he used to be the boss of a chicken collective." The professor lopped off several hunks of salami and offered them around. A brief nationalist movement had arisen in the early Nineties after the disintegration of the Soviet Union, he told me. Belarusian was declared the national language, and the country set out on the road to a privatized economy.

"But they weren't ready for the breakdown of the Soviet Union," the professor said. "For them, independence was a catastrophe. They saw Lukashenko as their solution." In 1994, elections were held, and Lukashenko received 80 percent of the vote on his promise to recreate a lost paradise. He would revive the old system, restore full employment, provide free health care, and officially reinstate the familiar Russian tongue.

"Idiots!" the professor said, shaking his head. "They were glad to return to Communism. There's no elite in Belarus to form an idea-oriented leadership. The Jews, maybe. But there aren't many now—the Nazis got most of them during the war and the rest fled. Any Jews still there want to get out."

Beyond the country's political and economic problems, Belarusians face a gruesome array of health hazards, the professor added with a look of disgust. Most of the radiation from the 1986 Chernobyl explosion blew downwind from Ukraine into Belarus, contaminating half the country's soil, possibly for the next hundred years. "Much of the food and water is probably still unsafe," he warned me.

As my fellow travelers continued their litany of Belarus' woes, the train rattled eastward, past the low hills and mist-veiled forests of the Polish countryside. Against this graceful backdrop, it was hard to picture Poland's neighbor to the east—backward, unlovely, and swept by the winds of Chernobyl. I envisioned Belarus as an island set adrift beneath a perpetually hovering raincloud.

As if reading my thoughts, the Czech stretched out both hands, palms up, his fingers spread in a gesture of futility. "Nothing there but ignorant people," he said. "The people has disappeared in their minds. They are sheep. No national identity, no history."

But, of course, Belarus does have a history, a tragic history of invasion, partition, and devastation that makes its current troubles appear not so much self-inflicted as the working out of some ancient curse. I'd caught glimpses of this past back in Detroit, while trying to flesh out a skeletal outline of events at Maly Trostinets. For 400 years, Belarus was laid waste by a series of wars before being divided in 1919, the western part ceded to Poland, the eastern becoming the Belorussian Soviet Socialist Republic. During the Second World War, the Germans leveled more than six hundred Belorussian villages and killed a quarter of the Republic's inhabitants. Not only did the Nazi army slaughter most of the Belorussian Jews, Hitler also designated the state of Belorussia as the site of a network of death camps—one vast, spreading graveyard for European Jews. Although the Nazi's grand plan was never fully achieved, one such site had been established in the forest near Minsk: the mysterious Maly Trostinets.

Transports from the ghettos and concentration camps of Europe began arriving in Maly Trostinets in 1942, the year noted on my grandmother's deportation record. Meanwhile, during a series of pogroms and transports to the forest, the entire population of the Minsk Ghetto was liquidated. The genocide ended two years later, when the Soviet Army marched into Minsk.

About this landlocked country of 10 million, the news was still bad. The government was dogged by allegations of money laundering, drug smuggling, and arms dealing to terrorist groups. Yet, in the U.S. the plight of Belarus was virtually unknown outside Belarusian immigrant circles. If Americans knew anything at all about the place, it was probably that Lee Harvey Oswald had defected to Minsk and married a Belorussian before returning to the U.S. to assassinate President Kennedy.

Arriving in Minsk, I slowly came to realize that the name Maly Trostinets, so unfamiliar to the rest of the world, was also virtually unknown in Minsk beyond the city's tiny Jewish community. Neither did it show up on the area map I purchased at a kiosk in the train station.

"I'm not surprised. No one knows about it," Marina told me later when I spread out the map on her kitchen table. She, herself, could not locate the place, she said, observing that Maly Trostinets does not appear in Belarusian history books.

A soft-spoken woman with anxious black eyes and curly black hair, Marina had met me at the train station. As we drove off in the Moskveech that had belonged to her father, we shifted back and forth between languages until it was clear that her English was better than my Russian.

Each time the tiny car sputtered, lurched, and stalled, Marina's face would redden. Her eyes would brim with tears. "I'm not used to driving," she whispered, as we turned onto Skorina Ulitza, the city's main street. At first glance, Minsk wasn't the shabby place I'd been led to expect by my compartment-mates on the train to Warsaw. What I saw through the fissured car window were Fifties-era cinderblock buildings in a clean, though gloomy-looking city, its streets all but deserted at four in the afternoon. In another respect, though, my companions' predictions proved accurate. Minsk was a time trip back to the USSR, beginning with the scale of everything. Skorina Street was seven lanes wide and lined with hulking gray office buildings, the holdover State-run department store monopolies known by the acronyms GUM and DUM (pronounced "goom" and "doom"), and signs plastered with patriotic messages. One billboard extolled Soviet World War II heroes. Another pictured President Lukashenko with his shiny head and bushy moustache.

So, Belarus has simply exchanged one bald-headed icon for another, I reflected, recalling my student days three decades back among the streets and squares of the Soviet Union with their ubiquitous statues and portraits of Lenin. But no, Lenin was here too, towering thirty feet tall above the courtyard of The President's Palace, as the executive headquarters was known. Other post-Soviet states might scrap their Iron Curtain artifacts, but in Belarus, Marina told me, gigantic Lenins still brood over every town and village.

"Do you like it?" Marina kept asking, her dark eyes begging for reassurance. I insisted I did like it. Eighty-percent of its buildings destroyed during the war, Minsk had reemerged as an orderly modern city. But like Marina herself, with her apologies and her pleas for approval, the place felt abandoned. Marina parked the car before a wedding-cake-shaped "Stalin Gothic" building. Cradling my arm, she conducted me to a sundial enshrined in the center of a marble fountain in the building's courtyard.

"Here you can see the distance to everywhere," she said.

Etched around the sundial's face were arrows pointing toward the major cities of the old USSR and indicating their distance from this deserted sidewalk in central Minsk: "Kiev, 573 km," "Moscow 700 km." The implication that the former Empire constituted the world made the city feel even more lost. Back home when I'd told people I was headed for Belarus, their eyes would go blank.

"Belarus?" they'd say. "Where's that?"

"Is that a country?

"Is it in Russia?"

Further on, Marina stopped the car to show me Minsk's only Holocaust memorial where it stood at the edge of a ravine surrounded by maple, chestnut, and linden trees. This was the site of a particularly ghastly pogrom known as "Yama," or "the pit" that was carried out in March of 1942. Replaying Babi Yar, the infamous massacre of Ukrainian Jews that had taken place only six months earlier, the Nazis rounded up 5,000 Jews from the Minsk Ghetto, marched them to the edge of this ravine, ordered them to remove their ragged clothes, then shot them or shoved them over the drop to be buried alive as bulldozers filled up the valley.

Had my grandmother been among those murdered at Yama, I wondered. A fenced-off section of the Ghetto had been reserved for a portion of foreign Jews who were not killed immediately. "It was very terrible for these foreign

Jews," a Belarusian survivor named Galina had told me back in Detroit. "They didn't know Russian. They couldn't speak to the guards. They couldn't speak to anyone." The foreign Jews would stand, mute and starving, arms extended through the barbed wire that separated them from the larger Ghetto. "They held out watches, rings, handkerchiefs, shawls. They tried to exchange anything for food." One woman put gold earrings in Galina's hand. "She didn't realize that we, too, had no food." In winter, Galina had seen the bodies of foreign Jews beyond the barbed wire, frozen and stacked like lumber. "Some of them killed themselves," she remembered. "After a while, we started thinking it was better to be a Russian Jew."

As I thought of that scene from the past, I made out the pale ghost of a swastika on the black marble menorah commemorating the Yama bloodbath. Vandals, probably members of Belarus' flourishing neo-Nazi movement, had spray-painted it here only last month, Marina said. Elsewhere on the monument, they had scrawled: "Holocaust Now," and "Death to Jews."

Incidents of neo-Nazi vandalism had increased in recent years, Marina told me. Earlier, a thirty-liter can of white paint had been splattered over the same memorial. Leaflets accusing Jews of crimes against Christianity had called for retribution. Anti-Semitic graffiti had shown up all over the city. At Jewish cemeteries throughout Belarus, memorial wreaths were often torched and headstones upended or shattered.

That night as I settled onto the red velveteen couch in the book-lined vestibule that served as a living and dining room in Marina's sixth-floor apartment on Kommunistchiki Ulitza (Communist Street), I spotted a globe of the world atop a bookcase. I stretched up and traced the route I'd taken here from Vienna, my finger inching east through Warsaw, then on to the Polish border. But a chunk of colored cardboard had worn off the globe. Belarus was missing. I replaced the globe on the bookcase and scanned the titles of volumes crammed into bowed shelves. There were collected works by Tolstoy, Pushkin, Gogol, and dozens of scientific tomes whose titles I couldn't translate. Later, as we sat at a table pulled up to the velveteen couch eating dumplings and spiced mushrooms, Marina mentioned that her mother had been a radiation specialist at the National Institute of Energy. She'd worked on the cleanup of Chernobyl shortly after the reactor blew up in 1986, then on and off for years until she fell ill with the cancer that had already spread throughout her body. Marina herself had worked in "the zone" for several weeks during 1987. Recently she'd suffered a bout of breast cancer. Her father had died of thyroid cancer the previous year. No one could prove that Chernobyl was the cause of her family's afflictions but, Marina told me, "Most of the people who worked there are dead."

The next morning Marina and I rode a bus downtown to the Museum of the Great Patriotic War of Belarus, where Marina's friend, Natasha, worked as a guide. Natasha knew the location of Maly Trostinets and had agreed to accompany me there. As we walked up the museum steps, Marina again took my arm. "I want to tell you something," she said in her gentle voice. "Natasha is Belarusian."

I didn't understand. Wasn't Marina Belarusian too?

"My country—yes. My nationality—I am Jewish," Marina explained. "Natasha is Belarusian." This was a distinction frequently drawn during my stay in Minsk. Marina wasn't religious. After generations of Communism, few Jews are. But ethnic divisions are carefully preserved. Until recently, Belarusian passports had been stamped with the bearer's "nationality." The stamp on Marina's passport had shattered her dream of attending medical school in the Eighties, and she'd found work as an engineer—a meaningless title, she told me, for her job was entirely clerical.

"Natasha is old friend," Marina said. "As children, we were in school together." But, as a Belarusian, Natasha might not understand my preoccupation with the Jewish victims of Nazi crimes. A quarter of the nation had perished during the war, Marina reminded me. Like most Belarusians, Natasha felt that Jews warranted no special place in a hierarchy of suffering. Over and over during my stay, I'd hear people make such statements with no evident malice or irony. "The War" is the dominant historical theme in Belarus, not the Jewish genocide that had taken place in the country's midst.

Natasha was a slight, pale woman with thin lips and a severe expression, which turned into a smile when she spotted Marina. We would take a taxi out to Maly Trostinets that afternoon while Marina was at work, Natasha announced in English. We would visit the monument—erected out there in the Sixties—that stood on a hill above an eternal flame. "It's a lovely place," she added to my surprise.

The taxi driver shook his head when we asked to be driven to Maly Trostinets.

"*Ne zniyou,*" he said. I don't know.

But Natasha gave directions, and soon we were headed south of the city on my first of two trips down the Partisan Highway. As my eyes scanned the fields of purple buckwheat and yellow cornflowers along the road, I wondered: Was this the route along which my grandmother had once been marched or driven?

Probably so, Natasha said. The old Mogolov Road, renamed Partisanski Prospect after the war, was the only route past Maly Trostinets. A few kilometers out of Minsk, Natasha directed the driver to turn off the highway and wait for us by a marshy field at the foot of a hill.

Natasha and I followed a rutted goat path up the hill past a splintered signpost that spelled out "M. Trostinets" in Cyrillic letters. From a distance, the pre-war wooden houses of Maly

Trostinets, with their vanished paint and sagging ridgelines, had looked abandoned, but as we approached the village, I spotted chickens skittering around the yards and leafy vegetables in the gardens. A pregnant goat lazed in the road. Here and there old people sat on porches or leaned on garden hoes. At two in the afternoon the younger generations were at school or at work, a world away in the concrete city a few kilometers up the highway.

"Was this the site of the killings?"

"*Nyet*," Natasha replied. No, the name "Maly Trostinets" had come to refer to the mass slaughters that took place, not in the village itself but in several nearby locations.

I asked some elderly villagers if they recalled the German camp or the convoys of human cargo passing by on the highway sixty years back, but most said they'd moved here after the war. One man with white hair bristling from underneath a faded blue baseball cap said his wife had lived here all her life. During the German Occupation, she had told him, villagers often heard screams in the night. But that was all he knew, and now his wife was dead. No one else could tell us anything.

As we walked back down the hill toward our waiting taxi, I was startled by an ominous, loud clattering—like the rattle of a machine gun. When I turned to Natasha in alarm, she laughed and pointed toward a stand of wiry brown reeds where a white stork stood, its head thrown back, breast feather puffed up, mandibles clacking.

"This bird brings good luck," Natasha said.

With the state of things in Belarus, I thought as the stork flapped its black-fringed wings and glided away, luck was the most its people could hope for. But I kept this to myself. Natasha plucked some reeds and held them out to me. These were the hollow "*trostniki*" for which the village was named, she told me, adding, "This is the plant of the Bible. The baby Moses was found among *trostniki*."

Back on the highway, our taxi passed stretches of birch and pine forest and fields carpeted with dandelions and feathery Queen Anne's Lace. Had my grandmother died on this road, I wondered. At sixty-eight, she might well have been among those too old or sick to walk, who were crammed into gas vans known in the Ghetto as *"dushagubki,"* or soul killers. Survivors remembered watching from behind the barbed wire as they passed—black metal boxes on wheels marked with the letters "MAN," the name of a German truck manufacturer. Their tailpipes were rigged to spew asphyxiating fumes back up into the box.

Had this been Berta's fate? Or had she already died before reaching Minsk, suffocated in an airless freight car along the way? Or perhaps my grandmother had been among the multitudes shot at the edge of the long forest trenches discovered after the Nazis' retreat. I still hadn't seen those trenches.

"Where are the graves?"

As if in reply, Natasha instructed the cab driver to turn off the road, and we entered a clearing. At the foot of steps leading up a grassy hill to a monument sat a stone cauldron the size of a truck tire.

"The eternal flame," Natasha explained. But the cauldron held only sand.

A black marble column atop the hill commemorated "More than two hundred thousand victims of Nazi crimes—Partisans and soldiers of the Soviet Army and local inhabitants."

No mention of Jews.

"They were local inhabitants too," Natasha said sharply.

As I opened my mouth to protest, the clanging of a bell distracted me. A cow was tethered to a nearby pine alongside a meandering path through the woods.

"The graves were here?" I asked, gazing into the distance where a flock of goats was grazing along the path.

"*Nyet. Nyet.*" Natasha shook her head. "This monument is not in the right place." The actual site of the mass graves was "a filthy place a few kilometers down the road." Scrunching up her nose, she refused to take me there.

That evening back at Marina's apartment in Minsk, Lev, the filmmaker with the wild Einstein hair, showed me the right place. When I again smoothed out my wrinkled map on Marina's table, Lev's finger stabbed at the blue mapmaker's stamp that recorded the city's population, latitude, and other vital statistics.

"That's where it is," he said. "You think the placement of the stamp there is a coincidence? No." He turned to me, his bushy eyebrows raised. "They hide the graves, the disgrace."

Several years back, Lev had gone to the site of the graves and filmed a documentary about Maly Trostinets. But the documentary had never been shown. State-controlled television refused to air it.

When I asked him why, Lev sighed heavily. Up went the eyebrows. He would give me a guided tour of the spot beneath the mapmaker's stamp. "You will not believe it," he said in Russian, slamming his palm down with a thump on the wobbly kitchen table. "With your own eyes, you will see." Then, promising to return on Friday, he marched out the door of the apartment. Marina turned to me with the bewildered look she frequently wore. Lev's combat boots sounded on the stairs.

On the warm, blustery morning of Lev's guided tour, I was again headed down the Partisan Highway, the same road Natasha and I had taken two days earlier. Marina was driving, with Lev in the back seat. Ina the historian made up the fourth in our group crowded into the little Moskveech.

I would finally see the mass burial site known as Maly Trostinets, Lev assured me—the place where my grandmother lay buried. The place Hitler had designated as the first of what was to have been a network of mass dumps for the human trash of Europe. But, Lev added, in the same mysterious tone he'd affected in Marina's kitchen, it wouldn't be what I expected. Again, he declined to elaborate, merely repeating what he'd told me that night: "With your own eyes, you will see it."

Like virtually every Belarusian Jew, Lev had more than a professional interest in the site of the documentary I would view only later. Although he himself had survived the war and the Jewish genocide by fleeing with his mother and sister to Kazakhstan, Lev's aunts, uncles, and grandmother had been prisoners of the Minsk Ghetto, as had Marina's and Ina's extended families. Their remains doubtless lay with my grandmother's in the depths of Blagovschina Forest, which was the basis of our unspoken kinship.

We passed the path to the village of Maly Trostinets, where the old man had told Natasha and me of screams in the night. Before us, beyond a field of dandelions, a fleet of canvas-covered trucks disappeared as they headed into a dip in the road, then reappeared as they climbed up the other side.

"Turn around. Look," Lev barked as the Moskveech topped the hill and headed into the dip. Peering out the car's rear window, I saw only the sloping road. "Because of this hill, a boy survived," Lev said, as the Moskveech emerged from the dip and the dandelion field reappeared. Then Lev told the only tale I'd ever hear of escape by a prisoner bound for the killing ground at Maly Trostinets.

"Two brothers were in the back of a truck. One little boy and his brother," he began. "The truck was carrying them to Blagovschina. The older boy knew they would be killed. The truck reached the top of that hill." Lev glanced back over his shoulder. "The big boy lifted up his brother. He heaved the little boy into the field by the roadside, just as the truck started down the hill." The soldiers in the truck's cab had seen nothing. The boy was found by Ghetto escapees hiding in the forest. Lev could attach no name to this story he'd heard while gathering material for his film, but if it was true, that dip in the road had provided the little boy his miracle.

The horrors of the Minsk Ghetto had been kept alive by a few thousand survivors. I'd even heard a tale of escape from the tangle of corpses in the Yama pit. But silence surrounded the gruesome events in the forest. There was only this wisp of a story. In the absence of human memories to draw on for his film, Lev had combined scenes from the present-day landscape with a voice-over narration pieced together from interviews with villagers and from a handful of uncirculated documents. These papers had been discovered by Ina's university colleague in the Belarus National Archives in 1995, a year after Russia had turned over the records of the former Soviet state to the new nation of Belarus. But when Belarus' state-controlled television stations had refused to air Lev's documentary, the silence surrounding the forest killings settled back in.

This silence puzzled me. Maly Trostinets had been a Nazi crime, not a Russian one. The Soviet state that had sometimes collaborated in Nazi crimes against Jews no longer existed. I studied the web of splattered insect corpses on the windshield, wondering: Why would the government of Belarus be reluctant to expose the sins of another country, another era? Why would they deny the physical reality recorded in Lev's documentary? Why had the film been banned?

"Three reasons," Ina began in her professorial voice. "First, this film is about Jews. Soviets hated and feared Jews. Soviet hatred of Jews was the same as Nazis', and this anti-Semitism persists today in Belarus in both subtle and not-so-subtle ways." By "subtle" anti-Semitism, Ina meant, for example, the kind of discrimination that had ended

Marina's dream of attending medical school in the Eighties. "Not-so-subtle" examples included the desecration of Jewish cemeteries and the ominous graffiti smeared across the marker at Yama.

"You saw the memorial—the swastikas," Ina said. "No one was punished. The authorities ignore such things. They maintain the illusion that nothing bad happened. Lukashenko has declared that he admires Nazi order and that we can learn from Hitler."

Not until the archival material turned up in the mid-Nineties had government officials conceded to Minsk's tiny Jewish community that Maly Trostinets had been a mass murder primarily of Jews. "It is time to tell the truth," Ina's colleague had written after viewing the archival documents. "Most of the victims were prisoners of the Minsk Ghetto, along with foreign Jews from the many countries of Central and Eastern Europe."

The documents also testified that the foreign Jews transported to Belarus in 1941 through 1943 had shared my grandmother's fate. Nearly all met their deaths at Maly Trostinets. Out of perhaps eighty thousand Jews imprisoned in the Minsk Ghetto, "Only several thousands of Belorussian Jews survived," one report concluded, "and only a few dozen foreign Jews survived." But the documents concerning Jewish deaths at Maly Trostinets had never circulated in Belarus, and the film Lev made, based on these documents, had been squelched.

"Anti-Semitism," Ina said. "But this is only one reason Lev's film cannot be shown." She cleared her throat. "Second reason," Ina resumed in her efficient tone. "People aren't familiar with what happened at Maly Trostinets. It was hushed up." In Belarusian history, the Jewish Genocide doesn't exist. The Soviet government blocked access to information and failed to raise the matter during the post-war Nuremburg Trials.

Here was another piece of the story that made no sense to me. What motive could the Soviets have for protecting the Nazis who had betrayed their trust, occupied their land, and slaughtered millions of their citizens? Why hadn't the Soviets raised the issue of Maly Trostinets at Nuremburg? Why had they protected a Nazi secret?

"Understand," Lev replied, leaning forward from the back seat, "this was not just a Nazi secret." He paused and turned to Ina, who was polishing her glasses with a handkerchief.

"The official number of people killed at Maly Trostinets is 206,500," she said.

"Yes." I'd heard that figure before, seen roughly that claim earlier in the week, chiseled into the monument looming above the dead eternal flame. Though Jews weren't specifically mentioned in the inscription, this number presumably included most inhabitants of the Minsk ghetto, as well as Soviet soldiers, Partisans, and all the foreign Jews.

But according to documents unearthed in the National Archives, Lev explained, human remains in the forest told a far different story. A sheaf of reports dated July 14, 1943, just two weeks after the Occupation ended, described the uncovering of thirty-four mass graves concealed with pine boughs—some of these graves fifty meters long. After measuring the graves' grisly contents, the investigators concluded that the remains of 476,000 people were buried in the forest around Maly Trostinets, vastly more victims than could be accounted for by the ghetto dead, the transport records, and the estimates of others the Germans had killed in the forest.

"That's more than twice the official figures," Lev said, stabbing his index finger in the air. "But the Soviet government prohibited the publicizing of this information."

"But these were German crimes," I repeated. "Why would the Soviets want to hide them?"

"Because," Lev said, "this number also includes victims of the Soviet Secret Service of the Thirties."

For years before the war, the territory alongside the highway on which we were traveling had been guarded by secret police, later known as the KGB. While making his film, Lev had interviewed elderly citizens of the nearby village, who remembered hearing frequent gunshots in the night during those years. Around the gravesites, Lev had found dozens of cartridges from pre-war Soviet weapons.

Ina nodded. "Stalin's police had used Maly Trostinets as a killing place in the forest, where the bodies were easily hidden. This was part of the mass extermination of the Intelligentsia whom the Soviets were so afraid of."

"You see," Lev said, "the Nazis came to a place already well prepared for killing Jews. Stalin's police were at Maly Trostinets before the war and killed a lot of people. The revelation of Nazi crimes would have unveiled Soviet crimes as well. So, at Nuremberg they didn't broach the subject."

Whether or not the 1943 estimates were accurate, I thought, if Blagovschina Forest had been a dumping ground for the bodies of political dissidents well before the Nazis arrived, the Soviets had a powerful motive for sealing their files on Maly Trostinets.

Lev nodded. "All during Soviet power, no one spoke of Maly Trostinets."

"The Soviet era is over," I protested. "Belarus isn't responsible for Soviet crimes, but still, this silence persists. Why?"

I turned to Ina. "You referred to three reasons why Lev's film was banned." I'd only heard two. First, the documentary would be unwelcome in an anti-Semitic country. Second, the long history of official erasure had kept Maly Trostinets out of the cultural memory.

"The third reason?" I asked.

"Yes, there is something else." Another reason the documentary cannot be shown. Another reason why Maly Trostinets remains a cipher, even in post-Soviet Belarus. Ina glanced at Lev.

"As you'll see," he said, "the location of the graves would be an enormous embarrassment."

Eleven kilometers southeast of the city, we reached the section of Blagovschina hidden beneath the blue stamp on my map. We turned left at an opening in the woods and followed another convoy of trucks with canvas-covered beds, like those we'd noticed out on the Partisan Highway. As, raising clouds of dust, the trucks lumbered along a rutted dirt road through the forest, I heard the faint rumbling of heavy machinery.

Enveloped in dust, the little Moskveech rattled along—past an empty sentry box with a sign reading "WARNING! NO TRESPASSING" in red foot-high Cyrillic letters—into the cool dimness of the forest.

I felt a surge of nausea as the thick, pungent stench hit. My hands went up over my ears as the grating and clanking grew louder.

"Shut your window," Lev barked, and I wound the handle tight, muting the noise and reducing the stink, just before we emerged from the forest into a vast clearing where we beheld entire mountain ranges of garbage and trash. Ahead, the trucks turned left to labor up a steep path toward the crest of the nearest trash mountain.

Here was my answer. The third reason why the Belarus government still protects the secrets of Maly Trostinets. The Holocaust killing field is now the Minsk city dump.

We breathed in the thick airless vapor and stared in silence as the convoy of trucks crept up the steep incline, then tipped the city's rotten cabbage and rusted fenders and broken chairs and dead cats onto the graves of Maly Trostinets. Somewhere deep beneath those heaps of trash, along with the bones and ashes of those quarter-, maybe half-million other souls, lay my grandmother Berta's remains.

We parked near the foot of the nearest garbage heap. Marina stifled a sob. "All those people," she whispered.

I'd anticipated that I'd grieve too when I first saw the site of my grandmother's murder, but I only felt numb. The scene through the rolled-up car window felt unreal, like an abstract painting: jagged lines, grids, fractured geometric shapes, mixed with splotches and smeary curves. Muted whites, grays and browns accented here and there by glints of light and blotches of darker hues; the psychedelic swirl of an oil slick on a puddle. Splatters and webby lines of blue around the base of one slope created a mottled effect, like a canvas by Jackson Pollack. A tangle of wire spilled over a ravine. Here and there, vapor rose from the earth and drifted like smoke.

Suddenly, the air was full of shrieks and vibrating wings as a flock of gulls appeared overhead.

Ina peered up at the birds, shading her eyes from the late morning sun. "*Surrealischeski!*" she cried.

"Hitchcock," shouted Lev, the filmmaker.

The gulls had shattered my protective shell of abstraction. As they rose in a mass and receded behind another trash mountain, the scene grew more real, more solid, my impressions specific. My stomach churned as I stared at brown liquid seeping from festering pools on the ground. Rot and dust and the sulfurous vapor of methane hung in the air. Coils of smoke rising from fires scattered over the mountains added the acrid odor of burning paper and wood to the sting of soot seeping through the car's cracked windows. Identifiable objects came into focus: twisted fenders and mufflers scattered over the clearing, a rag snagged on a piece of metal, rippling in the wind like a tattered flag.

Gradually, the people emerged. Of course, they'd been there all along, standing ankle-deep in muck near the base of the mountain—bent women in ratty headscarves and ill-fitting dresses, men in baggy trousers, one with a shirt tied over his nose and mouth like an outlaw. Further up, other clusters of scavengers sifted through the avalanche of trash. The pronged maw of a steam shovel scooped up thick sludge. A bulldozer knocked around tires, oil drums, and unidentifiable large objects.

Lev leaned forward from the back seat and called to Marina, who'd closed her eyes and was holding her head in her hands. He gestured toward the path the trucks had taken up the mountain. Hands trembling on the wheel, Marina aimed the Moskveech toward the path, and we plowed our way up on a carpet of trash.

"*Koshmar*," Marina whispered, "nightmare."

I doubted the car would make it up the steep grade, but I kept my mouth shut. Lev was aiming for the full effect, directing the scene he'd wanted the world to witness, the memory he'd tried to snatch back from oblivion.

Marina shifted gears. The Moskveech rattled and wheezed and, miraculously, kept climbing.

A dozen yards from the summit, a tire sank into the mud. The engine stalled. Lev draped his camera strap around his neck, unhooked the door's makeshift wire fastener, and leapt out.

"Follow me," he hollered theatrically as he sprinted the remaining yards up the mountain. Turning up the collar of my shirt in a hopeless attempt to cover my nose and mouth, I stepped from the car into a welter of foul-smelling feathers and took off behind Lev, nearly tripping over the rusted springs of a mattress. Marina was soon at my side, pressing the hem of her flowered blouse to her nose, while Ina kept guard at the car like a getaway driver. We stirred up black columns of flies that settled again like soot as we passed.

Here and there, gulls and yellow-billed starlings feasted on scraps of food, mixed with splintered wooden slats and leaves and paper—the whole mess strewn with ashes and chicken feathers. The wind picked up, scouring the outer layer of trash on the summit, where machines, like mindless gladiators, kept scraping and dragging and smashing. Our presence was ignored. The ecosystem of the dump toiled on—fire and methane, machinery and scavengers—all oblivious to the invaders scaling the hill and the little car stalled on the path.

When Marina and I caught up with Lev, he was standing at the edge of a cliff paved thick with bird droppings. The cliff overlooked a half-dozen more trash mountains. Lev was peering through a veil of blowing paper and plastic bags toward the city spread out in the distance, its wedding-cake buildings shimmering in the heat.

On the outskirts of Minsk, beyond the apartment blocks, the countryside stretched to the horizon, a peaceful mosaic of deep blues and greens. With the hand that held his camera, Lev made a sweeping gesture. "The graves are all over this place." The forest around and beneath the dump was riddled with burial trenches. During his filming, he'd discovered vast caved-in gullies nearby in the forest that grave robbers had ransacked for treasure. He'd found scraps of clothing, combs, toothbrushes, and many bullet casings. Once he'd unearthed a boot with a cache of coins, provision for a future, stitched into the insole.

"How long has the dump been here?" I asked in Russian.

"After the war," Lev said. He raised his camera, snapped a photo of the vista. "Right after the war they made this dump."

"But why? Why exactly here? Right over the graves?"

Lev's bushy eyebrows shot up. He shook his head. "This site wasn't chosen at random," he said. "Remember, this was an area the Soviets wanted to keep quiet about." It was the site of many political assassinations. Locating a dump here after the war was part of the cover-up, part of the scheme to keep people out. Just after the war, the forest had been isolated, supposedly as part of a military project. It had been surrounded with barbed wire and posted with signs that ordered, "STOP. NO TRESPASSING. THEY SHOOT HERE."

"That gave the impression that the place was a military shooting range," Lev said. "But no, it was already a dump. They didn't want people nosing around here."

I recalled the memorial a few miles up the road, the marble column on the hill I'd visited with Natasha.

"Is that why they set up that monument so far from the graves?" I asked Lev. "They didn't want people coming here?"

"*Da, da,*" he said, nodding vehemently. "The monument was erected in a place that's got nothing to do with the killings."

The three of us stood gazing over the city, the sun warming our backs, until Lev pointed down the slope, where a man was trudging across the path near the car, rooting out objects and dropping them into his sack. Lev jogged toward the man and called out a greeting. Marina and I tagged along close behind. As the man glanced up with expressionless red-rimmed eyes, my heart raced. The spirits of the place felt suddenly close by. Without a word the old man sloshed on across the mountain in his yellow rain cap and oversize boots.

"He's deaf," Lev said offhandedly. "I don't think he heard me."

As I watched the old man's figure receding, his yellow cap blurring into the rubble, I thought of my father, Proteus, the old shape-shifter, and my final glimpse of him vanishing down the alley pushing his cartload of relics. Although Proteus could not have known of this place, he must have understood what had befallen his mother after his failed rescue attempt. Perhaps his efforts to save my grandmother had been half-hearted. Maybe he'd waited too long. When the agent's yellow cable arrived in 1941, Proteus must have felt himself his own mother's murderer. Was this the image in the mirror that he fled? The unbearable knowledge that drove him from one protean incarnation to another and ultimately turned him away from the world?

"I want my body burned," his will had read. "I want my ashes taken out with the trash."

Shrieks filled the air, disrupting my reverie. A fresh cloud of gulls dove and receded, dove and receded, their sharp cries adding an eerie counterpoint to the low-pitched rumbling of machinery.

Lev had wandered away from Marina and me. He was snapping pictures—a box tumbling by, the clean-picked skeleton of an animal—a cat perhaps or small dog, a drift of feathers, a cart-wheeling newspaper. He scooped up a dirt-filled jar from the rubbish, shook out the dirt, and trudged back toward the summit, stooping now and then to ferret out some small fragment and drop it into the jar.

The earth was slick underfoot, and Marina slipped as we clambered down the mountain to meet Lev. I took her hand, helped her up. Her hand was cold, trembling.

"I feel it through my shoes," she murmured. Her soft voice trailed off. I felt it too. Numbness was gone, replaced by what I can only call an aching homesickness. We were standing on the horrors of history, leaning against one another in silence. There were no words for it.

Suddenly a shout rang out, and a thick, uniformed figure appeared from behind some barrels. The guardian of the dump. What had taken him so long? A nightstick dangled from the man's belt. Sunlight glinted off a badge on his navy blue shirt. Dark glasses masked his eyes. The man shouted again and hurried toward Lev, one hand hovering above his hip like a cowboy about to quick-draw.

A few yards from Lev, the guard stopped and shouted again. Lev glared back, eyebrows arched sardonically.

The guard stepped forward, white-knuckled fists hovering above his hips, but Lev stood rooted to his spot, looking like a giant glittery-eyed bird with his beaky nose, his tufts of white hair flapping in the wind.

With one hand the guard reached for his nightstick and flourished it, lunging forward and grabbing the strap of Lev's camera with the other hand.

Still clutching the jar and his camera, trying to free the strap, Lev lowered his head like a bull and butted the guard. Marina and I hung back a few yards. I glanced down the slope, gauging the distance to the car.

The guard slammed Lev on the shoulder with his stick, but Lev wouldn't let go of his camera.

From down the path came the sound of an engine starting up. Ina had started the car, and managed to turn it around. She was backing up toward us.

Hearing glass shattering, I turned to see Lev, still clutching his camera and strap in one hand. His other hand was empty. Near the guard's feet, shards of Lev's jar of relics were scattered along with its contents—fragments of newspaper, a length of green ribbon, a twisted spoon. The guard's beefy face twisted with rage.

"Run to the car," Lev shouted, unnecessarily. Marina and I were already running, with Lev close behind, snapping pictures as he ran.

Once we were all in the car, Ina coasted down the path toward the foot of the mountain, the red fire extinguisher bouncing around on the dashboard, the wipers flapping, scraping grime from the windshield. Gasping, Lev laughed like a madman. Suddenly, we were all laughing hysterically, though at what I wasn't sure. Lev pointed at the guard, who stood on the crest of the mountain, waving his stick like a Keystone Kop.

"What does he imagine he's guarding?" Lev wondered between snorts of laughter. "What does he think he's guarding with his ridiculous uniform?"

Shoulders shaking with laughter, Lev worked the wires to secure the broken passenger door. "What the hell does he think he's guarding?" he repeated. "He probably doesn't even know!"

We laughed all the way to the foot of the mountain, where Ina stopped the car. We all fell silent then, and turned back for one final look.

"*Koshmar*," Marina whispered from the back seat. "Nightmare."

"History," corrected Ina, the historian.

As we reached the clearing and headed back toward the road, a fresh wave of gulls wheeled overhead. I turned to watch their winged shadows flickering over the mountain of trash. I still heard their cries, growing fainter and fainter, as the Moskveech bumped along past the guardhouse with its looming "STOP. NO TRESPASSING" sign, and on through a half-mile of sunlight-laced forest.

As we turned back onto the Partisan Highway, Marina tapped my shoulder and pointed to the cloudless sky. A stork was gliding toward us, silently, white head and neck extended, black tail feathers spread, its long legs trailing like streamers. Ina stopped the car, and we watched the stork as it coasted down to a giant nest at the top of a telephone pole, folding forward like a hinge as it landed.

"This bird is our national symbol," Marina reminded me. "We say it brings happiness."

I smiled. "Does it bring babies too?"

"Yes, we also have this story," Ina said. "There are many legends about the stork, all happy ones. The stork is the bird of hope. And, perhaps because they return to the same nest each year, there's a legend that storks brought to mankind the gift of memory."

Hearing this, Lev again burst out in laughter.

"Memory," he muttered. Then, shaking his head, he added bitterly, "Our national bird."

I considered Lev's comment as I watched the stork settling onto its enormous nest. I'd come in search of my own history to a place where there were no historical records. I'd sought a memory in a land where the campaign to vanquish memory had been waged for over six decades. Before retreating from Russia in 1943, the Nazis had torched all their records, then dug up their victims' bodies and burned them as well to destroy the evidence. For the next half-century, the Soviets had carried on that campaign, blotting out even the memory of those erasures. When the Soviet Empire disintegrated, Belarus had been cast adrift, like that piece of colored cardboard missing from Marina's globe where her country should be. Now its leader clutched the helm of State with a rusty iron fist and protected the secrets of two dead empires. My journey to wrest a memory from the shadows had led me to this land where nobody remembered.

To conjure my grandmother into memory required something unshifting—a place, an image, a solid fact, yet the site of her murder had also been banished, buried beneath mountains of trash, then further obscured by the official blue stamp on the city map. My father, too, had rejected the past, even cast off his name, renaming himself after the shape-shifter of Greek mythology. To Proteus, memory had also become the enemy.

As we returned to the road and headed back toward Minsk, I watched the stork though the car's rear window until it was out of sight. I pictured my grandmother, Berta, as she may have looked as a young woman—her eyes maybe green, like mine. Maybe full of hope. But all I know of her story is that it concluded somewhere beneath those mountains of relics, layer upon layer of relics, flung away to rot or to burn or to blow, feather-light, in the wind.

Carolyn Kraus is Dorothy Lee Collegiate Professor of Journalism and Screen Studies at the University of Michigan-Dearborn. Her essays have appeared in The New York Times, Partisan Review, The Antioch Review, Threepenny Review, *and elsewhere. She has written as "Our Far-Flung Correspondent" for* The New Yorker, *and as an op-ed contributor to* The New York Times. *This story won the Grand Prize in the Fifth Annual Solas Awards.*

BILL GIEBLER

*≫ *≫ *≫

The Tea in Me

Transformation can be a long process.

PACKING

It looks like a dance floor, a thirty-foot-square section of smooth wood among the rough planks that make up most of the flooring, all surrounded by giant locomotive-like drying machines. I've been waiting at the cool, dark packing station just inside the front door of the tea factory, and alternately in the warm April Sunday morning sun just outside, for my packing shift. Packing represents the final step handled here at the factory, completing my education in the processing of my favorite tea.

At 4,600 feet above sea level in the Himalayan foothills of India's Darjeeling region, I'm at the 150-year-old Makaibari tea factory perched on a slope just below the town of Kurseong. I'm just over a week into my physical travels across northern India, but a dozen weeks into the personal journey that began with giving notice on a twenty-year career, and planning my solo wander across a land that has existed in my mind as a magical and challenging destination, no more or less real than Narnia or Brigadoon.

After an hour of waiting, four large full tins of finished tea from the sorting room—carried two-ladies-at-a-time—are dumped on the shiny floor, filling the air with the rich, dark vegetal scent of black tea leaves. A man, barefoot, wearing gray dress pants, a white t-shirt and, amusingly, a Starbucks baseball cap, shovels and sweeps the tea into a single well-blended mountain of the finest grade Makaibari Estate, First Flush Darjeeling Tea. We wait, he and I, for the inspector to ensure the quality of the grade, and then begin filling twenty-kilo foil-lined brown paper bags, one scoop at a time into the chute engineered into an upper corner of each bag. Easy at first, it becomes very difficult once the bag is over half full and has to be repeatedly shaken and shifted—the entire bag lifted and dropped—in order for the tea to settle and make room for more. We've been joined by a woman, swiftly scooping tea and maneuvering the large bags with an urgency and confidence that compensates for her diminutive size and arms that are, at their widest, the size of my wrists.

"She filled two in the time it took you to fill one," the foreman teases after watching my slow struggle with the process, "and then finished yours off for you." It's not true! I started two different bags, handing one off to each of them for the challenging final touches. It is true, though, that each of them has done twice the work I have. He smiles, "She says you should only get half pay."

Packing is the only part of the process that—as far as I've witnessed—employs both genders. The gender roles are strong, each stage of the process (plucking, withering, rolling, firing, sorting) is handled either by men or by women, never both. The process begins and ends with women, and the distinction can be drawn along the lines of precision. If the work is delicate enough that human hands are involved, they must be women's hands. The gross handling of larger actions (and larger machines) is done by men.

In any case, here I am, one man interested in experiencing each step of tea processing as my own process unfolds, far from home.

PROCESSING

Tea is both art and science. It is the careful, methodical refinement of a bulk raw material that is pure potentiality. If handled correctly, it can become a brilliant and universally captivating expression of this potential. It is a delicate and multistaged process, however. When it's harvested, how—and *how quickly*—it's processed, the precision of brewing, etc., all affect the degree to which the essence is optimally revealed.

I see this clearly from my position here on the tea estate, surrounded by dramatic hills carpeted with hundreds of acres of what many consider the world's finest tea. The drama of the place comes from the geography, the grade. Simply put: It is steep. These are young mountains, the Himalayas, and that must explain their boldness. These foothills burst out of the plains below with such urgency that a flat surface is nearly impossible to find. On a clear night I can easily see Siliguri, a plains city only twenty-two miles down Pankhabari Road, yet more than four thousand feet below me. The roads attempt to follow the ever-ascending ridges, and this is where the towns are. The tea villages and fields are in the startling, swooping valleys.

That's where I've spent these last several days, above nearly vertical fields of the robust little shrub, *camellia sinensis,* in a village homestay just down the road from the factory, the oldest one in the region, still processing tea today the same way they have for more than a century.

"Makaibari" is stenciled in white paint—each letter three feet tall—on the green corrugated tin roof of the rugged old building. Truly unchanged for well over one hundred years, even the machinery inside is pre-1900. The factory opened in 1859, not coincidentally the same year tea production began in the region. Mechanization came in the next few decades, and that's about it. The rest has happened day in and day out with very few changes over the next dozen decades. The place is run by the vital and eccentric Swaraj Kumar Banerjee, the "Rajah of Darjeeling Tea," a man in his early sixties, graying hair around his sharp, handsome Bengali face, and often a somewhat devious smile like a child with a secret. Known simply as "Rajah" Banerjee, he is the fourth generation Banerjee to run the estate, and the man responsible for bringing organic agriculture to India's tea lands, indeed changing the way things are done outside the factory in the fields.

Rajah and I were crouched in the dirt outside of his office one afternoon as he counted types of uncultivated flora growing between the bushes. ". . . three, four, five . . ." Then turning to me, "You have a brother? Same genetic make-up, same cultural upbringing . . . right?" I agreed on all counts. "Tell me, placed in a room together, facing, talking, how long would it take before you had a disagreement?"

"Two hours?" I considered.

"I bet it's more like fifteen minutes, but O.K." He resumed plucking fronds and flowers, all in reach from his squatting position between bush and building, all voluntary growth, ". . . six, seven, eight . . ." He stopped at fifteen. "*This,*" he declared, handing me the bouqueted cluster of flora, "is what happens naturally." He was referring to the stability of a complex ecosystem vs. the fragility of genetic homogeneity, like brothers or chemical-dependent monocrops. "*This* is what creates sustainability: diversity!"

Diversity is subtext, however, as are the words *mulch* and *dung* and *compost*. To distill Banerjee's ever-ready lecture to a single word it would be: soil. "Healthy soil is healthy mankind," is his mantra. The result is better tea, healthier workers, and a product that just might be reproducible for another 150 years, and then another after that.

Days later in his home, in a smoke-filled living room with two enormous taxidermied tigers and two very alive German Shepherds, I sipped sparkling wine with Banerjee and his wife, and their daughter-in-law and six-year-old grandson visiting from Bangalore. "My father was one of the greatest hunters in India," he proclaimed as I inspected the very large, catatonic, dusty creatures. "He took down eighty-six such beasts in his day."

I was glad to hear this placed him among the best of hunters, the notion that this might be an average performance made my stomach turn. "I think he might be singlehandedly responsible for putting these on the endangered species list," I said.

He smiled, accepting the jab, but was unapologetic about the contradiction. This man with his impressive legacy in organic agriculture and fair trade business practices, this champion of biodiversity, remained very proud of his family's legacy as well. Even those elements that depleted the local tiger population.

It's Makaibari's environmental record that intrigued me into coming here. That and the ad hoc homestay volunteer program. A love of tea, too, factors in. Particularly Darjeeling's lighter body, golden-brown liquor, floral astringency, and tannic bitterness. But I come without substantial expertise on the beverage, and my work here is not directly related to tea. I'm volunteering among the villagers—many employed by the tea company, but experts, each, in a single process, not a finished product—thus I'm not substantially progressing my tea knowledge save for a few shifts on the factory floor. My expertise on the topic of timing and handling comes from an uncanny sense of fellowship as we, leaves and I, are plucked from our framework and set on course to reorganize ourselves into something new. In fact, that is precisely my work here.

The story for both of us begins after the roots and branches have been well established; after the various feats, cultural and agricultural, that brought us to this point of readiness.

SUPPLY AND DEMAND

Three months earlier at a corner table in Boulder, Colorado's Dushanbe Tea House, I sat flanked by my sons, both of them smiling and joking and masking their competition over a shared scone and a small cup of Devonshire cream: sixteen-year-old Henry's self-assured attack on the thing, and Simon at thirteen demonstrating a more reserved—yet frustrated—politeness. Across the table, mirroring my *chai* sipping, sat their mother, my ex-wife CC, her tall frame and long brown hair framed by the tall windows and long drapes—pulled back to expose the cold January morning and the half-frozen creek outside. I looked forward to these family meals; they were good opportunities to catch up, but they tended to be scattered. We often failed to drop deeper than friendliness or remain on a single topic for more than a few uninterrupted lines.

That morning a new element was added to the mix: anticipation. There in my hands was a *Lonely Planet Guide to India* and a yet-to-be-opened card. On the table sat the handprinted gift wrap and raffia that had just come off this belated birthday present.

Our food arrived, just as the scone battle was won, and my two handsome sons dove into their breakfasts while they quietly watched me. I opened the card, a plain, store-bought birthday card, to reveal a $5,000 check and words that tumbled my heart in a way it is so rarely touched. "This is a thank you and an exuberantly offered investment in the second half of an already incredible life . . . now it is time to go and do something for you. Something a little crazy that feeds the soul and rocks the foundation." Here were words of gratitude and generosity in the handwriting of the woman I'd married nineteen years earlier, the woman with whom I was still raising these two remarkable boys. A woman now married to another man yet with whom I have a somewhat stilted closeness and friendship, like an honorary siblinghood—but clouded by the historical fact of deeper intimacy. Most of all, here was gratitude for a "decade and a half of doing things to ensure our security and happiness."

These words cut beautifully into the deepest wound from our divorce where my very loyalty to my work, my commitment to career in its conventional nine-to-five, day-to-day trappings, was the source of discontent for her. She couldn't "respect"—her word—that relationship. And even today, seven years later, the wound trembles. This was the single most painful communication in our divorce. At the time all I could hear was the ingratitude and irrationality of it. Here I was "ensuring our security," while she had left the paying work world in what was a long ascent to finding her true work, her passion. This search was honorable, but fettered me that much more, it seemed, to my office and my paycheck.

The searing word "respect" had long since been recalled, and time had erased my defensive reaction to it. I could see the complexity of our situation with greater clarity, and this gift testified that she could too. No doubt my career loyalty was honorable, but it was also sad and compromising, as it became a defining box so sturdy it began to sprout bars. I did want out but lacked the courage to make the break.

"We are gifting you with a trip to a place that defines WILD—human and otherwise," read the card.

India was not their idea, it was recognition of my number one travel dream. But India is not an extended weekend trip. It's not even a trip one can do justice to within the three weeks of paid vacation granted by my work. My mind raced with excitement and gratitude—*Was this level of generosity really happening?*—and doubt and even irritation. For in this gift was a directive, and in that was a lack of understanding, perhaps even a subtle criticism, of the demands of my career. *It's not this simple*, I thought. *You can't just say "go to India" and expect that my busy life will allow it.* My head spun with the responsibilities that would make accepting this gift impossible. There was work and the money and benefits it provided. There was Melissa and the stumbling, fumbling romance we were struggling through. And there were the kids.

"We will help you as 'ground support,' your cheerleading squad and the ones who keep the home fires burning." So, inherent in the gift was permission to temporarily downshift my family responsibilities. And with it, this excuse to maintain the status quo was removed. But still, I left the restaurant feeling both excited and uncertain how this would unfold and if I'd be able to pull it off.

It was three weeks later that I decided not only would this trip to India happen, it would be part of a more substantial breaking of the branch: I would quit my job of fifteen years (my career of twenty) and turn it all inside out. "I wanted my life," as in Mary Oliver's *Dogfish*, "to close, and open / like a hinge, like a wing, like the part of the song / where it falls down over the rocks: an explosion, a discovery; / I wanted / to hurry into the work of my life."

PLUCK THIS

Tea must be harvested at the right time. That is right now, April, for the finest Darjeeling, what is called "first flush" tea.

It starts in the hills where women pluck the emergent green tips. Yesterday I accompanied a few of these ladies as they harvested the fresh first flush leaves and buds. Baskets on their backs, strapped around their foreheads, both hands engaged in this rapid but specific plucking, many of these women exceeded—some by a couple of decades—my forty-two years. Carrying nothing but a small camera, I tripped and floundered behind them, scraping my legs against the firm branches of the tea bushes. I felt like a harbor seal hiking with mountain goats.

This place, the hills of Darjeeling, is like none I've witnessed. Each time I step outside, I'm struck by it. "Hold on," I'll say. "Let me take a picture." I say this because I keep thinking that somehow, *this time,* I'll be able to capture the magnificence of it, because, *this time*, the light is different. The light is often different: there's sunrise and sunset and there's mist. Sometimes the mist is so strong you can see only a few feet away, and like thick San Francisco fog it rolls over the place, a black-and-white filter stripping color out of the little that remains visible. Mostly it's the rolling blankets of clouds that amaze, flowing into the nooks of these recklessly steep hills, sometimes swallowing the entire town of Kurseong in its perch at the peak of the next hill. I'll muse as I sweat in the hot sun, that the people in town—less than two miles away—are cold and wet in that midday black-and-white fade. Sometimes the clouds are above me, but below the surrounding hilltops, transforming the landscape into an animated Japanese scroll painting.

A week and a half ago—the first Wednesday of April—I arrived in New Delhi en route to where I am now. The Wednesday before that was the middle of my final week at work, the last of some 750 Wednesdays I'd made my way into my office. Now on a tea estate on the other side of the world from my former job, my family and my girlfriend, I watched these durable, weathered women busily pluck tips from the bushes only days after the fresh leaves and buds had emerged. These first leaves of spring, the first flush, represent some of the finest tea and will command high prices for their delicate flavor.

There's a later "second flush," May harvest that is considered just as good by many. In fact, its richer "muscatel" character has always been my choice for a fine cup. This is a relief, too, because I fear I missed my own first flush and began to wilt on the branch a bit. A bright green leaf of potential, I believe I remained too long, especially in my job.

THE BRANCHES

It was confusing to find myself in a career, reasonably well paid, working for a company of good people driven to do good in the world, yet to be disenchanted. It was only my second company in two decades of nonstop forty-five-hour work weeks, commutes, cubicles, and eventually my own office. I ran the eco-friendly products division of the company, selling goods to consumers who wanted to be part of the solution, not part of the problem. This was not blood money, it was an honest, right livelihood. Almost.

There was compromise in every direction. The product *could* reduce energy consumption, for instance, but may itself be manufactured of nonsustainable materials and shipped halfway around the world. The consumer culture *could* be affected, inspiring people to live more simply or closer to the land—and likely was—but increasingly the job became one of failing budgets and discussions of profitability. My primary focus had shifted from eco-green to financial green and my interest faded.

I wilted. My potentiality began to droop. Not so much directly from the work, but indirectly from the stagnation that results by not finding passion in what I was doing. And the fear that kept me where I was, afraid to risk my employment, to jump ship, to reach out and find a better expression of myself. This fear deflated my spirit, and that rippled out into other areas of my life, other relationships. Like romance and family.

If the quality of output (my sons) is any testimony, my parenting is commendable. But exhausted and stagnating, I am often less present than I'd like to be, less attentive to their needs, less patient. Less aware in general, really, but nothing is more important to me than my sons: Henry as he forges his way, in the second half of his second decade, into a sense of self-reliance, yet still craving—in subtle ways—the parental boundaries of childhood. Simon, having just entered his teen years, asserting his own style despite the strong pull of his brother's character. Both of them unfailingly impressive in their brilliance and competence—in everything they attempted—yet too often disenchanted and discouraged—with school, with friends. With me.

The days or nights with them that were defined by my impatience and short temper are tragic moments in my parenting memory, burned in my mind. Thich Nhat Hanh says it's possible, firmly grounded in the present, to transform the past. He says, "the traces of a bad drought can only be erased by a bountiful rainfall, and rain can only fall in the present moment." I love and need this. But presence, a simple word and a simple act (or non-act), is so difficult to achieve—all the more so when palpably dissatisfied and restless.

Romance, too. Such a conflicted dance this has been for the last decade. Divorce, adolescent emergence (yes, at thirty-five), a constant dizzying centrifugal spin engaging woman after woman, and the breakaway and recoil that inevitably followed. And recent history, sharing this dance with just one beautiful and patient woman. Pulling, pushing; wanting in, wanting to escape. Desiring her in one moment and desperately needing aloneness and quiet in the next.

Six weeks before I left on this trip, Melissa and I went on a painfully ironic Valentine's Day walk. It was an unseasonably warm afternoon, and we were walking along a winding path between square, ordered backyards and rolling, golden open space. "Do you think we need to break up?" she'd asked in the office, prompting the walk.

Melissa is a beautiful woman, no less so that afternoon, and we are capable of coasting blissfully together. But not always. Too often the familiar tentacles of anxiety constrict in my upper chest when I'm faced with the pressure of our relationship. On the walk I explained to her that without knowing why, I felt an ill ease too much of the time. "I beat myself up trying to understand it, to find the reason. But really, the *why* of it isn't as important as the *fact* of it."

She stopped and looked at me, her blue eyes the color of a bottomless well of generosity, and asked, "What do you want to do?"

"I think we need to end it," I said, feeling a great conviction to keep away for the next several weeks leading up to my trip, and to go to India unencumbered by a relationship that competes for limited space in my limited heart. "To spare each other."

I don't know if I thought then of the half-dozen other breakups I'd engineered in the last few years, and the greater number of fade outs from undefined relationships. If so, I may have noticed the glaring common denominator. A few days later I would admit to myself a hope to take time away and to finally find the ability, some months down the road, to be in a relationship, and to find Melissa still willing to be in one with me. But if I had this awareness that Valentine's day, I withheld my confusion. We both needed my decisiveness. "Yes. I do think we should break up."

"O.K.," she said. I watched her lips—heart-pink against winter white skin—the symmetry of which had magnetized me for two on-and-off years. "I love you," she added. Then flatly, without venom, "Good luck, you sad and foolish man."

We kissed. I smiled, gently despite a torrent of conflicting emotion. My head smugly received the drama of the event and the clarity of the decision with a misbegotten satisfaction, while my heart raised one more dark, retreating step down into my gut.

Wilting on the branch, indeed.

We continued to see each another almost daily at work, and the attraction prevailed as it had before. We got back together—albeit somewhat tentatively—at the end of February, perhaps stronger (us), definitely still confused (me). And now, 8,000 miles away, I feel closer to her than ever.

STORM CLOUDS

After the first flush harvest there is a nonproductive period of four to five weeks, called *banji*. In his book, *The Rajah of Darjeeling Organic Tea: Makaibari*, Banerjee describes the climate during this period: "Fast moving rain-bearing clouds sweep up from the Bay of Bengal, and on collision with the Himalayan foothills, inundate the Darjeeling district with short but fierce bursts of precipitation." Ah, yes. I've stumbled back from Kurseong twice in these storms. He continues, "These are the awe-inspiring Norwesters. In a flash, dark clouds appear out of clear blue skies. The lashing is intense, with copious rain accompanied by streaks of lightning and deafening thunderbolts. God help those who do not unhook their electronics, as they blow up instantly. Within an hour, it is all over and the sun appears with clear skies. This is a magical moment. Overnight, the region is a riot of green and is abuzz with the emergence of all life forms."

This is when the emergent second flush shoots signal readiness to harvest a tea darker in liquor and fuller in flavor, the rich Muscatel Second Flush.

Certainly I've ridden out my own *banji*. A general climate of complacency hit with occasional storms of doubt, fear, and even misplaced anger when I'm stretched to my limit.

A bitterness sets in at these times, but maybe also a richness. Self-plucked late in the season, I now find myself halfway around the world, unemployed and alone, and ready to refine my character.

WITHERING HEIGHTS

The refining process isn't immediate, of course. The first and longest step is "withering." The leaves are laid out to dry under a mild air flow for about fourteen hours where they shrivel and lose about 70 percent of their moisture. They are beginning to decompose, to rot. At just the right time the following morning, the men overseeing this drying and oxidizing process drop the still-damp leaves through a hatch in the floor to the rolling machines below.

In this room, to the vibrating groan of monstrous machines, the leaves are churned together under moderate pressure. The mechanized rolling process hastens a more aggressive breaking down—the controlled death of the leaves—and is the height of the fermenting process, imparting the flavor style and caffeine. "This process of death," says Banerjee in his book, "releases the enzymes that are so essential for developing the aroma and infusion of the tea." Timing is critical to ensure that just the right amount of fermentation takes place.

What exits here is a shadow of its former self. Yet without the decomposition, the ultimate potential of that once bursting green leaf cannot be harnessed. For Darjeeling tea, the withering and rolling process takes less than one day. For me?

My last few weeks at home were hell. I'd given two-month's notice at work that was followed, not by the great liberation I'd imagined, nor a dark apprehension about my unemployment, but by a holding pattern. My life was a movie playing in slow motion, punctuated with dramatic scenes of worry as I wrestled the practicalities of the trip into place.

I'd given *myself*, on the other hand, only three days between my last day at the office and my flight. This proved insufficient for any physical response—call it let down—to my life's upheaval. My body, more aware of the situation than my brain, addressed the oversight with a profoundly inconvenient sickness (sinus infection, deep body aches, extreme exhaustion) for my last two weeks at home. Even as I readied myself and attended going away parties in my honor, I'd withdrawn. I began to emerge only somewhere between Newark and New Delhi airports.

Worry tackled me again in Makaibari by way of ATM failure. Days of marching up to the town of Kurseong to release my card into a machine and breathlessly await the bad news: "INCORRECT PIN," written in aggravatingly plain English across the screens of all four machines in the small town. Each time followed by a deflating sense of hopelessness combined with the familiar upper chest choke of my anxiety.

And then my homesickness. Part three, perhaps, of my decomposition.

My first Wednesday in the village I awoke from a long deep slumber, and after a moment of orientation, I lay in bed and cried. Tears running into my ears as I stared at the ceiling, or alternately as I stared with closed eyes into the beautiful smiling faces of Henry and Simon; and as I reached over, imagining the warm and comforting snuggle of Melissa's body. It'd only been a week, but add to that the vast distance, both geographical and cultural, and the fact that there were nine more weeks in my journey, and the whole recipe became a bit more than I could imagine.

Why am *I doing this? Why am I so far away from those I love?* I wondered. Somehow I'd imagined I could book a trip like this, like a twenty-year-old, and become that twenty-year-old. But that is a time all about outward growth, expression, and expansion. A time when we are immortal and eager to run from home and establish ourselves as adults, as independent in the world. A time to push away from those we love and go explore.

I'm not twenty. And while I certainly wanted to shake things up and push away from the constructs and confines of how I'd been defined, I did not want to push away from Henry and Simon and Melissa. My money situation had drained my inner reserves, and I was destined to settle into weariness.

Later that morning I headed off for my first volunteer teaching stint in the village school, a modest single-story building housing four small classrooms. Availing themselves of my assistance, the school director and two teachers retired to a small office and heated their early lunch on a tiny, shoddy stove.

As the scent of curried potatoes and fresh flatbread *roti* emerged from the stench of dirty fuel, I found myself among the sweet smiling faces of a dozen uniformed children, trying to explain the math assignments in slow English. Then I sat at the desk grading their work one at a time as they yelled "finish!" and brought their workbooks to me. Exhausted by it all, I played with the globe that sat, almost cruelly, in front of me. I wanted to see if indeed Chicago was closer to New Delhi than New York is (made curious by a shorter flight time), but all I saw, little finger and thumb stretched across the top of the small globe, was that I could not, in the northern hemisphere of this massive planet, be any farther from Boulder, Colorado. My eyes filled with tears again. Not "finish!" yet.

How much more withering will I have to endure before a good firing ends the emotional decomposition and sets me on my new course?

FIRING AND SORTING

For tea, the breakdown is brought to a sudden end as the leaves undergo a firing process, a tumble down five layers of a conveyer system through a large coal-fired oven at approximately 100°F. This takes just over thirty minutes, after which the tea is roughly complete and ready to brew, but needs to be sorted and graded.

It is then wheeled into the sorting room, the most magical room in the factory. Tin-lined wood floors and large sorting machines are bathed in natural morning light from tall east-facing windows, while a dozen or more barefoot women in brightly colored saris move about carrying various baskets and tins and handmade grass whisk brooms through the sorting process. The room is filled with the vibrating hum of machines and tea dust in the air, and the choreography of the process is delightfully theatrical. Even the sunken floor adds to this sense; it's like a black box theater—but a brightly lit set—with a thoroughly Asian performance art taking place. One of those theatrical endeavors whose brilliance titillates my senses, yet whose meaning escapes me: something about the meeting place of artisanal handiwork and larger-than-life technology, all in constant motion, a ritual dance of woman and machine alike. What flows out of this room, after hours of scooping, sifting, shaking and picking, is the beautiful fin-ished product of some of the world's finest tea.

SHIPPING AND HANDLING

This is the fantasy, of course. That by simply taking the leap, things will all be sorted out and then cleaned up the way the ladies clean up the sorting room after each batch. Will I be so deftly handled? I have nine more weeks of travel ahead of me before returning home. I await the firing that will end my deterioration, and then perhaps I will adeptly sort it all out, the next chapters of my adult life. This, I suppose, is the hope of any good pilgrimage: that we will find some clarifying truth to hang our next actions on.

This first flush tea, packed into these twenty-kilo bags and ready to ship out into the global market, will be brewed—and hopefully enjoyed—by someone, somewhere; the finally released, fully realized potential of that recently plucked-from-the-branch leaf. But perhaps it's too lofty an order. To take a wholly Indian view of it, it doesn't ultimately matter—as long as we do our best in any present incarnation of the process—because even the finest teas become compost and piss shortly after that first satisfying sip, ready to start over again.

What I do know is the branch has been broken, the withering is underway and what will emerge—well sorted, expertly prepared, and fully appreciated, or not—will be a version of me at least a little richer in character. And maybe that's enough. When I set out on this journey I wanted to know, returning to Mary Oliver's poem, "whoever I was, I was / alive / for a little while."

Bill Giebler lives and writes in Boulder, Colorado. His work on food, travel, and the environment has appeared in Organic Spa Magazine, Green Living Journal, Edible Front Range, *and more.*

❧ ❧ ❧

Masha

Two women, one skirt, and an untold story.

$\mathcal{T}$he first time I met Maria Konstantinovna, she was wearing a black leather skirt. It was Italian, brand new, and it was mine.

Masha, as I would come to know her, was a *dejournaya* in Moscow. Women like her sat on every floor in every hotel in the Soviet Union. They performed a range of duties—they served tea from a samovar that simmered behind their station. They ordered your phone call to America and came to wake you if it ever went through. They even washed lingerie and t-shirts, leaving the latter folded like fine envelopes, whiter than they ever deserved to be. They also handed out your room key with varying degrees of suspicion, charm, or ennui, and if you wanted to leave it for safekeeping, collected it when you left the floor. But allegedly, the real purpose of these hall monitors was to observe your comings and goings on behalf of the security apparatus of the Kremlin.

It was my second trip to Cold War Moscow.

One year earlier, I had arrived in Moscow with a new degree in Russian Studies and stayed in an old hotel in the center of town. On nights when I drank too much Georgian champagne, I crossed the street and walked alone past the cupolas and red brick walls of Red Square. Now I was back as a tour guide of sorts, a liaison, for groups of doctors who were on continuing education junkets. I was a translator, a babysitter, holder of boarding passes and whipping post if need be when tempers grew hot traveling around the Soviet Empire—which they often did. It was part of my job description to be cheerful, but when my busload of jetlagged gastroenterologists and I arrived at our hulking mass of a hotel, I despaired.

Our official Intourist guide told us it had been built in 1979 to house athletes and guests for the Olympics the following year. That much was obvious; it was a model Soviet vanity project, from the monstrous scale to the banners out front which erupted with optimism: "Onward!" they proclaimed. Across the street was a giant park devoted to the fruits of socialism, as well as a massive Space Obelisk. Inside, it was as sprawling and noisy as a city, and the air was dense with cigarette smoke and the grease from several restaurants.

Prior to my trip, a fellow tour guide had informed me that there were fiber-optic cables installed in every room, and that the entire twenty-fifth floor was devoted to surveillance. He claimed to have stumbled upon a wall of reel-to-reel tape recorders there. President Reagan had just given his Evil Empire speech, and the country was being run by an ex-KGB chief, Yuri Andropov. Paranoia was everywhere—in bars and on park benches where we changed dollars for rubles on the black market with people we had no reason to trust and who must have assumed we were listening to them.

As my new job paid little and I would depend on tips, I was eager to prove myself. But the first morning I woke up with a foggy head and aching limbs. So with apologies for being sick on day one, I loaded my fourteen physicians and their spouses onto the coach with their Russian guide and then repaired back upstairs, hungry for my bed. I peeled my clothes off and

crawled in naked. The sheets were coarse cotton and delightfully crunchy, and the duvet still held a welcoming hint of my
own body warmth.

I woke up to the sight of two men going through my suitcase at the foot of the bed. One man's arm was buried in a
zipper compartment; the other man was turned toward the
window, holding my raincoat up to the light.

"What are you doing?" I asked. Russian literature was full
of fever dreams, and I believed I was having one. The clarity
was dazzling—two guys in blue shirts, the older one with a
pale smoker's complexion and hair all neat like a little boy
on school picture day. The younger one had gray eyes that
betrayed a flicker of menace, as if I were the one intruding.

Startled, the older man dropped the raincoat into the
suitcase.

I was shivering and drew the comforter tightly around my
bare body, sleeping bag-style.

"Excuse me," he declared. "We thought you were out."

They scrambled out the door and soon I fell back into sleep.

The next day, while my group toured Lenin's tomb, I
sat on the bus sweating, too ill to move. I had not spoken of
my visitation the previous day. Many of my charges already
supposed they were being watched; some were amused and
some downright scared. They whispered to each other about
the presumed KGB sightings and enjoyed the Cold War
folklore. But they were all doctors and their American
guide was sick, so they insisted on taking me back to the
hotel.

I dragged myself through the lobby, into the elevator,
down the hallway that was thick with the rotten-fruit smell
of disinfectant. My feet carried me, quicker now, to my room,
to that delicious, warm bed. The *dejournaya* station was
empty. I had wordlessly passed her that morning, not stopping to leave my key. She had glanced up from her book and

smiled, which was unusual for a key lady. I had noticed her wide-set green eyes.

And there she was, inside my room, wearing my skirt. She was curvier than I, and the waistband stretched tightly around her middle. The leather pulled across her hips sexily, as if the utterly random act of wearing a stranger's clothes gave her an air of danger and power. She held a pair of black high heels that I had packed along with the skirt—I knew I would never wear them on my tour of Moscow and Central Asia, but they were new and expensive, and I didn't want to leave them in the closet of my shared New York apartment. Her own satin blouse was unbuttoned; the frayed remains of trim drifted around the cups of her bra, which, at least a size too small, pinched her ribcage and crushed her breasts.

"*Bozhe moi*," she said. Oh my God.

"It's O.K., really." What else could I say to this poor, mortified creature? "I just need to sleep."

"Just a moment," she said. One at a time, with two hands, she bent to place my shoes on the floor, toes pointed straight ahead like loaves on a baking sheet.

"Just a moment," she repeated, unzipping with shaky fingers. I turned my head so as not to see her Soviet-issue panties, hoping at least she wore some. She nodded deferentially, her face creased with shame. In what seemed like one move, she slipped on her wool skirt and stepped into her shoes. She shuffled her breasts around, rearranging them as if to make room in her bra, and fastened her blouse.

I waved her out the door, saying, "Don't worry, don't worry. Please!"

I scanned the room, flipped through my suitcase. Only my make-up case looked disturbed, with pencils, brushes and compacts strewn about the dresser. Strangely, despite my exhaustion and the fever that addled my brain, I knew I wasn't angry. Rather, I pitied her embarrassment at being caught. Whoever this woman was, she was now exposed and compromised, and I wanted her to know that I, at least, didn't care.

I fell fully clothed into bed.

When I woke up, she was sitting at her station and rose to greet me when I came down the hall. She seemed taller and more beautiful, having regained her composure, and must have been twenty-five or twenty-six, a few years older than I.

"Do you want tea?" she asked.

"Yes, please," I answered. "What's your name?"

"Maria Konstantinovna," she replied, using her patronymic rather than her last name. "Masha."

"I'm Marcia too," I said. In Russian, they sounded the same. "Is there anything to eat?"

She walked me back to my room, where I stripped down to my underwear and slipped into bed. Soon, Masha returned with rolls, cheese, and black tea. I drifted in and out of sleep. At times, I could hear the door swish open and closed or feel her swab my face with a damp cloth. Once I sat up to sip some tea and felt her hands bolster my shoulders, brace me as I lowered myself back to the mattress, and finally tuck the covers under my chin.

"I'm not working tomorrow," she said. I looked at her, puzzled. "I think you will be well enough to leave for Tashkent."

"Thanks to you, I think I will be," I said.

I had not mentioned my itinerary to her, but she knew. The next day would be our last in Moscow, as we were flying to Uzbekistan the following morning. In the room, the shades were drawn. There was still daylight behind them, but I had no idea what time it was. Loud voices erupted in the corridor, and Masha stood to return to her station.

"I'll be back in a few weeks. May I bring you something from America?" I asked.

She pressed the starched napkin that rested underneath the tea glass, and held her finger there while her eyes caught mine. I could see the corner of a folded square of paper, which I later slipped between my fingers and tucked into my wallet.

Within a month, I returned with another group of doctors, this time seventeen thoracic surgeons. At the airport, an agent had confiscated *Vogue* and *Newsweek*, but I still had the illustrated collection of Pushkin fairy tales Masha had requested. She wanted the book, she wrote in her note, to read to her young son. At the Russian bookstore in New York City, I had easily procured what was impossible to find in the shortage-ravaged Soviet Union. Of course, I brought a few extra things—a leather handbag stuffed with lip gloss, eye shadow, red licorice. The scene had never left my mind—her open shirt, the tattered lingerie, and her eyes that shifted around mine until that moment of comprehension and convergence: had our fates been reversed, I would have discovered the Italian skirt from the depths of her luggage. And I would have slipped it on as she had done to see myself reflected, just once, in something beautiful.

Right after checking in, I hopped the elevator to my old floor and found the on-duty *dejournaya*.

"Is Maria Konstantinovna working today?" I asked.

"She left," the woman answered.

"For the day, or for good?" I asked.

"I don't know," she said, and turned to rearrange the keys, inviting no further questions.

Over the next six months, I was back at the hotel several times with the book in my bag, but I never saw Masha again. In the winter of 1986, I returned to Moscow, this time with an American television network. Change was afoot, Mikhail Gorbachev was in power, and *glasnost* was the order of the day. I was low man on the nightly newscast I worked for, but in those days it still meant I had a car and driver. Snow fell gently, unstoppably, on the black Volga sedan. My old hotel seemed closer to town than I remembered.

She wasn't there.

Rounding the circular drive to leave, I recalled a brief embrace Masha and I had shared at the end of the one day we knew each other. I had recognized her perfume—Amazone—because it had come from my own bottle.

Over the years, I returned many times to Moscow. I went with Peter Jennings, Barbara Walters, and *60 Minutes*. Each time, I packed that book of fairytales, and each time I journeyed out beyond the Space Obelisk, past the All-Russia Exhibition Center, to the ever-forbidding hotel. Always a fool's errand, to be sure. And each time I got off the elevator, I swallowed harder as I confronted the empty space she once occupied.

After an eighteen-year absence, I recently returned to Moscow. As I packed, I slipped the slim, orange book into my suitcase. I was, frankly, surprised when I found it on the bookshelf, after six moves, a couple of renovations, and decades of neglect. The stories were in Russian so I never read them to my own kids, yet there it was, shelved patiently, a talisman to guilt, gratitude, and unfinished business.

Even though Moscow had changed beyond recognition, I hadn't. Nor had the feeling of dread and sensory overload I experienced when I got to the hotel where Masha worked the day shift twenty-seven years ago. The lobby was still garish, but now it was loud with Italian cafés and gift shops selling nesting dolls and amber jewelry. A large man in a suit would not allow me to pass beyond his checkpoint to the elevators, so I went to the front desk.

"Would it be possible to go to the fifth floor?" I asked the receptionist. "I'm researching a book."

"You are writing something on the hotel?" she asked.

"Not really. . . ." I hesitated. "Well, yes."

"What is the nature of your project?" she asked.

"Actually," I said, "years ago, I met someone here."

Her face softened. "I understand," she said, and turned. "Just a minute."

Within seconds, an official-looking woman approached me at the desk.

"Please leave your passport," she said, "and we'll go upstairs."

I handed it to the receptionist and was ushered past the guard.

"Do you still have *dejournayas?*" I asked.

"Yes, of course. It is not the same as it was. Mostly, they just take care of the floor."

"Can we please stop on five?" I ventured. She pressed the elevator button.

"Twenty-five is the only floor non-guests may see," she stated.

The doors opened.

There was no sign of tape recorders, only a fancy carpet runner and an eerie stillness that bore the echo of empty rooms. There was no *dejournaya*, either, and certainly no Masha. As we strolled back down the corridor, I murmured niceties about the lovely, modern décor.

Back in the elevator, I took out the book and turned to "The Tale of Tsar Saltan," the great writer's most famous children's story about the prince who saves the life of a swan, who in turn becomes a beautiful princess. The illustrations were simple but unremarkable, and I skimmed through the pages, stopping at a drawing of a bird flying across a starry violet sky. I closed the book and put it in my bag. It seemed that Masha had at last given it to me.

For all I knew, she emigrated, and I had passed her on a New York City sidewalk. Maybe she got sick or simply quit her job that day and was somewhere in Moscow now, her son grown. Perhaps she did vanish one night in that hazy time right before her country's sea change. I would never find out.

Masha was in my life so briefly it shouldn't have mattered. But to this day, I have not known comfort like the sound of her footsteps padding in and out of my hotel room as I sweltered with fever. I was twenty-three, in a strange land, nursed by the hands of a woman who, but for the clothes, might have been me.

Marcia DeSanctis writes for Vogue *and* Town & Country *magazines and is the author of the* New York Times *bestseller* 100 Places in France Every Woman Should Go. *She is a former television news producer who worked for Barbara Walters, ABC, CBS, and NBC News. Her work has appeared in numerous publications* including Marie Claire, O the Oprah Magazine, National Geographic Traveler, Creative Nonfiction More, Tin House, *and* The New York Times. *Her travel essays have been widely anthologized, including five consecutive years in* The Best Woman's Travel Writing *and four in* The Best Travel Writing. *She is the recipient of five Lowell Thomas Awards for excellence in travel journalism, including Travel Journalist of the Year in 2012 for her essays from Rwanda, Russia, Haiti and France, and two Solas Awards for Best Travel Writing.*

᪥ ᪥ ᪥

Love and Lies in Iran

Most people dream of spending their honeymoon
on exotic beaches. This newlywed couple opted
for a road trip through the land of the ayatollahs.

We raced through the darkness and didn't see it
coming. Mehdi sat erect behind the wheel, honking slower cars out of his way. But one car stayed in its
lane; it challenged his hierarchy. Mehdi honked, flashed,
tailgated, and when the other car slowly made way, he
barreled into the opening. Then something crashed, glass
shattered, and the other car's side-view mirror went flying
through the air, leaving a trail of silvery dust glittering in
its wake.

Mehdi laughed and kept going.

We sat in silence, and it unsettled Mehdi that my wife,
Gypsy, and I weren't laughing. He kept looking at us, anxious, it seemed, for approval, some kind of validation. And
then, suddenly, a car appeared next to us, honking, flashing,
pushing us to the edge of the road. Mehdi looked for a way
out, braking, accelerating, swerving, but the other car followed us like a shadow. He struggled for a while, then gave
up and slowed down. The other car cut him off, forcing us
to a stop.

It was after midnight and we were cornered on a dark road somewhere in Iran. This is where our honeymoon ended and the epilogue began. Without turning around, I whispered to Gypsy not to move or say a word. Then I pushed the bag with the money deeper into the legroom, until it was no longer visible.

The other car's doors opened and two women got out. The woman on the passenger side screamed into her phone and started walking in circles, glowering at us in the glare of our car's headlights. The woman on the driver's side went to the trunk of her car, opened it and leaned in. She was heavy-set and wore her headscarf in a rigid style, showing no hair. Mehdi jumped out of the car and raised his arms in disbelief. The woman pulled a baseball bat out of the trunk, straightened herself and slowly walked toward him.

I knew that a honeymoon in Iran with an American bride would not be without complications, and that my being a German journalist wouldn't help. When two governments are as mistrustful of each other as America and Iran, their citizens are made to feel the suspicion whenever they enter the other country. The fact that we were living in Berlin might have made us look a little less suspicious, but I was prepared. In my pocket, I carried a piece of paper with the phone number of the Swiss Embassy in Tehran, which, in the absence of a U.S. Embassy, takes care of Americans and their consular needs. Missing from my emergency plan was the wrath of the Iranian women.

We had been sitting in this car like exhibition pieces in a museum of the Iranian Revolution—in the front, Mehdi and I, two bearded men—in the back, Gypsy, a veiled woman. And suddenly the dominant male figure around which everything seemed to revolve in this country was gone. The man who minutes ago had his hands on the wheel was now standing in the street beseeching a woman who wanted to crack his skull.

When Gypsy and I made plans for our honeymoon, we weren't dreaming of lagoons and lonely beaches. We weren't drawn to riding elephants in India, or flying in a propeller plane across the Okavango Delta. We wanted to penetrate a hermetic country and find beauty behind its forbidding façade. We liked the idea of lovers subverting a state ruled by imperious men, and quickly fell for Iran.

The first conflict of our honeymoon erupted even before we departed, in the women's section of a department store in Berlin. We argued about a pair of shoes. To me, they looked like the shoes of a splay-footed ballerina—black and shiny, with ribbons glued to the tips. Their brand name was "Yessica," and I didn't like them. They made my wife appear small, with feet-like fins. I called them "mullah shoes." Gypsy bought them for seven euros.

We were standing in the middle of Berlin's hip Prenzlauer Berg neighborhood, and I felt as though the power of the Iranian mullahs extended all the way to the German capital. They had reprogrammed my wife.

I didn't know this side of Gypsy, this kind of submissiveness. She was born in the Dominican Republic and grew up in the Bronx, and she has the fearlessness of the underprivileged and Simone de Beauvoir's lust for arguing. She is also the daughter of a woman who used to carry a ladies' revolver in her purse, and who once shot into the ceiling of a bar where she had tracked down her husband, who had another woman sitting on his lap. And now Gypsy bought a pair of ugly shoes to please the mullahs, letting them decide when she was a woman and when a subject. I didn't understand. "You lack pragmatic intelligence," Gypsy said.

We knew that the dress code of the Islamic Republic of Iran was also enforced in Frankfurt, from the moment passengers entered an Iran Air plane. At the gate, we didn't notice it. We sat among Iranian women who only stood out because they were dressed more elegantly than the German women around them. But at some point they began to change. As boarding time approached, they slipped into overcoats and covered their hair with headscarves. They slowly disappeared.

A few Iranian women remained uncovered. They showed their hair, their necks, the shape of their bodies, and they weren't wearing mullah shoes. They walked around in high heels and didn't mind being followed by the looks of others. They seemed determined to hold on to their freedom for as long as they could.

Gypsy didn't dare to do that. She knew that, as an American, she would be watched with particular scrutiny, and she worried about offending anyone. She covered her head with a black scarf and pushed it back to reveal some hair, just as she had seen it in pictures of street life in Tehran. She knew the Iranian dress code in detail—she had been studying it for weeks. Sometimes during her many dress rehearsals, she would stand in front of me, covered in a headscarf and an overcoat, and ask if I was still attracted to her. I didn't care for the coat, but I became enchanted by the way the scarf framed her face, the mystery it bestowed on her.

Gypsy knew that liberal Iranian women are smarter at interpreting the dress code than the mullahs are at writing it. She admired their mastery at stretching the rules, how they played with the fact that the boundaries of the permissible are fluid on a woman's body. But she also knew that plainclothes officers walk the streets, harshly enforcing the dress code. In their canon, women are only allowed to show their face and hands; their feet, if they dared to wear open shoes, had to be covered by opaque stockings.

We entered the plane, and my Dominican wife, who was raised in America, lived in Germany and bears the name of a

vagabond, obeyed the Iranian dress code by covering herself
in an overcoat sewn by Chinese hands and a scarf bought from
a Kashmiri in India.

Gypsy understood the uncovered Iranian women and their
longing for freedom, but the German women irritated her.
She looked around the plane and none of them was wearing
a headscarf. She found it disrespectful. The men on Iran's
Guardian Council would have liked Gypsy, how she stood
there in her headscarf, her opaque stockings and her mullah
shoes, seething at the women of the West.

I kept quiet. In a strange way, I was indebted to Ayatollah
Khomeini and the revolution he instigated. My life would have
been different without him, shallower. I never would have met
the first love of my life. He pushed her toward me, and if he
were still alive, I would have to kiss his hand for it.

Her name was Mandana, which means "the everlasting." Her
parents took her and fled to Germany after Khomeini seized
power. We went to high school together, and she enraptured
me in a hotel room in Warsaw. I was eighteen and knew
nothing; she was nineteen and knew more. Our love lasted six
years. I could have liberated her father from the brothers who
kept calling from Iran, claiming they had found the perfect
husband for his daughter. But I kept her waiting, and she left
for Jerusalem with the one who promised to make her wait
no more.

Observing Mandana's father, I studied the inner conflicts of an Iranian man. He used to work as a bartender,
and had married Mandana's mother even though she was a
divorced woman from the West. He loved his black Jaguar
and a good whiskey. He worked tirelessly to give his beloved
four daughters the best education possible. And he lied for
me when he told his brothers that Mandana was already
engaged.

His name was Faramarz, and he could be as tender as his name suggested: the one who forgives his enemies. He seemed like a prototype of the modern Iranian man, but his modernity had its limits. He wasn't supposed to know that Mandana took the pill. He wasn't supposed to know that she was lying in my bed when she purported to be staying at a girlfriend's place. He wasn't supposed to know any of the secret deals his wife struck with his daughters.

He knew it. He knew everything. But he had to pretend he knew nothing. At the time, I thought he was living in a lie. Years later, I understood that the lie was his armor in defending us against the liars, the cover behind which he gave us freedom. I never thanked him for it, and it haunted me.

Gypsy knew this part of my past. She understood that Mandana had played a crucial role in shaping me into the man she took as her husband, and she was grateful for it. She knew that it was Mandana who had kept my life from falling apart when I despaired over my parents' separation, and that it was Mandana who had pushed me to mend my relationship with my mother. This journey was a passage into our future that acknowledged the past.

We landed in Tehran and entered a quiet country. Freedom of speech was quietly suppressed. Dissidents were quietly arrested. A nuclear program was quietly developed. We detested the regime, but we believed in the beauty of the country. We believed that the Iranian people were different from the men who pretended to represent them.

It was the spring of 2009 and we had no idea of the turmoil that was coming. We couldn't know that, only months later, people would take to the streets to protest the manipulated results of a presidential election, only to see their uprising brutally crushed. Many would be arrested, many raped, bludgeoned, shot dead. We didn't know the face of Neda Agha-Soltan yet, the student who would lie dying in a street in Tehran, blood streaming across her cheeks, a sniper's bullet in her chest.

The apparatus of the Islamic Republic of Iran received the American bride with theatrical coldness. The photograph in her visa showed Gypsy smiling, and the immigration officer might have liked it. But he didn't open her passport. It was enough for him to see the golden eagle and the gilded words "United States of America." He grabbed the passport, gestured harshly in one direction and said, "Come!"

He led us to a desk where two men in elaborately embroidered uniforms were sitting, frozen in straight posture. They carried themselves with an abrasiveness that suggested they were in charge of handling sensitive cases. I presented my German passport, but they waved me off. I pulled out our marriage certificate, but it didn't help that it carried the seal of the City of New York. One of the officers took Gypsy's passport and disappeared, the other pointed to a bench by the wall and said, "Wait!"

We sat on this bench like defendants. It didn't surprise us that the American received special scrutiny, just like Iranians are singled out whenever they try to enter the U.S. But we were convinced that they had vetted Gypsy before issuing her visa, and the same was probably true for me. We didn't have anything to hide and knew that our governments would be there for us if we needed help. But after twenty minutes in abeyance, we became nervous. We began to strategize how to react if they separated us.

That is the frame of mind where dictatorial regimes like to have their visitors. They give you time to think, and watch as you slide into irrationality. Gypsy was now a woman without a passport, stateless in an arbitrary state. The officer kept staring at us from behind his desk; that seemed to be his task.

Gypsy leaned over my shoulder and whispered, "My heart is going to jump out of my chest."

After a while, the other officer returned with Gypsy's passport. He placed it on the desk and took an inkpad and a sheet of paper out of a drawer. Then he asked for Gypsy's hand. Printed on the paper were two large and ten small squares. He took Gypsy's hand and pressed the tip of her fingers on the inkpad, then on the paper—the individual fingerprints in the small squares, the whole hand in the large squares. When he was done, he pushed the passport across the desk and smirked. He seemed to enjoy the fact that the American now had to run around his country with ink on her fingertips, like a criminal.

I waited for him to ask for my hand, but he wasn't interested. When I asked why he took Gypsy's fingerprints but not mine, he looked amused and said, "Because America does it." Our eyes locked and we both laughed at the absurdity of the games governments play.

Gypsy and I got on a bus that took us into the city, and the first thing we saw were the illuminated minarets of the Khomeini Mausoleum, piercing like lances into the night sky. Khomeini followed us wherever we went, always watching. Our hotel in Tehran was named after Ferdowsi, a revered Persian poet, but we only ever saw Khomeini. He gazed at us from the wall behind the reception desk, and on the way to the elevator we passed a Khomeini painting and a Khomeini bust, then listened to an instrumental version of "Careless Whisper" as we ascended to our floor. Even the elevator music was from the time of Khomeini.

We entered our room and saw two single beds, a picture of Khomeini hanging in the middle. We thought it was a misunderstanding. Perhaps they had given us separate beds because Gypsy had not shed her family's name. We went back to the reception and explained to the concierge that we were on our honeymoon and would like to sleep in the same bed. He gave us a mystified look and said that Iranian couples sleep in separate beds.

We dismissed this Iranian tradition and pushed our beds together under Khomeini's beard. Then Gypsy undressed in front of him. The ayatollah had to look at a number of things during our honeymoon. Maybe that is why he always stared at us with such a grim face.

The next morning, as we walked around Tehran to get a feel for life in the city, Gypsy caught a glimpse of her reflection in a store window. She stopped, spun around and said, "I look elegant." It was a tender moment that demonstrated how porous the mullah's banishment of sensuality from public life was. They didn't seem to understand that the shrouds into which they forced women are like frames that emphasize their beauty. Or maybe they did.

In the afternoon, Gypsy and I argued about something, and she went for a walk by herself. I shouldn't have let her go, but it seemed like a good way to release some of the tension the all-pervading restrictions had caused between us. After an hour she came back to our room, stirred up. She dropped her purse and said, "They're hissing at me!" She was talking about the men. Gypsy was used to this in the streets of Santo Domingo, but there was something playful about the hissing of Dominican men. They would explain themselves. The hissing of Iranian men was desperate, and they didn't say a word. Their speechlessness frightened Gypsy.

The men's desperation made me think about the unintended effects of the dress code. Coming from Berlin, where I had tired a bit of women with candy-colored hair walking around barefoot and holding bottles of cheap beer, I appreciated the proper way Iranian women dressed. But I wondered if the strictness of the code created a suppressed erotic tension in the streets. There was a sense of the men feeling strangled, of wanting to break out, and I could see myself as one of them.

Gypsy studied the women and learned how they pushed the dress code's boundaries. The closer she looked, the more skin she saw. She noticed women who pushed their headscarves so far back that they almost fell off their heads. She saw sleeves that ended at the elbow. She glimpsed skinny jeans under overcoats cut so tight that they revealed more than they covered.

Gypsy remained covered; she didn't want to be seen as the loose American. Every morning, she disappeared under her overcoat and closed it all the way up to her neck. She spent more and more time in front of the mirror, and despaired over how far she could go. One particularly hot morning, she stood in front of me and asked, "Do you think I have to wear the coat?" I thought so and pulled up her coat's zipper. Gypsy looked down on herself and, sounding crestfallen, said, "I'm oppressed."

I, in contrast, felt almost liberated. I was aware that there is also a dress code for men. (When you Google "male dress code," the suggested search automatically includes "Iran.") But I was in no danger of being targeted by the chastity squads. The very style that had often earned me teasing from my friends—crisply ironed shirts rather than t-shirts, no bright colors, and never, ever shorts—was in perfect sync with the mullahs' definition of decency. I also lacked the dramatically spiked haircut popular among young men, for which some of them have been arrested. I was behind the Iranian curve, though, with my rejection of Texan-size belt buckles, and bell-bottoms that seemed to come straight out of *Saturday Night Fever*.

In the streets, the visible women stood in stark relief next to the invisible ones. The women that I once heard two young

Iranian men call B.M.O.s—black moving objects—fluttered around completely covered up, showing only their eyes. "They could become pregnant and nobody would notice," Gypsy said. We soon learned that there are many things the invisible ones can do under their shrouds.

When one black moving object walked past us, we caught a glimpse of her uncovered feet in her open shoes. Her nail polish was a seductive scarlet. The discovery changed the way I looked at women. I began to understand the burning of Iranian men for a woman's ankles. They are the erotic zone in a disembodied country.

We began to see the abyss behind the veil, the revolts in the details. And then we saw two women prancing around the lobby of our hotel, dangerously uncovered. One of them had Cindy Crawford's hair and mole; she wore boots with heels capable of impalement. The other one had Amy Winehouse's winged eyeliner and aura of emaciation; she purred without pause into her phone. We saw this as our chance to join one of those infamous illegal parties raging behind Iran's closed doors, with dancing, alcohol, and other sins. But as we got closer, we stopped in our tracks. They were either transvestites or transgender women, pushing the boundaries in the safety of a hotel frequented by Westerners.

Deceit has always been the cloak of lovers in Iran, long before Khomeini seized power. The door of an old teahouse in the city of Yazd, an architectural jewel in the heart of the country, reminded us of that. In the old Persia, houses had separate door knockers for men and women. Men used a massive rectangular piece of iron to knock, while women touched a slender ring, announcing their arrival with a softer, gentler sound. But what was meant to keep men and women apart, opened the door for men who wanted to be with their beloved behind the façades of chastity. They knocked as women.

Khomeini didn't like the blurring of the line between man and woman, and he sought clarity. In 1984 he issued a fatwa allowing transsexuals to change their sex. To him, transsexuals were prisoners caught in the wrong body. He set out to liberate them and bestowed penises on male women, and vaginas on female men. It is a lesser-known part of the Ayatollah's legacy that the Islamic Republic of Iran has a budget for sex changes, allocating the equivalent of $122,000 for each person diagnosed with "gender identity disorder," the regime's term for transsexuality.

Khomeini became the god of plastic surgeons, and not just for transgendered people. The shroud under which he forced Iranian women reduced them to faces. He focused the male gaze on the one part of the female body that men could study in detail, and they were beguiled by the darkest eyes, immaculate brows, and beautiful noses. I liked the Iranian nose; there was something regal about it, mystical. But I made the same mistake as Khomeini. Many Iranian women don't want a nose that stands out from the frame of their scarf, a nose that exceeds the conventions of the West. They dream of a generic nose, a line in the face. This is how the Ayatollah created a promised land for plastic surgeons. For a few thousand U.S. dollars, they plane every bump in the Iranian face.

The operated women weren't hiding. We saw them everywhere: in the streets, in teahouses, at the mosque. They couldn't wait to exhibit their bandaged faces and show others that they were able to afford a small nose. The operated nose is the Iranian woman's Gucci purse.

And the nose was only the beginning. Step by step, plastic surgeons were conquering the body of the Iranian woman. After diminishing the nose, they moved on to pumping up lips and breasts to desperate-housewife levels. The veil turned out to be one of their best marketing tools, emphasizing the visible results of their work and covering the ones not to be seen.

The men, in a rare reversal, were beginning to follow the women's lead. Many of them are less educated than most women. They skip college in order to chase fast money, hoping it will enable them to purchase a captivating bride. But when it came to nose jobs, they were slowly catching up, showing off their freshly operated noses just as proudly as the women.

Gypsy shared my affection for the Iranian nose; she didn't like the operated men. Once, I saw her holding a rial bill dominated by a portrait of Khomeini. She moved her thumb across his face, as though she was caressing him. "He was a good-looking man," she said, gazing at Khomeini. She found his nose beautiful.

We traveled south and followed the road of addiction. The highway between Tehran and Kerman is the main artery of the drug trade in Iran, where an estimated 5 million people are addicted to opium and heroin. We didn't see any of that. All we saw was a dry, rocky landscape dotted by an endless gallery of portraits of supposed martyrs, sent to their death in the war with Iraq. Their faces lined the road like advertisements for an unnamed product.

At one rest stop, we saw a different kind of gallery. A truck driver opened the door of his cab, revealing that he was surrounded by pictures of half-naked women. When he got up, the body of another half-naked woman materialized, life-size and printed on the red cover of his seat. He had been sitting on her lap.

The mullahs have divided love into the allowed and the forbidden. Allowed love is a corset that suffocates lovers. That is why many seek refuge in forbidden love. Couples are not allowed to have sex before marriage, but if they do, there are solutions. Nobody ever asks the groom if he is still a virgin, and the bride can have her hymen stitched back together for a few hundred dollars.

Money is an important substance in Iranian love, a currency with the power to surpass the value of passion. The parents of a bride can demand a large sum for their daughter. The groom's family in return purchases the bride with a money-back guarantee, in case the marriage fails. A woman's value is meticulously assessed in the arithmetic of the law. In life, as a bride, she is most precious. But if she dies and somebody is culpable in her death and forced to pay blood money, she is worth only half as much as a man.

I gazed at Iranian love like a world behind glass. I was traveling around the country with a woman who had chosen me at a time when I had neither money nor the promise of it. I didn't have to pay for her, and I was allowed to find out if I liked sleeping with her before I married her. My love life began to feel like a province of privilege.

Sleeping with a man who is not her own can be deadly for an Iranian woman. An extra-marital affair can also lead a man into death, but he can rely on the masculinity of the Iranian state of law. In court, a woman's word, like her life, is only worth half as much as that of a man.

That was the other Iran. We didn't see it, but we heard of it. While we were savoring our honeymoon, seven women and two men were waiting to be stoned to death for adultery and sexual indecency. Their stonings were suspended, but when the time comes, the accused have to descend into a pit—the women down to their chest, the men down to their hips. The stonings have a strict choreography, and the stones must not be too big. Justice is supposed to descend slowly upon the indecent.

I have done things in my life that could have gotten me stoned in this country. My indecency had not gone unpunished, but I had gotten off comparatively cheap. I remembered the force with which a betrayed girlfriend once hit me in the face. I remembered the gentle stoning I received from Mandana. She threw the other woman's letters at me.

Later that night, Gypsy and I walked around Kerman and saw a house with two blinking hearts on its façade, melting into one. We suspected something wicked going on behind these walls, and sneaked inside. But the club of hearts was not a hotbed of vice; one couldn't buy love there, at least not the fast way. It was a wedding ballroom, but one with a twist. The Iranian hierarchy was turned upside down in this house—the women were celebrating upstairs, the men downstairs.

The bride was beautiful. She had eyes black as coal, and the classic Iranian nose. She was dancing in a strapless gown. I never saw her; I wasn't allowed to go near her. Gypsy told me about her, after a group of giggling women had taken her upstairs. I was sitting downstairs with the other men, staring at our juice glasses.

I felt dirty in this aura of purity. The separation of men and women and the banning of alcohol and lust were the opposite of everything that was welcome at our own wedding. We had placed the voluptuous Turkish woman next to the divorced German man, hoping for attraction. My bride danced with other men. We drank Dominican rum in large amounts, and at five in the morning, a gay male friend was passionately kissing a woman.

All that was taboo in the lonely hearts club. The women offered Gypsy sweets; the men were brooding in their juice quarantine and ignored me. I felt like inciting them to storm the women's floor, but I learned that there were other ways for them to find solace. For Shiites, Iran's overwhelming majority, marriage can be a wide-open field, at least for men.

There is room for up to four wives in their marriages, and if that is not enough, the husband can expand his portfolio with "temporary marriages." This kind of marriage may last up to ninety-nine years, but the more popular version lasts only a few hours. That is why Iranians also call it a "pleasure marriage."

The pleasure is the man's alone. He is not obliged to tell his wife about a temporary marriage, and all he has to discuss with his pleasure wife is the price. No written contract is required, which is also a pleasure for a man in a country where his word counts twice as much in court as that of a woman. If the man wants to, he can strike a temporary marriage agreement that includes how often he wants sex. The woman, however, is not entitled to any sexual demands, and she must not be married. She only has to be at least as old as Aisha when she became the third wife of the Prophet Muhammad. Aisha was nine.

The temporary marriage affords men a diverse sex life, where no adultery and no children out of wedlock exist. The wives in temporary marriages are usually divorced women, who are damaged goods in the permanent-marriage market. They need the money, and hope that the man stays with them for more than an hour, perhaps even leaves his first wife. They discreetly signal that they are available for a temporary marriage by wearing their chador inside out.

Wherever we went, we realized that this is not the norm but, rather, a possibility. It felt like a wand invented by a male-dominated regime trying to show a way out to the very men it is stifling, and we were reminded of that at the lonely hearts club, where the pleasure was the women's alone.

It was almost midnight, but there was still light inside the shop. An elderly woman wearing a black chador stood in front of a white wall, perfectly placed between portraits of Khomeini and Khamenei. When I stopped to take a photograph of her with the ayatollahs looking over her shoulder, she gestured for us to wait and called to someone in the back of the shop. Out came her smiling daughter, and a perilous conversation ensued. She told us about her forbidden love.

I cannot write where we met her; there would be terrible consequences if the guardians of Iran's order found her. She had a lyrical name and spoke good English; she liked the language and literature of her country's supposed enemy. She was in her early twenties and hungry for unrestricted love. But she was afraid they might come for her. There was always the fear of being arrested for the crime of having a boyfriend.

She told us about the night everything changed. She remembered it clearly, the time, the place, the sweet taste of ice cream on her lips. They had waited until night fell, thinking they would be safer under the cover of darkness. They drove to a quiet street, with her at the wheel, pretending to be sister and brother. They had just stopped when another car slowly passed by, with two men inside staring at them. After a while, the car came back and stopped behind them. The two men got out, approached their car and dangled handcuffs in front of the ice cream-eating couple.

The men weren't wearing uniforms and didn't identify themselves. They didn't have to. The couple knew that if they said a wrong word, they would be dragged to a building that everyone in the city knew—the prison of forbidden love. After their arrest, the parents would have had to pick up their indecent children. They would have had to pay a fine and sign a pledge that this will never happen again. "We don't have the right to eat ice cream," the young woman said, tears welling up in her eyes.

The mother looked at her daughter and took her hand. She didn't understand a word, but she seemed to know exactly what the daughter was telling us. Then she threw her thumb over her shoulder, pointing at Khomeini and Khamenei on the wall behind her, and shook her head. We went back to our hotel room and turned Khomeini's portrait around, making him face the wall.

It was the saddest night of our honeymoon, but something changed as we lay on another tradition-defying bed. A delicate confidence was seeping into the way we looked at the country, especially the women. There was a subcutaneous seething, a quiet determination to turn their rage into change—with a baseball bat if necessary. It reminded us of something a man had told us at a teahouse. We were cautious not to discuss anything with the slightest political undertone, but we eagerly listened to whatever people wanted to share. What the man told us sounded incredible at the time, but his words kept coming back to us as the mothers and daughters of Iran came into sharper focus. He said, "The women will bring the mullahs down."

The man with the golden microphone stood in front of a wall and sang. A small crowd of people gathered around him, looking enchanted as they listened to him. This made the man dangerous. He sang only love songs, but a policeman pushed through the crowd, bent over the loudspeaker and lowered the volume. The man smiled and kept singing. A few minutes later, two other policemen came and unplugged his microphone.

We were standing in a street in Shiraz, and the Iranian police state reminded us of its fearful nature. Shiraz is the city of poets, the heart of romantic old Persia, but we came only for Hafez. Iran's most beloved poet had written with breathless passion about love and lies in the time of despotism, and it moved us. He called himself a "serf of love," drank heavily, and dreamed of soaking prayer rugs with wine. Hafez lived in the fourteenth century, when mosque and state were one and the mullahs ruled with an arbitrary fist similar to the Iran of the twenty-first century. We read his poems and felt as though he was still alive.

Preachers who preen in prayer-niche and pulpit,
when in private, quite another matter do they practice
than they preach!

The Hafez mausoleum is a place of pilgrimage for lovers. Newlyweds come from all over the country to be close to Hafez, and we followed them. We placed our hands next to theirs on the cold marble of his tomb and listened to them recite the Qu'ran's first *surah*. While they vowed to worship Him alone, we whispered a worldly wish, desiring a child.

There was something about Hafez that made people feel safe. At no other place did we see so many couples touch each other—holding hands, embracing each other, exchanging chaste kisses. And in the park surrounding the mausoleum we saw men that, former president Ahmadinejad once claimed, don't exist in Iran. Following the trend of the time, they had carefully modeled their hair to look like ransacked birds' nests. But something was different about them. Their eyebrows were a little too perfect, their t-shirts a little too tight, their nails a little too filed, and one of them sat on another's lap. We sat with them for a while, and one of them confided to Gypsy that they were "admirers of men." Then we saw some of them look at two policemen walking by as if they were their secret fantasy.

Young men and fire. A lot of them seemed to be playing with it, especially in matters of love. But the gay men reveling in Hafez's shadow, despite being persecuted by a homophobic regime, seemed almost privileged when we came across another generation of young men. On the road from Shiraz to Isfahan we stopped at a white building adorned with Iranian flags; it seemed to be decorated in celebration of something. Inside were the tombs of three soldiers who had fallen in the war with Iraq. It was a shrine to their deaths, silent on their lives. On the pristine white walls surrounding the tombs were photographs that documented their transformation from soldiers to martyrs. The first images showed nervous, smiling young men up to their chests in murky water, each holding a rifle over their head like a monstrance. The last images showed bodies that were missing something. An arm. A leg. A head.

In Isfahan we wanted to let go of all this. The sadness of having ice cream. The danger of golden microphones. The decency guards wielding feather dusters at the mosque, tapping women they deemed insufficiently covered. The air was clear and the night warm, and we felt like tourists again. But the men had a way of drifting toward us. We walked across the Bridge of 33 Arches and watched a man having his portrait drawn by a street artist. When the man noticed us, he pointed at the drawing and asked, "Beautiful?" He was unhappy with the size of his nose, even though the artist had drawn it smaller than it actually was. We sat down for our own portrait, and the artist, giving us the Iranian treatment, drew our noses smaller than they actually were. When we said goodbye, he reached out and shook Gypsy's hand. He was the first man in Iran who touched her.

Under the bridge was a teahouse with a beautiful view of the river, the glow of the city reflecting on its surface. Teahouses are the Iranian substitute for bars, a placebo for those who want to talk and mingle in a country where drinking alcohol is forbidden. The place was bustling with large groups of friends and families, and watching them engage in passionate discussions, it became obvious why the regime had shut down teahouses around the country. It was there that we met Mehdi and his brother Muhammad. They brought us saffron ice cream and told us about each of their difficulties finding a bride.

Mehdi and Muhammad were in their early thirties and their father was getting nervous that his sons still weren't married. He was putting pressure on them. The problem was money—they had too much of it. Coming from a wealthy family, the brothers felt that what attracted most women to them was their buying power. It's the luxury problem of privileged men in a society where brides come with a price tag. "Maybe I should marry a foreigner," Mehdi said.

As a man with a foreign bride, I was not in a position to argue against marrying one. But I didn't want Mehdi to give up on an Iranian bride, and I told him about the women in New York I had pursued in vain. Claiming that Gypsy was an exception to the rule, I said that, over there, I often felt that a man's value partly depended on his net worth. Gypsy put her hand on Mehdi's and nodded. He looked at her in disbelief.

We talked late into the night and wanted to take a photograph to remember it by. Gypsy placed herself between the brothers, but they didn't fit into the frame. They kept their distance from the woman in the middle and stood next to her like soldiers at roll call, arms pressed against their flanks. I motioned for them to get closer to Gypsy. The brothers looked over their shoulders, as if planning a crime, and then, beaming, moved in and put their arms around Gypsy.

The man I came to call Little Shah didn't want to be in the picture. He had heard us speak English and hovered around our table, but now he kept his distance. Mehdi knew him; he was a regular at the teahouse. His English had a tinge of an American accent, which he seemed to cultivate, and he watched us like somebody who knew us. He was dressed in a black pinstriped suit with a shiny veneer of neglect, as though he had not taken it off in a long time. He wore it like his past.

His name was the same as that of the last Shah of Iran, Mohammed Reza. When we went for a walk along the Zayandeh River, which irrigates the fields and dreams of the people along its banks, he followed us and told us his story. He said he used to work as a journalist and, as punishment for writing the truth, was thrown into jail for several years. Now he worked at a police station. He cleaned it.

I viewed the Little Shah in the conditional. He had a black briefcase that he hugged like a pillow and said things that make a person cautious in a surveillance state. He told us that he had seen us in the morning near our hotel and overheard us speak German and Spanish, and he tried to impress us by speaking a little bit of both. He knew what had recently been on the cover of *Der Spiegel*, a magazine I have written for. He wanted to know if I had brought a laptop and foreign newspapers.

Maybe he was an unrefined spy; maybe he was just a ragged man cleaning the dirt of those who had broken him. I didn't know what to make of him. We said goodbye, pretending to be exhausted from our honeymoon, but the Little Shah wasn't done with us. He asked us to give him just a few more minutes. He sat down on a small brick wall, pulled a school notebook and a fountain pen from his briefcase, and wrote a poem for us.

> *People tell me that windows*
> *have no feelings and no heart.*
> *But when a window fogs up*
> *and I write the words*
> *"I love you"*
> *on the glass,*
> *the window begins to cry.*

The following night, we went back to the teahouse. Mehdi had asked us to meet him there. He wanted to drive us to a popular spot in the mountains that he said has the most beautiful view of Isfahan. As I sat down on the passenger seat, he put a plastic bag full of money between my feet. I looked at the bag in amazement, and he laughed and said inside were the day's earnings from his uncle's business.

As we drove out of the city and saw it turn into a sea of lights behind us, Mehdi tried to impress us with his racing, pushing other cars out of the way. We ignored it, until everything came to a stop and we saw the woman with the baseball bat walking toward Mehdi. She was taller than him.

The road lay in front of us like a stage in a play about a future Iran. In the spotlight stood a man at the moment when everything crashed and his hubris caught up with him. Mehdi raised his arms higher and pleaded with the woman. But she didn't say a word. She held the bat in front of her chest like a scepter and stared at him.

Mehdi slowly retreated, came back to the car and reached into the bag with the money. He grabbed as many bills as he could, walked back to the woman and waved the bills in front of her, begging her to take them. The woman lowered her bat, turned around and got into her car. She sped off and left Mehdi standing in the street with a handful of money, a small, humiliated man.

Mario Kaiser is a writer of narrative nonfiction whose work seeks to expand our understanding of social justice and human rights. His stories are based on long-term immersion in environments that are difficult to access, illustrating how government policies and social disruptions affect people's lives and long-term prospects. After graduating from the University of Bonn, Kaiser received a master's degree in journalism from New York University. A former reporter and editor for Die Zeit *and* Der Spiegel, *his*

work has also appeared in The International New York Times, Guernica, Narratively, *and* Transition. *He lives in New York City. "Love and Lies in Iran" originally appeared on the website Narratively and won the Grand Prize Silver in the Tenth Annual Solas Awards. You can follow Mario at @MarioKaiserNYC.*

ERIN BYRNE

❧ ❧ ❧

Spirals: Memoir of a Celtic Soul

This trip to Ireland was a strange kind of homecoming.
If you do not bring the kind eye of creative expectation
to your inner world, you will never find anything there.

— *John O'Donohue,* Anam Ċara

A shell-shaped spiral emerged in my center when my
child-eyes first beheld the rugged cove outside the cottage where I was born on the west coast of Ireland. The clear
wavelets lapped over gray-blue rocks and my little pink toes,
and washed into my fragile senses. This shape was all around
me as I grew—*mollusca*, seahorses, and *Scolelepis Squamata*
(the bristleworm, slender bluish green, which swims in spirals
when disturbed)—and I collected many to set upon my shelf.

The Gaelic tongue curled into the whirls of my ear, to
the spiral ganglion, sending the sound to my brain when
my mother called me home across fields of high grass (*gabh
isteach!*) or in my own voice raised in song (*amhrán*) or when
my grandmother (*máthair mhór*) murmured her love, saying,
"*Tá grá agam duit.*" The lonely tones of a *uilleann* pipe chased

the wind through mist-kissed air to rustle the leaves of the wild cherry tree I climbed.

When I was four years old, my mother held my newborn sister in her arms and I put my hand upon her small head, smoothing her silky black hair.

"See this place where God breathed life into her," my mother said. "Right here on the top of her head it was; see how her hair grows around and around the spot. It happened just the same way with you, love."

She cupped her hand on the top of my head and smiled.

My grandfather took me for long walks along leafy lanes. One autumn day he pointed to a falling leaf.

"Watch the wind waft it down in spiralesque whooshes, darling," he said. He reached down and pulled the ribbon from my head and my long hair lifted and fanned out and wrapped around my face. The sound of our laughter rose and was carried off.

He put his gnarled finger on the tip of mine and whispered that the spirals there were my very own print, with none other like it in the wide world. He told me about limitless galaxies that danced in space in the very same shape, and magnetic fields that drew objects together. He showed me rings upon a freshly chopped tree trunk, and tendrils of flower stems and vines that grew in loops.

Some days at dusk, I stood on the shore and watched for my father's boat on distant waves. He'd told me that the oceans ushered their tides in and out in a spiral motion, and I trusted the sea to return him to me in just this same way.

Smoke snaked into my nostrils from a peat fire in the hearth of our cottage, then again in another cottage, then again in another, illuminating, cooking, warming, and ever burning—smoldering overnight then blown to orangish life in the morning. The smell wound around my red-bright heart while my family slept and waked and worked and ate and stared into those licking flames; we were warmed outside *and* in.

I remember arcs of sparks leaping from fires.

A strange thing happened to me when I was fourteen, walking home late one night across a high plain in County Kerry. Across the black ink-spill of sky I saw fires on far horizons. My spirit flew backward over decades, centuries, millenniums to a night halfway between the spring equinox and summer solstice. I was standing inside a circle of gigantic stones and there were fires everywhere. The warm earth pulsed under my bare feet and a restless breeze raised the hair on my arms. A heavy cloak pressed my shoulders. (I knew, of course, that it was white.) My raised hand held a dagger.

Bealtaine, the fire festival.

I was at the place of seventeen pillars, Drombeg, called Druid's Altar, over in County Cork, miles from my home. I knew the bonfires were the burning of winter bedding and floor coverings, and some saw witches jumping through flames in ethereal ecstasy while others performed rituals to protect people from otherworldly spirits. It was the Bronze Age. As I stood surrounded by the stones, spirals sparked from the fire and sprinkled down from shooting stars straight into me.

And just as suddenly as I'd appeared at the bonfires, I was at the gate of our cottage—my hand on the latch, my feet on the path. It was like something out of a story, it was, that apparition of myself. Even now when I think of that dagger, I am filled with fright. Have I been *gifted with a faery life?*

It sounds strange, but the spirals I felt that night remained inside me, wrapping around time and place, turning memory to experience and experience to memory, in spite of time's insistence otherwise. What is this shape that laps around and around my awareness of the real?

These ancient symbols existed before the written word. Before the pyramids emerged in Egypt, in a place called Newgrange on the eastern side of Ireland, the people sensed something quickening inside their bodies when they looked up at the swirling of the heavens. They sought to imprint this upon their stones, to show order coming out of chaos. The spiral's mystical powers were thought to repel evil spirits from entering tombs, and the stones of Newgrange were covered with these curving carvings.

Bees danced in a spiral near their hive, revealing the source of honey I collected as a young woman. It was for the making of the mead: ambrosia, honey-wine, the nectar of the gods, which promised pleasures of the palate and the flesh, and quickened the mysterious pulsings of arousal that were beginning to stir in my blood when I felt the touch of a certain young man.

My people always felt this force whisking through their beings, so they carved, painted, and drew it upon their treasures: jewelry, tools, precious metalwork, and always the stones.

What does the shape signify? The self-expanding out or the natural world reaching in? The spiritual balance between ourselves, the sun, and the cosmos? Land, sea, sky or the Holy Trinity? The constant spiraling of the soul through death, initiation and rebirth? The answer is unknown because myths and spiritual ideas in Celtic culture were passed down one generation at a time, through ritual, storytelling, music and dance, but never the written word—these secrets were too sacred.

One thing is sure: Theories and sophisticated stories were spun to explain our existence, and we Irish developed brilliant minds and unparalleled lyrical grace that remained unsullied through centuries of enslavement.

Throughout my years in Ireland, the green ribbon grew like stardust out of a magic wand, sparking in one long line that looped up and around and through my eyes, ears, skin, hair and heart, tingeing my life with magic.

Childhood passed swiftly. It seemed suddenly I was a grown woman living in America, married into a clan who kept Irish traditions by producing a never-ending stream of children, celebrating life's end with four-day-long wakes, and declaring love often with kisses on the lips and long-winded, sentimental toasts.

Now my home is Washington State where the rain keeps everything green, but I pine for patchwork farms and roads lined with wild fuchsias. I think of Ireland so often that this country intertwines with that country until both places are one.

The ring I wear has three spirals, the *tristele*, a tiny silver reminder of what winds within. This shape is, to me, *álainn*: beautiful. I chose it to decorate my home: My favorite upholstered chair is covered with gold threads of spirals, the rug beneath my feet is bordered with wavelets of them, and a print upon my wall of van Gogh's *Starry Night* has in its center an undulating starswirl in greeny white-blue—all around my house spirals pirouette. There is even a calligraphic curlicue at the top of the first letter of my own symbolic name.

I see widening gyres in my mind's eye, next to me on life's journey, gently rolling or flying forward. Through times of poisonous loneliness, stinging sorrow, or the dark grip of grief, they illuminate my path like a chain of tiny emeralds pulled across an expanse of black velvet, making visible the invisible, making brighter the divine.

These sixth-sense Irish arabesques steer clear of the English in me and skirt the Scottish, but cling to my Americanness. Their motion is ceaseless, their repetition reassuring—up and down and around and around again and again, these Celtic spirals, spinning on their predestined course. They are mine to keep; when my spirit leaves my body they will fly with me.

I came again to that Kerry coastline years later and the vortex inside me lit up like phosphorescence. As I stood on the bluff over Ventry Bay, out of the corner of my eye I saw tips of long strands that ignited and flashed from auburn to silver as the breeze again swirled my hair around my shoulders.

I returned, with my husband and sons, to fields where black-and-white cows lounged in front of rugged castle and cathedral ruins, to the land of the navigator whose name I gave one of my strapping sons, and the place that holds the illuminated manuscript the other son is named after. The taste of soda bread dripping with butter and honey orbited my tongue, taking me back to simple meals with many bodies wedged around a rough-hewn table inside a country cottage.

John O'Donohue, Irish poet, philosopher, and scholar, wrote that the eternal world and the mortal world are not parallel, but fused, as captured in the Gaelic phrase *fighte fuaighte*, woven into and through each other. I felt this fusion when I returned alone at night to that megalithic circle.

Drombeg sat silent and stoic upon its high plain, the stones shimmering silver in the moonlight. I had heard when the site was excavated they found the remains of an adolescent wrapped in a thick cloth inside a pot in the circle's center. I stood again inside the circle remembering the raised dagger and the hair on my arms rose: What had happened the night I crossed over?

When all is said and done, how do we not know but that our
own unreason may be better than another's truth?
For it has been warmed on our hearths and in our souls, and is ready
for the wild bees of truth to hive in it, and make their sweet honey.
—William Butler Yeats, The Celtic Twilight

I ask: Is a soul decorated only with the times and places that the body inhabits? Is not the lace we are made of more intricate and complicated than that, woven of what exists within our senses *and* what we sense from our existence? Is yours forged within the confines of reality? Mine is not.

For I was not born in Ireland, nor did I grow in many cottages there, or climb the wild cherry to the echo of the *uilleann*. I first set foot on Irish soil when there were slivers of silver in my reddish hair and my sons were nearly grown. But when I arrived, it was—to every cell in my body, each neuron in my brain, and all the sensors in my spirit—a homecoming, a return. The coils inside me glowed and sizzled as I *remembered*—in the truest sense of my experience of memory—a past I didn't possess.

Unreasonable to some, perhaps. But whether placed there gingerly by my ancestors—for I am surely of Irish heritage—or, stranger still, through a series of previous lives spanning thousands of years, these curls cling sweetly. I suppose there is a way to test the truth of this.

Into my soul, which has been honeycombed with golden spirals, I invite the bees.

Erin Byrne is the author of Wings: Gifts of Art, Life, and Travel in France, *winner of the Paris Book Festival Award and the Next Generation Indie Book Award, editor of* Vignettes & Postcards from Paris *and* Vignettes & Postcards from Morocco, *and writer of* The Storykeeper *film. Erin's travel essays, poetry, fiction and screenplays have won numerous awards including the Reader's Favorite Award, Foreword Reviews Book of the Year Finalist, and an Accolade Award for film. This story won the Grand Prize Silver in the Sixth Annual Solas Awards. She has taught writing at Shakespeare and Company Bookstore in Paris and on Deep Travel trips, and is host of the LitWings*

event series at Book Passage, Sausalito, which features writ-ers, photographers, and filmmakers. Her screenplay, Siesta, *is in pre-production in Spain, and she is working on a novel set in the Paris Ritz during the occupation,* Illuminations. *Follower her at www.e-byrne.com*

AMY GIGI ALEXANDER

☙ ☙ ☙

Oranges and Roses

A planned trip to Paris changes with sudden grief,
and changes again with the discovery of
Africa on the outskirts of the city.

Women stand above me, brightly colored *boubou* dresses blending into an African origami screen blocking my view. Hands, like undecided hummingbirds, hover over my heart, swiftly moving to my eyes, covering them with damp palms. Children tied to their mothers' backs watch, as I lie on the thin mattress in the tiny apartment, wooden bones of crates underneath pressing into my back. I feel the slap of hands hard against my calves, hear the metallic ring of the spoon as it stirs an elixir of powder and mango juice. I drink the glassful greedily, juice running down my chin, tasting the sweetness mixed with clay, dirt, earth.

Glimpses of the room through the crowd of women: verdigris-green walls splattered with tea-colored stains, sporting faded posters of a Senegalese paradise. Plastic bags of fruit and spices hang from the ceiling, an occasional cockroach dancing among them. Cherry pink satin drapes hang crookedly at the window, dirty glass framing a view of the largest African street market in all of Paris. The sweetness of carnations and the lushness of rotting fruit argue and push their way into the apartment. Street sounds blend and float up: the lilt of the melodic languages of the Ivory Coast blending with clipped French and rap music, forming a background chorus to the cluster of women in the room, who call to one another loudly, as if they are far apart.

Rocking, singing, the women close my eyes and cradle my head, guiding me to sleep, to an earthy rainforest I once knew that is far from this green room. I travel until I touch reddish rainforest earth, hear shifting animal sounds, smell bitter coffee beans roasting in fired gourd pots. Prompted by the creaking of delicate strings of a hammock sighing with my weight, following the echoes of stone hitting stone mashing yucca roots, I re-enter jungle time, and dream.

How I'd come to this bed, this room, this apartment, this tiny piece of West Africa located on the edge of Paris felt almost like another dream, too.

I'd been on a multi-year journey around the world, and having spent more than half a year living and working with an indigenous tribe in remote Panama, I wanted to experience something different: Paris. When the day finally came to leave, I walked through the village, finding it hard to say goodbye. Embraces exchanged with women in circus-colored dresses, grinding corn by the river in lean-to kitchens, sheltered by shiny slick palm roofs. Prayers spoken with holy men on horses adorned with collars of fruit, braided with sugarcane stalks. Accompanied by barefoot children in wet party clothes, I walked for a day through a downpour to the nearest village, where a 4x4 truck sat waiting to take me to a plane, sending me far from such a rare and untouched world.

Halfway to Paris, on a layover in Dubai, the news came that a flash flood had destroyed the part of Panama I just been in. Torrential rains and manmade erosion had made the river of my memories swell almost overnight. Dams broke, leveling villages, leaving people clinging to trees, eventually swallowing them whole. Only the night sky remained the same, still dressed in midnight, strung with stars of alabaster pearls. Hours later, boarding the plane for Paris, eyes burnt from tears, I was filled with longing for a place that no longer was. The pull toward the City of Light extinguished, I would arrive in Paris blinded by grief, blind to the most beautiful city on Earth.

Paris. It had begrudgingly welcomed me with rain that streaked the sky like scattered silverfish. I searched for the Paris of my imaginings as the taxi from the airport took me through city streets, but all I saw was cool cement and stone, attended by molding statues and bedraggled pigeons. Brisk Parisians, dressed in a monochromatic blur of black-charcoal-mushroom-brown rushed by homeless tent villages reflected double in glassy mirrored windows. Finally arriving at my rented rooms, I stood in a puddle in the street as the taxi pulled away, my shoes crushing crumpled red geranium petals that had fallen from the balconies above.

Cathedral bells outside my pied-a-terre rung each morning while it was still dark, sending me out into rain-drenched streets, dodging flowing gutters, wandering in search of something that would make me feel the soulfulness of the people I had just lost. My loss, incompatible with the touristic-laminated veneer of the Michelin route, allowed me to avoid the café where Hemingway ate his meals, the standard photograph from the top of the Eiffel tower.

It was on one of these wanderings that I discovered the Grand Mosque of Paris. Turquoise pools filled with cerise hibiscus blooms. Walkways tiled green and gold, a stylized forest floor. The *hammam*, staffed by women who had looked at my face wet with grief without questions as they willingly scrubbed a years' worth of jungle dirt away. Pinkish, glistening, I had emerged from the *hammam* blessed to witness the sun finally unveiled, glinting white and yellow lights off the Mosque minaret, its spiral tower reaching to God.

While I'd been being pummeled and scrubbed raw, the street outside had come alive, not just with sunshine but with the sound of drums. The pavement was a blur of crowded commotion, held back by police. Everyone arched toward the drumming: fast, furious, exuberant.

As the procession turned the corner onto the avenue and came into view, the crowd had roared in angry French, shaking hands and fists, a few among them spitting or mumbling curses. Their catcalls were drowned out by dayglow orange bullhorns, trumpeting songs in a melodic language alternating with French.

What was this? A parade?

"It is the Africans. They are allowed to legally protest today about their status in France. Many of them are here illegally." A man standing near me had replied to my silent question. "Stay away from them. They are dangerous."

The protesters were so close I could trace the flowery details of their long robes of bright batik, see the folds of the complex crossword of fabric covering their heads, black skin shining brightly against the white marble of the Mosque. I watched their happiness as they sang and danced, pausing now and again to state their case, voices resolute. They were the first people I had seen here who seemed alive, real. My hands lifted the ropes dividing the crowd from the Africans, and I ran, flying, toward the protesters, ignoring the shouts of the police, ignoring everything but the joyful drumbeats.

"*Soeur!* Sister!" The protesters had called out to me as I entered their group, breathless, giddy from the realization that I'd just broken the law. Everyone hugged me, kissed me on the cheek, smiled. My shoulders and waist were wrapped in a piece of African batik, and I held onto it tightly as I attempted to copy the curving moves of their dances. The beating of the drummers forced my feet and arms to move in ways they never had before, past the City Hall and the Sacre-Couer Basilica, through the Jewish Quarter and Montmartre.

We moved, swirling and dancing through the streets of Paris, a Paris I had never seen before that afternoon. And what a way it was to see it: not a rushed blur from a tour bus, nor a route suggested by a stuffy guidebook; instead, a view from the center of the street. Traffic stopped and statues gazed as traffic lights blinked in unison, fountains timed their water show with our steps, and parks bloomed. Paris, at last, was no longer gray and sullen, but had come to life. And so had I.

Goutte de'Or, Drop of Gold, was our final stop: the African quarter on the outskirts of central Paris. People greeted us with explosive exuberance, handing us flowers and cakes smelling of peanuts and sesame, dancing alongside us until we reached the center, an enormous outdoor market filled with hundreds of people. The drumming got louder, the singing flashed faster, spinning the dancers into streaks of violet and orange batik, turbans touching. With a throbbing head and blistered feet, I pushed my way out of the mass of music and neon to the comfort of the sidewalk.

Surrounded by endless food stalls and grocers, the scent of food was overwhelming. *Cinq centimes*, sugar cookies frosted with peanut butter, cooling on racks in front of Senegalese bakeries. Rainbows of fish, metallic against slabs of ice, pink eyes glassy. Ochre bundles of spices, hot-pink coconut candy, shining stacks of iridescent white tripe. Crowds stood around open-backed trucks, watching the butchering of goats and chickens. Sizzling chunks of meat twirling on wires over hibachi grills. Men carrying silver canisters of hot sugared mint tea, cups clattering on carts. Ropes of green plantains mixing with dark red bananas hung from rafters. Baskets of green mangoes leaning against celadon melons stacked in crates. Clusters of dusty pink grapes resting delicately in sky blue paper.

The Islamic call to prayer sounded out, followed by church bells. Then sirens sounded. Shutters marked with graffiti suddenly closed. People disappeared. Blending. Fading. Left was the lingering smell of fish and peanuts, shopkeepers' blank expressions, the rustling of goats and chickens as they shifted legs, having gained a little more time.

I stood alone.

It was then that I recognized a woman from the protest: wide face with equally wide-set eyes, thick arms in bangles, dress of acid yellow, black stripes. She stood staring at me from the doorway of a restaurant, its façade painted in an oceanic mural of moonscape waves. I found myself pulled toward her, as if strung along by an invisible fishing line cast from within the mural of watery blue wilderness.

"Welcome, welcome! I am Binta. Come, come!" she exclaims, opening the door and quickly grabbing my hand to pull me inside.

I introduce myself, but she moves her body impatiently, jiggling protest from her arms to her hips. "Sister! You are the one who marched with us. I already know who you are."

The street is suddenly pockmarked with police vans with grated metal windows and officers running darkly past the windows like quick daggers, helmets shining black. Binta swiftly locks the door and shuts the crusty blinds, motioning me to follow her to the back of the restaurant. My anxiety surfaces just for a moment, but her smile reassures me as we walk up a rusted metal staircase, her chatter effortlessly moving from French to English.

Once upstairs, Binta opens a door to a tiny apartment, the color of a greenish copper penny. The room is tightly filled with a dozen ample women wearing voluminous dresses of shimmering sorbet polyester, a display of batik fireworks golden and green, lounging on mattresses spread out on the floor. The jangle-jangle flash of gold bracelets mixes with babies and toddlers swaddled in between folds of flesh.

"There is no room for me." I protest. "I will just stay downstairs until the trouble is over."

"No." When Binta says it, her eyes narrow, her yellow-and-black dress puffing up like a bumblebee. "You walked with us. You will eat with us. This is our way, *terranga*, to be welcoming. Welcome to Senegal!" she heartily laughs, as she moves babies off of a mattress to make space for me.

We both sit down together, Binta beside me. A woman brings us a bowl of water, and I reach out to take a drink, causing wild laughter amongst the women. Binta takes the bowl from me, motioning for me to wash my hands, then dry them with a washcloth. The water smells of oranges and roses, the washcloth sour and ripe. Binta leans forward, taking the cloth from me, and I breathe in more of the same smell: she smells like oranges and roses, too.

Stories begin, Binta first. As she tells me about Senegal, her home, several women get up and begin to make tea in a tiny kitchenette serviced by a single hotplate. Binta tells me whom she left behind: children, parents, family. A journey by boat from West Africa to Spain, she was one of the few who survived the trip. Traveling by night on foot, by bus, by truck, hiding until she reached France. And then joy, to arrive here, at Goutte de'Or. Her luck at finding a job, learning English, saving money for her children. Her words are punctuated by the clatter of spoons mixing with the whistle of the kettle, and when her story is finished, a dozen teacups magically appear, brimming with hot mint tea.

"And you? Why did you join us? You are different, not like the rest," Binta says, her hand squeezing mine tightly.

"I came here because I thought Paris would be beautiful, but it isn't. I've been terribly sad." Crying, I tell them about the extraordinary people I had left behind in Panama. The flash flood that took them away. Their bright dresses. The ring of their language. The night sky from my shared hut. How I don't want to say goodbye to that mountain, that village, those people. How I don't want to forget. How they taught me how to live in the moment, and now, their moment was gone.

When I finally look up, it is to silence: the women stare at me and the children are gone.

"We don't believe in showing our sorrow with tears." Binta wipes my face with a cloth. "Tears take your power away. Tears are not good for children to see." As she says this, the women begin moving the mattresses against the walls, rolling the bedspreads, clearing the teacups. It must be time to go. I get up, confused, embarrassed. Everyone pushes me to sit down again. Binta presses harder than the rest.

She tells me that they will do something to help me, a ritual.

"You helped us, and now, we will help you. Death is not the end, it is just different. You must keep the relationship with your friends forever. To do this, we will call a *jabaran-kat*, a healer. You will stay." Binta says the words firmly, yet her expression is warm and her hand is still holding onto mine.

For a moment, I feel my familiar grief, sharp, the spaces where the people I once knew now empty. But then I turn her words over in my mind: death is just a different place . . . I don't have to say goodbye.

"O.K." I say softly. I want to say more, but no words come out.

An hour later, the tiny apartment is a flurry of activity, the women a blur of cleaning and cooking. A long green plastic mat is brought in, rolled out into the center of the room with the mattresses laid around it. The kitchen has moved onto the balcony, where hibachis roast meat so spicy my nose itches. Like new puppies, the children have returned, bundled in blankets, some asleep on my lap. Men sit on plastic lawn chairs in the hallway, drinking tea and reading newspapers, while teenage boys stand in the doorway shyly watching me. Binta stands in the center of the room, her wide face beaded with sweat as she waves her plump arms, shouting orders to everyone all at once. Windows opened to the street below, sirens gone, market stalls bustling, rap music filling the apartment.

When the *jabaran-kat* arrives, I am nervous, afraid to even look at him. Perhaps he knows this, for he never speaks to me, and disappears after a long conversation with Binta, spoken in low and soothing tones. Binta comes and explains to me all the things we will do: a meal, with special foods; bowls of water outside the door as offerings; and the women will sing all night. But she says the most important thing tonight is that the *jabaran-kat* has given me a gift, so that I will not forget my Panamanian friends, but remember them even more so than when they were alive.

Never once do I consider leaving and going back to my lonely pied-a-terre: I know I am in the place I need to be. The colors, laughter, and spiritedness here remind me of my friends I lost in the flood, of their connection to one another and to me. Tonight, there are no strangers, only friends.

The meal is served to the men in the hallway first, individual dishes scooped up, piled high on a single communal dish. Once the men are done, dozens of women file into the apartment, until they fill all of the mattresses on the floor, propping up sleeping children along the walls or tying them to their backs with long strips of cloth. Chipped floral platters are placed in the center of the green mat on the floor, lit by a single bare fluorescent bulb, which casts an unappetizing purplish glow on the meal of rice mixed with meat.

Binta sits near me, full of advice. "Eat with your right hand, never your left. Use only three fingers to scoop up the food into your hand. Only eat the food nearest to you. Do not touch the mat with your feet. Do not point your feet toward anyone."

Everyone waits for me to eat first, but there are no forks, spoons, or plates, and I wonder if they have been forgotten. Soon I figure out cutlery isn't coming. I pretend to take a few bites, and the platters are quickly emptied by expert hands, rings glinting, red-polished fingers grasping bones and meat. Laughing gaily, telling jokes, clapping hands, shouting louder and louder across the room. Many hours later, when toasts are being made with swigs from jars of thick soured yogurt, I discover the gaiety they have been showing is false. They believe their happiness will encourage the dead to go their next destination.

As women begin to sing and clean up after the meal, Binta takes me out into the hall, showing me shallow pans of water lined up at the door. "We put these here when someone dies suddenly in the night. It keeps them from entering the house. For you, the *jabaran-kat* did not know what was best. So he put them here, to protect you."

I stare at the tin pans of water, not fully understanding, yet overcome at the trouble that they have gone to ensure my peace of mind and the peace of a people they don't even know halfway around the world.

"You all have done so much, Binta. I don't even know you." My lips feel swollen and thick as I stumble over the words.

Binta leans down to straighten a pan, her eyes tearing. "I know you, Sister. You open yourself to people. They open to you. Come. It is time for the gift *jabaran-kat* brought for you."

As we turn away from the hallway, there is a sharp bitter taste on my tongue matched with a heady perfume clinging thick in mid-air. Oranges and roses again. Binta and I walk through the cloud of scent, back into the center of the crowd of singing women, their babies gurgling wisdom wide eyed, toward a single mattress set high on wooden crates.

I sit, Binta beside me, guiding me. Two glasses are poured of mango juice, each mixed with brown powder. I drink the first quickly, spilling it on my face and blouse. Sweet, raw, the bark of a tree. The second glass is harder to finish, the green room now mixing with smells of the jungle: sharp and distracting, a fast moving kaleidoscope of palms, cherry pink satin, the smear of batik.

"Sister, finish it all so you will not forget." Binta's voice slides in, slow motion.

I drink it all, and fall down to the ground, listening to the cicadas playing their rainforest sonata.

The room, damp, steamy, seeming to perspire, rivulets of sweat running down the walls, over my legs, dripping onto the floor. Crowding around me, the women's patterned dresses moving like book pages quickly turned. Their voices singing louder and louder, lifting me high, out the window, across a blue-black sea, deep into the jungle of Panama, to my friends who run to greet me. They tell me I smell of oranges and roses. I tell them tonight, we are together forever.

Amy Gigi Alexander is a geo-cultural explorer and writer who explores place through memoir-infused non-fiction, magical realism, and psychogeography. Her work has appeared in numerous anthologies and publications around the world. She divides her time between San Miguel de Allende, Mexico, and adventures—wherever they take her. This story won the Grand Prize Gold in the Ninth Annual Solas Awards.

❧ ❧ ❧

Discalced

Some things never change, and that is a good thing.

Ever since I started camping in tents, I have enacted a nightly farce. On the advice of desert dwellers who warn that I will step on scorpions or even rattlers if I walk barefoot in the dark, I arrange my shoes by the tent flap so that I may step into them if my bladder wakes me in the night. And when my bladder breaks into a dream, my mind is far too blurry, too resistant to shaking its sleep state, to steer my feet into shoes. Recklessly I advance barefoot to my chosen spot, and over treacherous decades I have stepped on nothing livelier than a stray thorn. The only advantage to this charade is that my shoes are waiting neatly for me at dawn. I was startled, therefore, to crawl out of the tent on New Year's morning, 2006, and discover only one shoe.

As usual, I was hiding out from the holidays at a ranch along the Gulf of California, arriving before Christmas and leaving after New Years' hangovers had cleared from the highway. This time I had pitched my tent at the edge of a small dry lakebed that a hill cut off from the coast. Shoes don't wander off by themselves, but nonetheless I initiated a search, scanning the lakebed, then prowling the more secretive scrub on the hill, though I could think of no agency that could get them there from my tent. The rancher was a close friend, I knew his family well, and I ruled out anyone's practical joke. Switching to hiking boots that were the uncomfortable alternative, I held my tongue until midday, hoping the shoe would wander back. Then I mentioned the disappearance to the rancher.

"You didn't leave your shoes out at night?" It was a pseudo-question.

"Yes," I replied.

"A fox took it."

"A fox?"

"Obviously."

"I have been leaving shoes unprotected in the desert all my life," I protested, "and never even heard of the problem, let alone losing a shoe."

"You're lucky," replied Lico. "Foxes steal shoes whenever they can. No one knows why, but they love them. They're regular Imeldas."

I returned to the tent site, looked in vain for paw prints in the lakebed and scoured the thorn bushes father afield, the enormity of this turn taking hold. There is probably no shoe I have owned in my life, except for the lost shoe's mate, whose vanishing could produce such a disproportionate pang. This pair of shoes, as it happened, represented a conscious turn in my self-presentation to the world, and this theft was the latest plot twist in a most unlikely saga.

The shoe's defection could even be the revenge of its breed on a lifetime of being ignored, for I had always and deliberately worn the plainest of lace-up black or brown Oxfords, void of the least splash. Shoes, I held, should be comfortable and anonymous. I hated shopping for them. I wore a pair until it disintegrated, then grudgingly bought another. Once, in Cologne, a shoe literally came apart in the street and I had to hobble in one shoe and one sock to the nearest Schuhgeshäft before I could go back to being a tourist.

Scorn of footwear was part of a more general bad attitude toward clothing. Being praised for what concealed you was, by implication, being told that the self underneath was unworthy of comment. People preoccupied by fashion were by definition superficial, and no number of snappy dressers worth knowing had tempered my stance. I didn't need a shrink to tell me how this prejudice had come about. To be sent into public as a small child, undersized among peers, in a little suit jacket, neck-clutching shirt, tie, and short pants because one's mother thought it was "cute" was to permanently despise dressing for display. To be maternally nagged about appearance when one became old enough to drape oneself was to dress with scorn for any flourish and, as a statement on formal occasions, to deliberately underdress. By the time a fox made off with an attitude-changing shoe, the mother whose obsession with finery had backfired was fifteen years in the grave and a son's rebellion had become mere unconsidered habit.

But I began to reconsider shoes, at least, when I met Fernando. Owner of two women's shoe stores in La Paz, Fernando was obsessed with all footwear. Several times a year he flew to shoe conventions—in Guadalajara, in Monterrey, in Los Angeles—where the world's leading manufacturers of shoes strutted their wares, and I knew that for Fernando this was more than the acquisition of inventory. The shoe, forever confined to the shape of the human foot, mediating between its tenderness and the world's hard surface, like the pantoum or the sonnet, expressed the infinity of the human imagination. After thousands of years its incarnations were still changing, its forms still emerging and adapting. To be present where breaking trends, motifs, and profiles converged from the globe's extremities was to partake of the mind's own far reaches in one of its thousands of specialized pursuits.

During each of his three visits to Aspen, Fernando bought multiple pairs of shoes, and I was fascinated by the secrets he showed me in my own town. The leather insoles of American shoes made a fine show from the heel to the arch and were replaced by synthetics in the unseen part that stretched to the toe, whereas Brazilian leather insoles maintained their integrity all the way. Italy once made the world's finest shoes, but due to labor costs, the Italian shoes he bought in Aspen might have been commissioned from China, which turned out a gamut of footwear from the highest quality to the plastic slippers that flooded the world's markets. Because of globalization, breakthroughs in style were less associated with countries than with individual designers who might not be working in their homelands—say, a Chinaman working in Italy.

In Fernando's company, I was interested in the phenomenon of shoes without being interested in shoes. He offered a glimpse into one of the world's unsuspected corners, revealing secrets that literally sustain us, meanwhile confirming the idiosyncrasy of each person's reality. We meet in an agreed-upon world, a commons where we interact, while remaining lone citizens of a willfully chosen, wacky universe of our own. Fernando and I shared visits to the realm of classical music, a mutual obsession, but I inhabited a world of deserts and he walked in a world of shoes. Within our separate kingdoms we were both connoisseurs, even fanatics. Fernando's presence made me shoe-conscious, and though I didn't upgrade my clunkers, whenever we were to meet I inspected them for presentability. Since I had switched to the kind of convenience material that didn't take polish, I held them under the faucet and dried them with paper towels. I knew that Fernando looked at a person first from the ankle down, forming a judgment, and I was sure that he suspected me of soul rot. I also knew that he was as fascinated by men's shoes as by women's. How much better shod I would be if he sold them—why didn't he?

"Men hate to buy shoes. They wear them until they give out. Manufacturers know this and don't bother to change the styles. Men's inventory sits in the stockroom taking space that could be filled by women's shoes, which turn over once a season. I don't sell men's shoes because there's no money in it."

I was in a poor position to object, but suddenly an opportunity opened up: Fernando and I planned a month-long trip to Spain, Morocco, and Portugal in the fall of 2005. We would inevitably be hitting shoe stores on a daily basis, and if Fernando didn't select the perfect shoes for me himself, his very aura would infuse me with the juju to buy my breakthrough pair.

I watched Fernando deploy his keen eyes and probing fingers in Madrid and Marrakech, and when we hit Sevilla I got serious. I even had a certain street in mind. A self I could now hardly imagine had spent three years of the mid-Sixties in the nearby province of Cádiz, playing nightclub piano with an Andalusian band, and we made numerous expeditions to Calle Sierpes in Sevilla to visit a musical agent who got us gigs and kept our papers in order.

As the name suggests, Sierpes is one of the terms for snakes and the street was indeed serpentine: narrow, twisting and dark, lined with small shops and dense with vendors, many of them gypsies, selling their wares in the street. Sierpes had an unsavory reputation and a Salesian monk once told me he was afraid to enter it. Without God on my side, I was drawn to Sierpes rather than frightened, for Franco's police always kept order and the only Spaniards who frightened me were the police themselves.

One of my first acts when we reached Sevilla was to take a nostalgic walk down Sierpes, and I discovered that it had been widened, straightened, and turned into a pedestrian street for upscale shopping. Clothing stores abounded and every third showcase was full of shoes. This was hardly the Sierpes I had known, but neither was I the person Sierpes had known. I liked that alloy of continuity and disruption: a passing tourist instead of a young musician, a street that represented indulgence and consumerism instead of tyranny and want, yet the same person in the same place.

We entered a store and inspected. I realized Fernando couldn't actually select for me, but he approved when I picked up an ankle-high arc of mahogany leather, somewhere between a shoe and a boot, and paraded the pair around the store. I liked the way they looked, felt and—though I knew it wouldn't last—smelled. I kept them on my feet and had the store box the bituminous Oxfords I hoped I would never wear again.

Mission accomplished, or so I thought, but when we had crossed into Portugal and I was exploring downtown Porto with Fernando, pausing as usual at every shoe store window, my gaze was caught by a pair of Oxfords of the shape I always wore, except that they were cobbled from leather of three tones—chestnut, tan, and cream—in an aerodynamic configuration. They were simultaneously the old and the new me.

"In a style that doesn't lend itself to style, they have style," I said to Fernando, a phrase that comes off crisper in Spanish and which he liked well enough to repeat later. They fit perfectly and were immediately my lifetime favorites. I refused to take them off and had the store box my fresh Sevillian bootees. The latter joined the battered Oxfords in the small traveling bag I had deliberately kept light to spare my lumbar, and when we reached Lisbon and I lifted the bag from our rental car, my spine tweaked, then my back went into spasm. It was bitter to be laid up in a pension the following day while Fernando was out climbing the five historic hills, but advances in style have their cost.

I saw Fernando to his plane in Madrid, then returned south for a solo visit with old friends in the province of Cádiz, staying with my namesake Bruno, now a lively young man of twenty-three. Wanting to fly home with a single light carry-on, I asked Bruno to box everything I didn't need—reading matter, purchases in Morocco, all shoes but the Portuguese favorites—and ship it to my address in Aspen. That would give the package six weeks to reach me before I left home for my annual half-year in La Paz. I gave Bruno more euros than I thought the postage would cost, and when he remarked that I had surely overestimated, I told him to spend the balance on beer.

I became increasingly anxious as the box from Puerto Real failed to reach Aspen. Friends in La Paz wouldn't receive the Christmas presents I'd bought them in Morocco. Where, above all, was my link with Calle Sierpes? Had Bruno spent every euro on beer? I headed south in my Portuguese Oxfords, not having received the package from Puerto Real. The ranch where I spend the holidays is unreachable by road and I tried not to touch seawater with my precious shoes when Lico's skiff reached the shore. I was newly protective of my feet as I commuted gingerly through the dust. And it was because of that charged, convoluted, trans-Atlantic preliminary that I was so traumatized the morning that I pictured some vixen barking, "Portuguese leather. Happy New Year!"

On leaving the ranch, I commented to Lico that I was keeping the other shoe. "There's nothing like throwing one away to turn up the other."

"Good idea, because we're all over these hills looking for cows. We could stumble into it."

Not the least of ironies was that after my life's single binge of shoe buying, my first obligatory act on reaching La Paz was to buy a pair of shoes. To avoid accusing Bruno of not sending the package, I waited a few more weeks, then sent a note mentioning that the items I had left never arrived. My friends in Puerto Real had not entered the age of email and it took more weeks for my handwritten note to cross the ocean and for the reply to come back. In the meantime, a relevant email arrived from another source: the friend in Aspen who forwarded my mail. A mysterious package had arrived. It was too beat up for him to make out the return address but it looked somehow foreign. Should he forward it?

I emailed back, "It's from Spain. Open it and tell me what's in it."

The following day I received the inventory: assorted books and maps, a couple of colorful wool caps, a small box wrapped in Arabic newspaper and three shoes.

I hit Reply. "Three shoes? Not four shoes? Three shoes?"

"Three shoes," he confirmed.

"What color?" I added to the e-mail chain.

"One brown and two black."

My new sensibility reeled. I was down to one Portuguese shoe, one Sevillian shoe and the two black clodhoppers that had already spent years on my feet before I flew the Atlantic. I wrote again to Spain. Had only three shoes been put into the box or did one somehow slip out of the battered package en route? Bruno had found only three shoes, had wondered at it, but had mailed everything I had left, following instructions "to the foot of the letter," the Spanish equivalent of English's equally inscrutable "to a T" and, in this instance, unwittingly appropriate. The only suspect I could think of was a small street dog that Bruno had adopted, which might have had vulpine tastes. But Bruno lived in a second-floor apartment, the dog only went out in his presence, and surely

Bruno would have noticed if the cur had trotted beside him with ankle-length shoe leather in its mouth.

Lico, meanwhile, found no three-toned Oxfords in the cactus. "After months in the weather, probably chewed by a fox, by now it won't match the other even if it does turn up," he said. "At this point you're safe in throwing the other shoe away, unless you plan to have it bronzed."

Fernando's hilarity hit new heights. I should ask whether the Sevillian bootee that reached Aspen was a left or a right: perhaps I could assemble an Iberian pair. It was, furthermore, my fate never to have stylish shoes, even as it was Fernando's destiny ever to be natty from head to toe. I was a follower of St. Teresa of Ávila, founder of the Discalced Carmelites and frequent visitor to Sevilla, who flaunted the worst peasant sandals of her day. I was a permanent member of the Secular Order of the Discalced, an ordained lowlife in footgear. Or so I record Fernando's verdict, shod still in my bituminous Oxfords.

Bruce Berger's books about the intersections of nature and culture in desert environments include The Telling Distance, *winner of the* Western States Book Award, *and* Almost an Island, *an account of thirty years' experience in Baja California Sur. For three years he was a contributing editor with* American Way, *and his essays have appeared in* The New York Times, The Yale Review, *and* Orion, *and have won the Ralph Kreiser Nonfiction Award and the Sierra Nature Writing Award.* "Discalced" *won the Grand Prize Silver Award in the Third Annual Solas Awards and was published in* The Best Travel Writing 2009.

CAMERON MCPHERSON SMITH

෴ ෴ ෴

Ghost on Ice

He spent a month—in winter—
on Alaska's North Slope.

I knew that polar bears tore apart cabins every winter, so the first crunch—the sound of a large animal
stepping carefully in deep snow—stopped my breath. The
second crunch tripped a dozen primal alarms, jolting me
out of my sleeping bag to stand with the cocked 12-gauge
aimed at the door, the plywood cabin's weakest point. A
month before I couldn't have found the gun's safety switch,
much less brandished the big Remington like Rambo, but
when you go to Alaska, alone, in winter, you learn about
guns. It was nearly forty below, but I didn't move for the
next ten minutes as the crunches slowly circled the cabin.
*It knows I'm trapped. It's patient. I have to do something.
I have to act.*

When I'd arrived in Barrow to begin my month-long winter expedition on the North Slope, everyone—from visiting
sea-ice scientists to native hunters—had warned me about
polar bears. And everyone had different advice: they hunt at
night, they hunt in the day . . . they don't go inland, they go
inland all the time . . . you can deter them with a warning shot,
no, they don't care about guns, they just keep coming. The

only consensus was that polar bears were smart—smarter than a lot of people.

One Inupiat hunter, Billy Leavitt, swept aside all speculation as we tore down an ice road in his battered pickup. The sixty-below wind-chill roaring through his window cooled Billy nicely but just about froze me solid.

"Nanuq—the polar bear—does what it wants," he explained, smiling as he spoke in the long vowels and soft consonants of Native American English. "You can't predict it. Nanuq doesn't speak. If it wants to eat you, it don't matter what kind of gun you got. It's not in the world of man."

Billy gestured at the flat white landscape rushing by. "If you go out there, you're in the polar bear's world. You just got to live with that."

"Out there" was Alaska's North Slope, a windswept flatland that expanded for miles before knuckling up or dimpling down here and there. The nearest mountains, or even hills, were a hundred miles south. But up here, 300 miles north of the Arctic Circle, where Alaska was drawn to its uttermost northern tip, the land was flat and open, cloaked by snow most of the year. In the short summers the snow soaked into the tundra and countless shoelace streams trickled into countless shallow lakes. To the north the land ramped down to the Arctic Ocean, its surface frozen for much of the year. I'd come to explore this wilderness alone in winter, dragging a sled containing my food and other supplies. My last expedition, to Iceland, had been three years before—too long. I needed to get out. I needed to breathe again, to fight for my life again.

I have to act. But I was paralyzed, imagining the polar bear crashing violently through the doorway like they crash into seal dens. Death would come faster if I didn't resist. I have to act. It could be waiting for me to come out. But I have to act. Are you prepared to kill? Yes.

In record time I dragged on my clothes and cracked the door, squinting against the snowlight and wind before leaping outside. Knee-deep in a drift, I sighted down the gun's fat black barrel, swinging it from side to side. Nothing. No bear. Only blowing snow. Blood roared in my ears. Cold knives carved into my face. I edged around the corner of the hut, still sighting down the barrel. Nothing. Then I saw prints in the snow. Laughing, I let the gun barrel swing down. Caribou tracks. Caribou! Paralyzed by herbivores! I went inside to make breakfast.

Later I headed out for firewood, part of my daily routine. There wasn't a tree within 300 miles, but the little hut overlooked an Arctic Ocean beach where driftwood piled up in summer. Tramping down to the snowed-over beach, I stopped to turn full circle, scanning for polar bears.

Wood pointed out of the snow here and there like the prows or rails of sinking ships, twisted and splintered by shifting sea ice. This wood had journeyed far, entering the Arctic Ocean either from Siberia or one of the great Canadian rivers that drain forested lands hundreds of miles east. Some pieces came free easily; others were permanently frozen in, curving down through the snow like tusks. I used an axe to hack out the wood and chop it to pieces. Sometimes the axe bounced off the icy wood with a clang, as though I'd struck metal. Bent over the work, I felt uneasy, watched like prey. I began to behave like an herbivore, compulsively popping up to scan for predators.

Kneeling to examine natural wonders—a crack in the sea ice, or a galaxy of glittering snowflakes blowing like a stream of stars funneled between two snowdrifts—I always felt watched. I didn't feel more comfortable as time passed. A bear could be watching me, learning my patterns. Each day I felt more vulnerable. I was terrified of becoming complacent. Exercising vigilance for my very life charged my spirit. I was alive again.

But I was an infant in this brutal world, where a breeze might corkscrew the temperature down to seventy below, which is about one hundred and forty degrees below room temperature and freezes exposed flesh in seconds. My food froze before I could get it to my mouth. My heavy boots, and drifts of deep, ash-fluffy snow, demanded a new gait. And Nanuq was always in mind, subtly factoring into every decision. I was re-learning the basics: how to eat, how to walk, even how to think.

My master for this re-education was Cold itself, a ghost, defined only as the absence of heat energy. Great heat is tangible, pressing like stacks of smothering blankets. Great cold is its opposite, a vast absence, the earth's blanket stripped away, empty space in arm's reach, ready to brand and sear, wither and cripple. All accomplished simply by an absence of energy. Cold is death, either approaching or upon you. You calculate every action to elude it. I wore gloves in my sleeping bag, ready to hop out in any emergency—like the hut catching fire, or a polar bear tearing down walls—without losing my fingers.

Fiddling with sound recording equipment, or my tripod and cameras, I learned how to work with my back to the wind, how to windmill my arms to drive blood back into my fingers, and how to run in place with the Remington slung over my shoulder.

In the evenings the driftwood blazed and popped in the hut's little iron stove, collapsing into piles of irregular cubes with pulsing red cores and blackened corners. They radiated pure bliss into my opened palms, warming my blood and they my very heart. Some of the wood burned cool, hissing and spitting saltwater, the pale green flames edged with white.

After a week alone I began dragging my sled back to Barrow for more film and supplies. From a jetliner this land was a featureless white blur, but on the ground I found it endlessly varied.

Sometimes I crossed fields of sastrugi, waves of snow arranged in orderly ranks, one after another. To cross them I trudged up one side and then loped down the other before the 200-pound sled could bomb down and break my legs.

Sometimes I traveled on sea ice, my boots crushing a million ice flowers, spiky, two-inch crystals that stuck up in bristling clusters. Cracks in this part of the frozen ocean were small, only inches wide, but shot as far as I could see. They formed when the moon drew at the sea beneath the foot-thick ice.

I also crossed frozen lakes, the black ice, six feet thick and hard as bottle-glass, screeching under my crampons. I often knelt to examine shapes that seemed to move beneath the surface. Through the thick, irregular lens of frozen water, spectral gray bubbles seemed to wobble if I moved my head from side to side, and I did this to keep them in their surreal, drunken motion. Some were big as balloons, others like marbles. Deeper forms were blurry. In some places, multitudes of star-white points clustered like rising soda fizz. And there were isolated specks, lonely as interstellar dust. The surface of the space-black ice was often broken by inch-wide cracks that shot and jagged like lightning bolts hurled from the sky and caught in the ice. Most of the cracks were filled with snow and the broad gray slots dropping into the ice looked like curtains or gray guillotines. Occasionally the scenes would be obscured as a gust-driven swarm of sparkling grains slid across the ice.

I knew that each bubble and crack, each ripple in the ice, had a story, was information. But this was an encyclopedia I could not read. I didn't know the language. I hadn't observed enough.

Once I spent ten minutes gazing into the ice. Had I been on a mission to devour miles and make records, to compare myself with other people or turn this wilderness into a race track, these treasures would have gone unnoticed. I would have trampled over them while columns of numbers—representing calories, miles traveled, ounces of fuel consumed, miles yet to go—ticked and streamed in my mind. I'd played that game before, dragging my sled like an automaton across the lifeless, 100-mile wide expanse of Iceland's Vatnajokull ice cap. It had been a good challenge, serving its purpose, but I had a different quest, now—to learn the language of the ice. So if I traveled slowly, I didn't care, and it took me nearly three days just to haul my sled twenty miles back to Barrow. By luck, Billy Leavitt picked me up just outside town and drove me in.

"It's too warm this year," he said. "When I was a kid it would be seventy below even before the wind-chill!" I couldn't imagine it.

Standing in a hot shower, almost incapacitated by ecstasy, I dimly wondered how the native Inupiat had adapted to this land. Hundred-below wind-chills, blinding billows of drift snow, the world's largest land predator . . . what were these folk? How could I understand them? An opportunity at some glimpse of understanding arose. I learned that the Inupiat Messenger Feast, "Kivgiq," would take place over then next few days, and that I could attend. Kivgiq was a social, economic, and cultural gathering of native people from across the Arctic. I couldn't miss it. Rather than re-supply and rush back out, I stayed in Barrow for the three-day spectacle.

A thousand or more natives from across Polar Alaska and Canada had gathered, children, adults, teens and the elders, who told the legend of the Messenger Feast.

When the Inupiat were young and learning to live in this place, life was hard and they hunted all the time. But when they knew how to live, Eagle Mother taught them to drum and sing and dance, and how to build a large feasting house.

She told them to invite neighbors to listen to the songs, and dance to the drums. The invitations were delivered by Messengers, who also made requests of the invitees: here is what the sponsor of the feast, respectfully, wishes from you.

Drums—fifteen at a time—beat slowly, directing the subtle movements of dancers' bodies, a shoulder shrug, an arm or wrist gently turned. The slow beat was the invitation to let go, to be taken by the spirit of the dance. After a time, suddenly, like a bomb, the pace and volume increased—BOOM BOOM BOOM . . . BOOM BOOM BOOM—accompanied by wailing and chanting, as the dancers were taken, stamping their boots hard, locking their bodies in stiff postures of shock or terror. Sometimes there were sweeps, syncopated paddling motions, the communal pursuit of a whale. Sometimes arms were hauled joyfully towards the chest, pulling in a whale, sustenance for a whole village, starvation staved off or another season. There were pantomimes of hunger and plenty. Conflicts were acted out, and resolved. And there was always respect for the land and its animals, the gravitational center of this culture around which all else revolved.

These performances were as important to Inupiat survival as any harpoon or kayak; they were instructions for a proper life. How did they survive here? I'd asked. It was a question only a wholly urbanized person could ask. How did they survive here? Easy. Keep your population low. Don't mow down your resources. Manage the plants and animals so their populations will be healthy for your descendants, as your ancestors did for you. Be respectful of the land. It is not rocket science.

And have a sense of humor! Some of the greatest applause at Kivgiq came for "Eskimo Elvis," a dancer outfitted in a caped jumpsuit, sunglasses and pompadour. "E" rocked the crowd with a fusion of Inupiat and Elvis moves complete with a karate-kick ending that sent the crowd through the roof.

Kivgiq ended with solemnity, but laughing was just as important. Life is short, after all.

Soon I was pulling my sled again, south and east from Barrow, out for more lessons. Thirty-below temperatures left my
facemask caked with ice by the time I crawled into my tent in
the evenings. The snow crunched and squeaked underfoot, as
if I were crushing styrofoam blocks with my boots.

One day I spotted a Thing ahead. I couldn't identify the
shape, but it was an object in the snow, its outline different
from anything else in the snowscape; although there were
plenty of regular shapes here, like the legions of sastrugi, this
one didn't belong. It stood up from the snow, whereas most
everything here seemed to lay low. And the color wasn't right;
it was an off-white, almost yellow. When the color registered,
my most primitive alarms were tripped again—polar bear!

But it didn't move, and soon I was close enough to see
that it was wood, and then the shape resolved into a dogsled.
I stepped closer. It was almost entirely swallowed up by the
snow. The wooden walls were peeling, and rusty nails bent
out here and there—someone had salvaged pieces from it.
I wondered when it had been abandoned, and why. Was it
months ago, years? Decades? A hundred years? In this dry
environment, wood might easily last that long. And this thing
might be here for centuries more. It reminded me that it was
us humans who came and went, while the things we build
remain long after we've moved on, like ghosts.

One morning a stiff wind drove the temperature down to seventy degrees below zero. The wind rushed through my face,
bypassing skin and muscle to directly attack the bone. It felt
as though a screwdriver had been jammed between plates of
bone in my skull and was prying them apart. Stunned and
gasping, as though I'd been punched in the face, I crouched
with my back to the wind, raising my neoprene frostbite mask

and lowering my goggles. I could only function here when completely insulated from my environment, like an astronaut on the moon. In this sense, my appreciation for the environment was filtered. It was different than when climbing on rock, for example, when my fingertips were a direct interface with the natural world, taking in, as Craig Childs has written, "a limitless flow of information" from every crack and crystal. And it was different from scuba diving, when my entire body was submerged and in contact with fickle currents and temperature gradients. In the Arctic my body was insulated from these sensory inputs and learning was slower. It was alright, though. I would come back. There were riches here.

On my twentieth morning in this frozen world the Earth rolled another fraction and the rind of the sun flooded up and over the snowy horizon, a syrupy slash of bloody red and molten copper. Turning from the roiling blaze, I saw that the snowscape was now an irregular checkerboard of hues. A million wind-scalloped hollows brooded watery green, cold cups patterned regularly between battalions of small wavelets and whips of windblown snow that stood up a little, their peaks catching the light and glowing as if lit from within. The snow radiated a misty pink and the expanse of delicate shades leaping away from my boots in all directions seemed so buoyant that the entire snow-capped tundra might just rise and gently float away, an immense flying carpet. For a moment I forgot the cold and the wind and allowed myself to believe that I was in a magical place.

I recalled the wonders of the past weeks. I'd watched a herd of caribou trample the snow to get at the tundra beneath, and I'd been entranced by the lunar stare of a snowy owl perched on a distant hummock of snow. I'd come across dozens of arctic fox trails, frantic scatters of paw-prints that bounded across crystalline snow before abruptly changing direction, or commencing gigantic loops.

Once, I'd heard the Arctic described as a "wasteland." Having walked slowly here, having taken time to kneel and wonder at the wolverine and caribou tracks or lemming nests, I knew that this was the evaluation of someone who had been here but had never really opened their eyes. Perhaps they had flown over in a jet, or torn along the surface in a snowmobile. But nobody who'd taken the time to walk here, to get down on their knees and learn, could call it anything less than a thriving biome. Cold, yes, but without question thriving—crackling like the ice under my boots, electric with life.

Cameron McPherson Smith has traveled from the equator to the Arctic, reporting his experiences in many magazines, including Archaeology *and* South American Explorer, *and in the book,* They Lived to Tell the Tale: True Stories of Modern Adventure from the Legendary Explorers Club. *He returned to the North Slope in Winter 2008 to fly a paraglider over the tundra, and in Winter 2009 to SCUBA dive beneath the sea ice. He is currently completing* The Frost Giants, *his account of several winter expeditions to Iceland. "Ghost on the Ice" won the Grand Prize Silver in the Second Annual Solas Awards.*

❦ ❦ ❦

Fish Trader Ray

My Amazon man, as large as life.

"Sitten ze down!" The German's livid face was as red as an equatorial sun setting through the pollution haze of a third-world metropolis.

Flora and I looked at each other. She winked, and we wobbled the canoe back and forth with our newly acquired hip-shaking samba dance moves. Again. It was too delicious to be exacting revenge on the pissy photographer, who was tightly gripping both sides of the pencil-thin canoe. Murky, chocolate-brown river water splashed into the hull. This sent him into full-throttle hysteria.

Should we tip him overboard? I could tell Flora was thinking the same thing. No one would know. We were in the heart of the Upper Amazon Basin on a remote, flooded tributary.

He had shown up the day before. Ray had sent him. A photographer on assignment for a travel magazine. He had a lot of expensive camera gear with him.

Ray had also sent me to stay with Flora. I had arrived one week ago with a hammock that I hung from the rafters of her tiny hut. We'd hit it off, having more in common than one would suspect between a tribal Amazonian woman and a middle-class California chick. We were the same age and had the same men issues. Daily I went out on the river with her three young children to catch fish in handheld nets. We would carefully flip the iridescent wriggling fish from the netting into tightly woven, waterproof baskets. Flora sent these to Ray via the weekly mail *panga*—a long, narrow, motorized canoe. Ray was a tropical fish trader.

It was a two-day boat ride from the jungle port town of Leticia, where I had come from, to Flora's hut. I had wanted to spend time deep in the Amazon Basin. That meant getting off the well-trafficked thoroughfare of the Amazon River and into its backwaters.

Fish Trader Ray was the man for my Amazon plan.

I had met Ray in a hotel lobby in Bogotá, Colombia at the beginning of my South American odyssey four months earlier. Fantasies of rubbing shoulders with a bunch of colorful characters straight out of Graham Greene and Gabriel García Márquez novels were the extent of my travel plans. And of course, to experience the Amazon and go to Carnival.

I landed in Bogotá on a $125 round trip ticket on Avianca Airlines from Miami. I spoke zero Spanish but managed to find a dingy yet elegant hotel with high ceilings, fans, and gleaming hardwood floors in the colonial part of town. I was immediately enthralled by the mustachioed men with battered leather briefcases drinking *café tinto* and holding their morning meetings in the overstuffed lobby chairs, and the plain-faced Catholic nuns from missions deep in the *selva* sipping from green glass Coca-Cola bottles. Then there was Ray—a big, loud twangy-talking Texan, who looked like he desperately needed something cool to drink, wearing a pastel-striped shirt with sweat stains under his armpits.

Desi Arnaz and Carmen Miranda were my only window into Latin culture. Oh, and the crazy nonstop partying Brazilians I had met the year before in Paris. Expecting salsa and rumba dancing in the streets with sexy ladies crowned in tropical fruit hats, I was dismayed to find Bogotá a slummy and polluted place populated by sullen citizens shuffling down the sidewalks. At 8,600 feet in elevation, this dreary city was chilly and overcast with *nada* a Busby Berkeley fruit hat in sight.

It had been a frustrating arrival, and I was piqued.

After checking in, I wandered into the streets to find my first local meal. There were no restaurants, just a few hole-in-the-wall stores in this rundown part of town. A gang of young Colombian toughs in flared jeans was milling about on the corner, eyeing me. The soundtrack from *West Side Story* played in my head: "When you're a Jet you're a Jet all the way, from your first cigarette to your last dying day."

Gulp. Chin up. I crossed the street toward them. "*Hola,*" I said with false bravado, making hand gestures to indicate I was looking for food. They were as surprised as I was by my forthrightness. Surrounding me like a military escort, they marched me to a stairwell leading down to a dive with six tables. In unison they poked their heads into the place and yelled, "*¡Abuela!*" A darling gray-haired woman about half my height appeared from behind a beaded curtain, gave me a welcoming smile, and gestured for me to sit at one of the plastic flower-print-covered tables. The gang departed, but not before they all kissed their grandma on both cheeks and formally shook my hand. The woman handed me a menu, and I recognized one of the items offered: *tostadas*.

"I'll have an order of that," I said.

Savory smells emanated from the tiny kitchen. The short *señora* shuffled out from behind the clacking curtains and set a small plate of plain toast in front of me. Where were the tortillas, meat, cheese, guacamole, topped with sour cream?

I had just learned my first gustatory word in Spanish. Tostada=toast.

With two pieces of toast in my grumbling belly, I headed back to the hotel tired, grumpy, and ready for a hot shower and a long nap. I turned the water on full blast and within minutes the small bathroom steamed like a sauna. As I stepped into the shower stall, a strange gurgling sound grabbed my attention. Peering through the mist I was horrified to see a waterfall gushing out of the toilet onto the bathroom tile and out the door in a steady rush across the mahogany bedroom floor. No matter how many towels I threw down to block the flow, it was unstoppable. Without thinking, I wrapped the last towel around me, scampered out of the room and down the grand staircase to the reception desk.

The clerk was shocked that I was standing at the counter sporting only a bath towel. "Americans can be so inappropriate and such attention-getters," I'm sure he was thinking as he tried not to look me up and down. My bosom was barely covered as I fluttered my hands and flapped my arms to communicate that there was an imminent disaster happening upstairs. "A flood! The toilet! Hurry! In my room!" I squawked like a parrot.

I now had the full attention of the clerk and everyone in the lobby. But nobody understood. The urgency was completely lost on them, yet they certainly found me amusing. They laughed as I continued to gesticulate that there was a serious problem and it was not me dressed only in a towel.

The sound of splashing water got them to focus. A river of water cascaded down each stair like a liquid Slinky. Now they were looking at something besides me.

I slumped in one of those overstuffed chairs in the lobby, completely ignored, and waited for them to fix the toilet and mop up the mess.

"Looks like a rough day, young lady." The large bulk of the man with the stained shirt I had seen earlier stood above me with a concerned look on his face, his thinning sandy-gray hair slicked back in an impressive helmet. "I'm Ray Johnson and you obviously don't speak Spanish. Can I help you?"

He didn't seem lecherous and reminded me of a mix of Sean Connery and Santa Claus, so I hiked my towel up a little higher and confided, "This is my first day here. Where can I get a good meal?"

"The hotel restaurant has quite decent fare. May I take a fellow American to dinner? Not now, of course. . . ."

I giggled, relieved to be speaking English and tugged at the towel again in a futile attempt to cover an inch more of my legs, self-conscious about how I must seem wrapped only in a towel.

The hotel staff moved me to a drier room, where I lingered in a luxuriously hot and uneventful shower. I gussied up in a new pair of jeans and a crisp, cream-colored linen blouse, and met Ray in the dining room. A waiter with a white napkin draped over his arm took our order. Ray counseled, "Colombian food can be very starchy and bland. They cook with a lot of yucca, which has the texture of a stringy potato without flavor. They also add fistfuls of cilantro to every dish. Try the *carne asada* with a hearts of palm salad. Have a beer, Argentinean Malbec, or a Chilean cabernet, if you like, but I don't drink."

"What are you doing in Bogotá?" I asked after we had ordered and I sipped on a lush, garnet-hued cabernet.

"I'm a tropical fish trader, along with other commodities, and I'm here to drum up buyers."

I nodded as a waiter bustled by with a fragrant, steaming dish. I could smell the cilantro. My stomach rumbled.

"Why are you in Bogotá?" he asked.

"This was the cheapest airfare destination I could find to South America. I'll be traveling for a year or two."

"So where are you going on your South American grand tour?" Ray asked with a grandfatherly twinkle in his milky sea-blue eyes.

"The novel *Green Mansions* inspired me to travel the waterways of the Amazon Basin and explore its green veil. I also really want to go to Carnival in Bahia, Brazil and samba dance in the streets. I think the cheapest way to get there might be down the Amazon River."

He thought this was hysterical and laughed till he wiped tears from his eyes but finally responded, "You might be right, but do you know how long the river is or where you are going to launch?"

I answered seriously, "It's two thousand miles to Belém in Brazil and I'm going in via the headwaters of the Rio Napo in Ecuador, just like the Spanish explorer and conquistador Francisco de Orellana did in 1542. Orellana's voyages served as partial influence for the Werner Herzog's film *Aguirre, the Wrath of God*. I've done my research."

He tried to stop grinning and said, "Well, you must come visit me on your way to Brazil. Leticia is a trading outpost in Colombia on the Amazon River bordered by Peru and Brazil. I live there with my common-law Yagua wife, who's from the Red Macaw clan, and our passel of kids."

He seemed sort of old to have a young family, but I kept that thought to myself. The waiter brought our dishes. The savory aroma of grilled rare meat was irresistible. Silence reigned for a few moments as we both ceremoniously picked up our silver-inlaid steak knives and dug in eagerly.

"How did you end up in the Amazon?" I stopped chewing long enough to ask.

Ray waggled his fork at me and said, "In the 1950s I was a photographer for *National Geographic*. We were down here making a film when our plane crashed in the jungle. Everyone survived, but I got malaria and was too ill to continue on with the film crew. Besides, I fell in love, several times, and stayed in Leticia. Been there twenty-one years."

"That's about when I was born," I said.

He chuckled and carved into his blood-red steak while still talking. "Thought I could discover an unknown tribe and make a name for myself by filming them. I'd canoe far up the rivers and ask around, hear rumors about tribes that were still virgin to the white man's eyes. I even encountered an isolated clan up near the Orinoco River delta on the Venezuelan border. They didn't cook me and even initiated me into one of their hunting trip rituals where they blew snuff up my nose with a blowgun. It knocked me out for hours, and terrifying giant anacondas and toothy, yowling jaguars populated my hallucinations. Oh, and I threw up. A lot."

Mouth gaping open, I stared and asked in disbelief, "You took psychedelic drugs with a cannibalistic tribe?"

He shrugged and said, "I didn't know. Thought it was cocaine or something, though the blowgun was a lot longer than a straw or a rolled-up dollar bill. I was in like Flynn after that experience and slept in the chief's hut, completely convinced I had found the lost tribe until one night, swinging in my hammock, I noticed light glinting off a Coca-Cola bottle hanging high up in the rafters. Boy, was I disappointed!"

"After that, I started taking tourists and scientists into the jungle since I knew it so well. Funny things happened. One lady botanist was terrified of piranha and continually obsessed about them. I reassured her they were not in the middle of the river we were traveling on but schooled in the eddies along the bank. Right then, we hit a wake and a piranha flew from the water, arced into the boat, and landed on her head, latching itself onto her forehead. Getting that fish off was one of the biggest challenges of my life. I didn't know whether to laugh or cry as I pried the piranha's pointy teeth apart. She made me deaf with her screaming. Fortunately, it was a flesh wound. The fish didn't take a big bite since there's not a lot of skin to bite into on the forehead."

"Ray, that's impossible!" I laughed.

He shook his head and said, "You wouldn't believe how weird it can get in the Amazon."

He continued, "At that point I decided it was too difficult being a tour guide, so I put the word out among the various indigenous tribes that came to Leticia for supplies, that I was buying exotic birds like macaws, toucans, and Amazon parrots. There was a big market in the States, but that ended when so many died in quarantine because of avian diseases. And you couldn't sneak 'em in anymore after customs officials upped their security checks because of the escalating drug traffic out of South America. So now, I do fish."

Several months later, still tenaciously heading to Carnival in Brazil, and having canoed down the Rio Napo in Ecuador that connected in Iquitos, Peru, with the mighty Amazon River—even mastering Spanish out of sheer necessity since my flummoxed first night in Bogotá—I scrambled up a muddy embankment to the dock leading into Leticia, looking for Ray, who I thought could introduce me to the "real" Amazon.

The early morning sun was already blazing on the Amazonian frontier town as I walked the wooden sidewalk that went back toward Leticia. Electric Blue Morpho butterflies burst from the rain puddles while mangy mongrels skulked about, picking at piles of fish bones haloed in clouds of botflies. Indians in feathered headdresses and ear plugs, their skin painted in red achiote, hustled past on their way to the open-air market, carrying spider monkeys, black caiman, emerald-green macaws, and even a terrified hissing jaguar kitten, trussed on poles or trapped in basket cages swinging from the Indians' blowguns. One shirtless *mestizo* in ragged soccer shorts had a twelve-foot anaconda draped around his shoulders. He caught sight of me, and before I could wave him off, he wrapped the snake around my neck, holding onto the back of its head so it couldn't bite, and asked for money for a photo. The reptile was uncomfortably weighty and smelled of snake urine, which has its own distinctly unpleasant pungent odor. As I looked at its skin, I noticed ticks bloating out from underneath its scales. Repulsed, I wiggled out of the snake's tightening grip. Bursts of gunfire, coming from a ramshackle bar perched on stilts overhanging the river, punctuated the cacophony at the dock. This roughshod town assaulted all of my senses at once, invoking Hieronymus Bosch's paintings of hell.

Salty sweat poured down my face, stinging my eyes. I managed to make my way to the deserted main plaza and sat, panting, on a bench under the pathetic shade of a scrawny palm tree. Scratching under my shirt, concerned one of the ticks had hopped off the snake for a warmer host, I wondered how to find Ray. He didn't have a phone or an address, and had simply told me, "When you get to Leticia, just ask for Fish Trader Ray."

I motioned to a young boy kicking a ball across the otherwise-empty plaza. "¿Dónde está Fish Trader Ray?"

The boy looked puzzled and then asked, "Pescadero Raymundo?"

He motioned for me to stay where I was and ran off down a side street. Minutes later, Ray appeared on an exhaust-spewing motorcycle with his wife and several kids hanging off his wide girth like a bunch of ripe bananas.

Ray hesitantly greeted me, but then a huge smile broke across his face and he embraced me in a sweaty bear hug, introducing me to his family. He said, "You found me. I almost didn't recognize you. You've lost a lot of weight since we met in Bogotá and your clothes are pretty beat up. Still going to Carnival?"

We all sipped Coca-Colas at an outdoor café, the kids playing with a shiny black rhinoceros beetle that scuttled in the dirt under our table. The frosty, curvaceous bottle in my hand yielded the most delicious, sugary-sweet, icy-cold soft drink I had ever quaffed. Surprised that he had paid for our drinks in dollars, I asked him why, and he explained, "The dollar is more common than pesos because of the drug cartels coming through here to the States. Leticia is a hub for outlaws, contraband, and cocaine."

Ray entertained me by pointing out CIA agents trying to blend in as American businessmen in dark suits, their bulging necks and biceps giving them away.

"Why are they in this godforsaken place?" I asked.

He raised his eyebrows and talked out of the side of his mouth in a whisper. "You don't want to know. They protect the drug trade and make sure the government officials are cooperating."

"My tax money is paying for that?"

This further heightened my desire to get out of town pronto and return to the green tangle of the jungle. Give me poisonous bugs, blood-sucking bats, carnivorous fish, and strangling snakes anytime over men with guns.

"Ray, I really don't want to stay here. I'd love to spend time with you and your family but this place scares me. Do you have any suggestions for how I might get farther into the backwaters of the Amazon? I want to see the rarer flora and fauna, and then head toward Brazil and Carnival. I've been practicing my samba steps. . . ."

He nodded sympathetically and said, "Leticia is a very dangerous place. There's a mail boat traveling downriver leaving late this afternoon. My buddy Marco, the captain, will drop you off at Flora's, about a two-day boat ride from here on one of the more obscure branches of the Japurá. She collects exotic aquarium fish for me and loves visitors."

Ray walked back down to the wharf and got me settled into Marco's twenty-foot-long panga. He waved goodbye with his weather-worn Panama hat, surrounded by his retinue of barefoot children and his short, stoic, native wife. Another gunshot emanated from the stilt bar, as if a starting pistol was announcing our departure. Leticia quickly—and thankfully—faded into the distance. That town was no place for a young woman—unless she was plying her trade.

The sunset across the twenty-one-mile width of the Amazon River was a fantastical light show of tangerine spectral colors. The languid water's surface shimmered in a coppery-peach glow. I curled up on a lumpy sack of mail, appreciating the tranquility and dreamily watched as the constellation of the Southern Cross faintly appeared in the gloaming of twilight.

We chugged along the sluggish waters of the Amazon River with dozens of other craft, from slipper-size dugouts paddled by plumage-bedecked natives to rusty cargo container ships struggling upstream to Iquitos or Pucallpa. My only company in the stern of the boat was a wild peccary in a slat cage who, thankfully, gave up squealing after a few hours, and Marco's pet capuchin monkey, who made a game out of looking for nits on my scalp. His gentle preening soothed me during the hazy, heat-baked days. I had to lie on my pack, as the mischievous monkey also enjoyed digging through it with his dexterous digits—squeezing out the toothpaste or chewing on the soap bar. His most naughty and annoying trick was absconding with my silky underwear, placing it on his head like a beret and keeping just out of my grasp. We shared a passion for cashews and boiled palm nuts that I cut up and fed to him. He was too cute to be mad at for very long, especially when he innocently batted his coal-black eyelashes at me.

Toward the end of the second day we detoured up a coffee-colored river confluence and into narrower tributaries, finally arriving at a small hut on stilts above the riparian jungle terrain.

There was no terra firma to disembark on, so we motored right up to the porch railing. Marco introduced me to a compact, smiling woman with bright white teeth, mocha-toned skin, and peculiar pale green-blue eyes that flashed an invitation of friendship. Flora reached down, gave me her calloused hand, and hauled me up from the boat's rim into her twelve-square-foot thatched roof shack. Marco confirmed he would come get me in a week and hook me up with a ride to Manaus midway between Leticia and the mouth of the Amazon River in Belém, where a bus would provide transport to Bahia in about three days. "Just in time for Carnival!" he emphasized as he shoved off, in a hurry to get back to the main river branch and visit his family. The monkey screeched goodbye with a furrowed brow as he watched me, and my pack contents, fade into the dusk. He was wearing something on his head. . . .

Flora seemed pleased to have me as a guest. She was isolated here with just her three young children, all under age five, for company—her only social life the occasional visitor Ray sent or the infrequent passing trader. The tribe she came from lived much farther upriver, and she never saw them. I never asked why she lived by herself, but I got the impression she was an outcast due to her mixed blood.

She spoke passable Spanish, so we communicated easily. I agreed to contribute to the food kitty and also help her with household chores, fishing, foraging, and childcare.

When we weren't out fishing we cooked, swept, wove baskets, and lounged in the hammocks, sharing stories. And braiding my hair. The kids were fascinated by my back-length blond tresses and fooled with them constantly. I teased that they should open a beauty salon. This sent them into giggle-fits, as the only women for many miles in this riverine no man's land were Flora and I.

Flora's tipsy canoe was the only way to get around. Carved out of a single tree trunk, it floated just a half-inch above the waterline. Balance was essential when we sat, stood, or paddled.

At night, after the children were asleep, we'd slip into the dugout with flashlights and glide silently into the lagoons surrounding the shack, looking for black caiman. Their eyes glowed a spooky citrine-green in the distance like iridescent marbles hovering right above the obsidian-dark waters. We'd quickly shine the flashlight into their eyes to mesmerize them before they disappeared below the surface. Then we'd paddle over and gently tap on their prehistoric boney heads. This would break the spell and, plop, they'd sink underneath the inky water.

That was about it for nightly entertainment.

My visions of the magical realm of the jungle that *Green Mansions* had stimulated were real. How glorious the gigantic, two meters in diameter, Reina Victoria lily pads were—each one a universe inhabited by jade-green frogs and giant-legged bugs—and how strange and mythical the pink river dolphins appeared, quietly rising up and sinking back into the muddy malachite waters as our canoe wove through the mesh curtain of vines and drifting roots. I was finally living the fantasy that had inspired the long and arduous journey I'd taken to get here. Traveling through Flora's watery world was worth every bug bite and petrifyingly scary moment.

Over her brazier set on the floorboards, we shared meals of smoked monkey stew, boiled palm nuts, dried pirarucu—the largest freshwater fish in the world—and my favorite: grilled capybara—the world's biggest rodent. We also did what women do all around the globe—we talked about men. Ironically, she had the same boyfriend problems I did. Hers was a bigger dilemma, as she also seemed to get pregnant and have children by the various Casanova traders who canoed past.

The week at Flora's passed quickly. I was ready to travel onward to Carnival, especially once the sour German arrived the day before I was to leave and put a crimp in our fun factor. He took up half the hut with his camera gear and shoveled all the stew onto his plate leaving a thigh bone and some sauce for the rest of us. He spoke in a bullying baronial tone of self-importance ordering us about like servants, but Flora needed the money he was paying for her guide services, so I couldn't shove him over the railing and feed him to the caiman like I wanted to. Thankfully, Marco showed up when promised and had consigned a boat ride to Manaus for me. I hugged her wild, spunky kids goodbye and promised Flora I would stay in touch with her via Ray and return to visit her special watery world someday—maybe with my own future children in tow.

I did arrive in Bahia on the first day of Carnival as Marco predicted and danced nonstop in the streets for a week. Several pair of shoes were worn out as I tried to keep up with the battery of booty-shaking, sexy samba mamas who paraded around town 24/7 in their stilettos, towering headdresses, skimpy costumes, and mile-wide electric smiles. Shimmy, shimmy, smile, rotate, wave to the crowd; then run, run, run to catch up with the frenzied drum bands on the motorized parade floats and shimmy some more. It reminded me of the moves Flora taught me to prepare me for Carnival, standing up in her tipsy canoe, scaring that silly photographer. Shimmy, shimmy, shake, shake, giggle, guffaw! Sisterhood discovered deep in the Amazon.

The Amazon and Carnival faded into a blur of further larger-than-life adventures traversing Iguaçu Falls and the glaciers of Patagonia, over the Atacama Desert to Bolivia, and months later, flying home from Ecuador—a full circle from where I began my Amazonian quest.

I went back to California and started an import business. For seven years I commuted to South America, and whenever I could find a flight from Colombia or Peru to Leticia, I'd take a detour and visit my friend Ray and his growing family. Leticia held a certain backwater charming seediness that grew on me the more I explored the region. Flora had married one of her Casanovas and moved to Iquitos, and I never saw her again.

The last time I saw Ray was thirty years ago, right before I sold my import company. He was hoisting me into the cargo hull of an unpressurized plane on a dirt runway filled to the gills with odoriferous planks of salted pirarucu fish. Throngs of Indians pushed and shoved to get on the plane that provided the only transport to Bogotá on a random schedule. Luckily, they were much more diminutive than Ray, who tossed me like a football, launching me over the indigenous feathery finery and head first onto stacks of smelly fish. As the plane sputtered and the propellers whirred, we lifted upward. There was Ray on the runway below, large and pasty white, enthusiastically waving his sweat-stained Ecuadorian Panama hat, grinning and squinting upward toward the blazing orb of the sun. His kids taller, his wife shorter. Fish Trader Ray. My Amazon man. Straight out of a novel.

Lisa Alpine is the author of Wild Life: Travel Adventures of a Worldly Woman *(Foreword Reviews' Gold Medal winner, INDIEFAB Book of the Year Award, and Best Travel Book 2014 North American Book Awards) and* Exotic Life: Travel Tales of an Adventurous Woman *(1st Place North American Book Awards winner and BAIPA Book Awards Best Women's Adventure Memoir). She is currently crafting stories from her recent trips to Albania, Cuba, Morocco, Armenia, and the Republic of Georgia for her upcoming books* Blessed Life *and* Dance Life. *She divides her time between Mill Valley, California and the Big Island of Hawai'i. Read her monthly online magazine about travel, dance, writing, food, and inspiration at www.lisaalpine.com. This story received the Grand Prize Silver in the Eighth Annual Solas Awards.*

NANCY L. PENROSE

Flamenco Form

She found her calling in Spain.

I am a traveler in search of flamenco. In a nightclub in a cave in Granada, I sip Cruzcampo beer and watch and wait for the music to begin. Stools scrape, tables shift, and that narrow room grows crowded. Fellow tourists. British accents. A small stage; a backdrop of wrinkled cloth. In the front row, chic summer cool of the Spanish—young women in tight bodices; men in dark shirts.

This is not my first time in Granada. I passed through thirty years ago, an American student in a hurry to return to classes in France after Christmas in Spain. I had no time to explore the great Moorish palace of the Alhambra, no time to find the music. Now I have returned, deep in middle age, to fill this void in my repertoire of travel. And that afternoon, headed to my hotel, sated from a day within the splendors of the palace, I saw a flyer for the evening's performance: simple, black and white, an address, a time, four names, and the word FLAMENCO. I sniffed treasure, something real, authentic, an antidote to shops with jumbles of bullfight posters, Don Quixote t-shirts, plastic castanets. And in the flyer, I tasted the promise of passion: I may dress like a good girl but I have the soul of a diva.

A man rises and takes the stage. Locks of black hair curl
to his shoulders. Pudgy cheeks and jowls. The singer. With
his opening wails of aye, aye, aye, he wrings the air with grief,
his face twisted by the pain of the tale. He sings to the peak of
one word, weaves and warbles around the top before riding
down the slope of sound to rise again, stretch the air, pulse to
another peak, all on that one word. In his voice I hear the cries
of the muezzin calling long-ago Moors to prayer, Sephardic
half tones, the threads of an Indian raga pulled through centuries of Gypsy wanderings. I do not understand the words
but my heart takes the tears, the ecstasy. His head drops at the
end of the song. He looks up to the applause as if surprised to
see us.

Flamenco was born of a brew of outcasts: Moors and Jews
sent into exile, death, and hiding in 1492, the Christian Reconquista of Spain complete. Queen Isabella and King Ferdinand
claimed the Alhambra as their own. The Gypsies, who already
lived life cast out, took in the newest exiles. Ancient cultures
and sacred memories melded a music with strong and complicated rhythms. The uneven beat of the twelve-count—not
the familiar 4/4 count of Western time—is common. The
names of the song forms are music—*soleás, siguiriyas, livianas,
bulerías*—containers for words that hold the anguish of love,
loss, exile, hunger.

Two guitarists step onto the stage and sit down. One is tall,
gray hair pulled back in a ponytail. The other is roundish with
the beginnings of a bald spot. Hands wrapped around each
guitar neck, fingers baited to strike, they nod to each other
and begin. Single sparkling drops of sound. Tight squeak
of finger against string. Filigree of high notes against a wall of
bass. Knuckles knock the face of the guitar; wood body, wood
drum. Fans of fingers snap open and waves of *rasgueado* break
and roll through me over and over and over. I try to enter
the music, imitate the clapping, the *palmas*, of the Spanish in

the front row, hands perpendicular, fingers spread. But I am clumsy in the attempt, unable to find footing in the uneven beats, like missing the last step on a flight of stairs. The singer's voice enters. Wood and flesh grow the notes, send them forth as pearls flung to the audience. Shouts of *olé* burst from the crowd.

A break at the end of the first set. Guitarists and singer mingle with the summer cool at the front of the room, kissing hello to friends come to share the evening. I go outside for fresh air. Above me, the red rocks of the Alhambra, ramparts lit by moonlight. I had seen their reflection in a courtyard pool that afternoon; rough exterior stones meant to hide, shield, deflect commoners' perception of beauty and wealth within. Mirrored against the gruff red in the surface of the pool, marble pillars webbed together by stucco. And the walls of the Palacio Nazaríes dense with patterns of foliage and flowers that swirl and curl around the script and wisdom of the Koran and flowers and foliage and script and tiles that twine and line memories of the days when Jews and Moors and Christians lived and worked and mused together in Granada before the Reconquista, before the Inquisition.

The poet Federico García Lorca, favorite son of Granada, was haunted by the cruelties of the Inquisition, enraptured with the passion of flamenco. His hometown was his muse, the music his model. Lorca wrote that, "Granada is made for music, for it is a city enclosed by mountain ranges, where the melody is returned and polished and blocked by walls and boulders. Music is for cities away from the coast. Seville and Malaga and Cadiz escape through their ports. But Granada's only way out is its high natural port of stars. Granada is withdrawn, enclosed, apt for rhythm and the echo, the marrow of music."

The break ends. The dancer takes the center. She is dressed in a simple black blouse and long red skirt. Her hair is pulled

back into a tight bun. Lines at the corners of her eyes and
mouth do not mar her beauty. She cocks her head to the right,
lifts her chin. One hand rests on a hip. The other is raised
to the top of an arc above her. The audience is still, poised.
With a stomp of heels she announces her beginning and flies
into a swirl of skirt and snapping fingers. She lights a stac-
cato of *zapateado* that sounds like a woodpecker gone mad in
the forest. Blur of black leather heels and toes. She flings to a
stop. Skirt pulled to thigh she spins a slow circle. She stamps
once, twice. Her fingers are flowers; her arms snake against
the pounding rhythm of heels on wooden stage. The singer
joins in. His voice curves around the flick of her hips, shapes
the music she dances. She locks him in a gaze that smolders
then snaps to face the gray-haired guitarist, who leans into her
passion and responds with a roll of chords like a well-muscled
bull in the ring. This was what I had craved. This was why I
had come. I fill those shoes with her. I fling my soul into her
wild and complicated rhythms, into the sensuous arch of
her back. I feel the jolt of heel against floor, lick of skirt against
legs, heat of music in my own breasts.

The whirling, swirling, snapping, pounding, strumming
crest and recede. The audience jumps up, clapping, cheering,
shouting, screaming our *olés*. Dancer and singer stand frozen,
breathing hard, lost in each other's gaze, then turn to bow to
the audience, special nods to the front row.

I walk back to my hotel, beside the river, beneath the ramparts of the Alhambra on the hill above. I have the treasure;
how do I carry it home? Will life on another continent destroy
what I hold? How will I stop the black press of the mundane?
Pat Conroy wrote ". . . once you have traveled, the voyage
never ends, but is played out over and over again in the qui-
etest chambers, that the mind can never break off from the
journey." I take heart.

I use my mind and body to continue the journey. The spirit
of Granada echoes in the stomp of my heels on the wooden

floor of a dance studio in Seattle. My shoes are black leather with a saucy little notch above the heel. I've learned how to flick my skirt on the kick turn at the end of a *paseo*, how to slide my hands against my hips at just the right place in the music. My feet ache from the arc of the shoes. I stepped on my own toe last night. My body struggles against the foreign form of the twelve count—1 and 2 and 3 and uh 4 and uh 5 and—but I soar when my teacher tells me "That's it! You've got the idea!"

New CDs are stacked in my living room: Paco de Lucia, Carlos Montoya, Gypsy Soul, Sabor Flamenco. I've rented the Carlos Saura video, bought a book called *Song of the Outcasts*, read Lorca's poetry and written in imitation: I have docked within the music and the long reach of my senses has explored its depths. I dance at the fringe of this universe but the treasure holds me captive.

Nancy L. Penrose writes essays about science and travel. Her work has been published in Shenandoah: The Washington and Lee Literary Review, 1966: A Journal of Creative Nonfiction, Drash: Northwest Mosaic, Ekphrastic Review, *several collections of* Travelers' Tales *titles, and the anthology* Burning Bright: Passager Celebrates 21 Years. *She is the co-author, with Khoo Seow Hwa, of* Behind the Brushstrokes: Appreciating Chinese Calligraphy, *and is co-author of a forthcoming book from the University of South Carolina Press on Louisiana sculptor Angela Gregory. Her website is www.plumerose.net. This story won the Grand Prize Silver and Women's Travel Gold in the First Annual Solas Awards.*

෯ ෯ ෯

Red Lights and a Rose

He discovers the meaning of paradise.

I was thinking about paradise, a word so often flippantly tossed around in churches and mosques, at Club Med resorts and on Norwegian cruise liners. The word could be powerful, but we've made it soft.

It was 1:00 A.M., an hour before closing. A bottle of Heineken hung from my left hand and a pen from the other. And on the stage before me were six women wearing black high-heeled shoes and black thongs, dancing as if they thought paradise were far away indeed. They danced with remarkable disinterest, each clutching her respective pole, moving their knees and hips with the same tired pep as an old Volkswagen about to break down. One woman kept her hand around her navel, self-conscious of her stretch marks. For her, the pole was a shield she used in a vain attempt to hide herself. This was anything but an erotic sight. It was more like witnessing a subtle form of torture.

Is paradise a place we stumble upon only after death, where, if we are to believe some Muslims, seventy-two virgins await, ready to indulge us in sensual pleasures?

"Pretty Woman" played on the sound system and I finished what was left of my beer. An American businessman-type with a Texas drawl sauntered in and found a seat. Now four of us guys were in a room with eight girls, six on stage and two sitting among us. It didn't take long for the Texan to find the prettiest of the bunch, a woman in her early twenties who had quit her job as a bank teller about two months before. She was not here because her family was poor; she was here because she wanted to be rich and men like the Texan would pay well to spend the night with her. She was quiet, polite, and intelligent, and I had no difficulty imagining her working in a bank. But now she looked so small next to this big man. Her dark eyes stared straight ahead—straight into the wall—as he put his arm around her and began to caress her shoulder. I thought of a quiet animal caught in the claws of a hawk, too frightened to move as it prepares to be swallowed. But she was here voluntarily.

Is paradise, if we are to believe some Christians, largely an individual enterprise where, by simply believing in Jesus but otherwise going about our lives as we normally would, we will find ourselves in celestial glory after we die?

Back on the stage another woman, Ann, was about to rotate off. A twenty-seven-year-old mother who speaks Thai, three tribal languages, and a few words of English, she had been working here one and a half years to earn money for her extended family, most of whom live in a poor village seven hours north of Bangkok. I had asked Ann if she likes her work—I knew some women did—and she replied with a tired smile that said she did not. She danced and prostituted herself only because providing for the needs of her family was her top priority. Her seven-year-old daughter remains in the village, in the care of her grandmother.

The lights were dim and the music loud, yet it was conducive to note-taking (in Asia to write a book, I was taking a lot of notes about a lot of places). Just before Ann stepped off the stage and returned to my table so that we could continue our conversation, I made a note to ponder the idea of paradise as "right relationships." Later, back at my hotel, I would write, "Paradise is not indulging in selfishness, it can't be bought with money, it can't be had without including the poor. It will not descend so long as we sit on a couch watching television, or stand among pews singing songs. We enter into it neither by driving planes into towers nor by hoarding storehouses of grain. It is deeper than 'feeling good.' And it is wider—much wider—than personal salvation."

This was my second night in Soi Nana, a square three-story structure with the feel of a frat house. Or was it more like that ride at Disney World, Pirates of the Caribbean? Yes, that was it. Nana reminded me of a Disney World ride: Pirates raucously chasing screaming women, people living out of bounds, with ogling eyes, on a quest for ill-gotten treasure. Yo, ho, ho, a pirates life for me! But here many of the swashbucklers were upper-middle-class businessman from the West, strolling in and out of clubs with names like Spankys, Lollipop, Carousel, DC-10, and G-Spot. And at less than two dollars, which covered your first beer, it was considerably cheaper than Orlando.

Over a three-day period I would visit several clubs in Nana, all of which were pretty much the same. They were like trash compactors, all of us pressed too tightly together, fighting the heat and humidity, sensing that intimacy was strangely recyclable here. It was a raucous environment indeed, with so much careless movement that hearts were easily broken. At least this is how I read the looks on the faces of several women, and later what I would hear them say.

And yet it was here, in a minefield of flesh and dreams, where black cats prowled on sheet metal awnings in search of geckos, where satellite dishes pulled in ESPN that overweight German tourists watched as girls nestled compliantly into their girth, where sound systems belted out the likes of

Billy Ray Cyrus so that girls could rock their bodies to the rhythm of "Achy Breaky Heart" . . . it was here that I stood on the verge of discovering something new about paradise.

With few exceptions, Nana was not a place of desperation. It was something more playful and ambitious than this. When the ladies weren't sitting with patrons they were often in the back room giggling together, as though they were kids enjoying a late night at a friend's house. There was an atmosphere present that would have had an appeal even if everyone had been fully clothed.

Nor was Nana merely a place where money was exchanged for sex, since hundreds of women brought their dreams to work. They sought a quality Western man, someone with whom they might live happily ever after. And so a clearly demarcated border between business and friendship did not exist. It was easy to see why men who might not seek a prostitute at home might do so here. The girls radiated playfulness and innocence, and made you think you simply had a friend. You never knew when you'd be met with real affection.

But, you never knew a lot of things, and vision is difficult when the lights are dim. There was something unsettling about all this flesh, as if it had been so exposed that it managed to become ghostly. The music was the most real thing here, or at least the clearest, and so I tethered myself to it in an effort to see well. The musicians and I were old friends, friends I hadn't heard from in ages, and I listened to every word they had to say because they reminded me of a place and time that tonight I couldn't afford to forget. Music is rarely as potent as when it's heard in a strip club.

In its moral ambiguities and brokenness, Nana was a place where you saw everything in a new way. Flesh wriggling on poles was an unusual teacher, not the kind that demanded rote memorization of facts and figures but one that instead employed the Socratic method, asking questions of the student to which the student had to craft an answer. And the women were not merely teachers from afar. They often came over to sit a while. They were scantily clad, sometimes naked, but many of them were keen on leaving sex behind and simply sharing a story and hearing one in return. The place was all about human connection—its possibilities, failures, and dangers—and this is precisely why I sensed that something of paradise was here, just waiting to take shape.

I recalled my first visit to Bangkok four years earlier. I don't remember her name anymore, but she was a go-go girl in Patpong, another adult entertainment district, and it was there that we met one night and sat in a corner of a club. She was completely nude, as were the other thirty-some women in the room, and I think this may have been why her eyes were so striking—with no clothes, the body was left unadorned, and her eyes, so earnest and intense, contained a power they otherwise might not have. I could think of only one parallel in my experience: looking into the eyes of a Saudi woman, who is fully draped in black fabric except for a slit at the eyes.

She was in her mid-twenties and had seen many men, she said, but I was different—why? I fumbled over an answer. It might sound strange, I told her, but after watching so many men who did not seem loving enter these doors, I decided to enter them as well, and invite someone out for dinner. "Would you like to join me for *pad thai*?" I asked. She said yes, but her shift wouldn't end for three more hours. After about an hour, she was called to take the stage, where she would join three other ladies to (there is no delicate way to describe this) shoot bananas from her vagina and then pop open bottles of Coke, also with her vagina. For the last hour her eyes had looked broken—broken, but not defeated—and now they begged for trust. "Please don't go," she pleaded, "I come back soon." Of course I would wait, I said. Then she stood up to leave. With her eyes looking at the stage, she appeared nervous, perhaps even pained, and for several moments she didn't move. When finally she did take a step it was not toward the stage, though she would be up there in only a few seconds; rather she turned back toward me. She leaned close to say something, her eyes still begging.

"Please don't watch," she whispered.

Walking around Nana now, four years later, I remembered her and wondered how her body and spirit had fared with the passage of time. But while I could still remember her eyes, I knew I wouldn't be able to recognize her even if she were still in the city. I couldn't even remember her name. I hoped that if I were to meet someone again tonight that I would remember her—her story, her name, her face—for many years to come.

It was about midnight, in a sea of bubbliness and hardness and crassness, when I met Fon. She was dressed in jeans and a white t-shirt, had a tattoo emblazed on her right arm, and sat on a stool at the door to a club, urging men to peek through the curtain and enter. She snagged my arm as I passed.

"Come inside!" she screamed, just as all the other girls outside all the other clubs would scream. But Fon seemed particularly obnoxious.

Tired, I said I was on my way home and needed to sleep. But she persisted, "No problem, five minutes, drink one beer."

"No, really," I said, "I'm almost out of money. I've got to go home."

"No problem, I buy," she responded, and then slipped into the club. She emerged a moment later with a cold Heineken and an extra stool.

"Really, I don't have money to buy that drink—I will *not* buy that drink," I said, suspecting some catch in her offer. But she was clear: the drink really was her treat.

We exchanged biographies. She was twenty-four years old, from Phuket, and had been living in Bangkok for two months. Her boyfriend died three years ago in a motorcycle accident. As for the tattoos, she got the first at the age of fifteen and now had a total of five, all of which she pointed out to me. The last one cost a whopping 7,000 baht—the equivalent of $175.

Fon was an enigma, not because of her generosity— three times this week I would invite prostitutes to dinner to hear their stories, and each time they would insist on covering the bill—but because talking to her was like trying to start a cantankerous car, one that might turn over but then croak a moment later. She was not quiet, nor was she unsocial; she simply chose to be difficult. "Who are you?" I wanted to blurt out several times. But I will never know. And maybe neither will she. Kind one moment but caustic the next, she was incapable of prolonged conversation and kept much of herself locked away.

The conversation wasn't the smoothest, but after some time it suddenly fell headlong into a jarring pothole. "Do you want to fuck me?" she snarled. I winced at both the question itself and her tone, which really was vicious—like someone maliciously running fingers down a chalkboard. She was admirably blunt, but I had no idea what she was actually saying. Was this a test, or an invitation? Was it the voice of a wounded woman who wants to be attacked so that she can attack back? Whatever it was it didn't even intimate love. It screamed of its absence.

"No," I said, suddenly feeling more worn out.

At 2:00 A.M. Nana closed. The neon lights were extinguished and the people—giggling and screaming ladies, all sorts of men—spilled into the street, where they plopped down at food stalls or hailed taxis. The area swelled with energy—something like the halls of a high school on the last day of the year when the final bell rings—and it was contagious. I let the rush of people go ahead of me because I wanted for just a moment to experience Nana void of its people. When the crowd had passed and it was just Fon and me left in the courtyard, what I noticed most was the litter strewn on the ground. And I felt that not all the trash was visible because some of it had walked out, buried in the hearts of all who had spent time here. I knew that more wholesome venues get trashed as well, but here the litter made me think that joy does not come cheaply, and if it does come cheaply it will not likely stay. I thought of the word "sex industry" and felt keenly that the emphasis here was on industry. I thought of a construction worker wearing his work boots, factories polluting the sky, and laws trying to regulate it all. I thought of a wilted flower, a poisoned spring, nature in decay. And I thought how ugly is the floor of a place that sees innocence as a marketable asset. The whole environment was an odd mix, a troubling mix, a place that if not now would later call out your tears to cleanse yourself. And maybe in some odd way you'd even feel that your tears came from someplace else, that because they were not entirely your own they were not merely personal property, that they were meant not only to cleanse yourself but also in some very small way to bathe things like this trashy courtyard.

Fon asked if I was hungry—I was—and recommended a family-run food stall a couple blocks down. We ordered hotpot and pulled meat and vegetables onto our plates as a downpour swept through the area. When the rain passed Fon invited me to see her apartment, which wasn't very much farther down the street.

The first thing I noticed when she opened the door of her one-room efficiency was the bed, neatly made and occupied by a stuffed animal. It was Tweety Bird. The walls were decorated with posters of Western boy bands and Leonardo DiCaprio. On a Buddhist altar beside the bed were two open bottles of Strawberry Fanta, some peeled fruit, and joss sticks. And for an entertainment system she had a portable CD player and tiny speakers. Sitting down next to Tweety, Fon pulled a shoebox full of pirated CDs out from under her bed. "Do you like Enrique Iglesias?" she asked.

Fon was a rough personality—tattoos, a stud in her tongue, a callous sneer reflecting her many, many sexual encounters with men. But her room was that of a child.

I met Fon for a late breakfast about noon the next day. The night before we had talked about my love of news, and this morning she presented me with a copy of the *Bangkok Post*. She also offered to let me stay at her place the rest of the week for free rather than spend money on a hotel. "I wouldn't bother you because I work nights when you sleep," she said, "and I sleep in the day while you away. Really, no problem."

I didn't see Fon the rest of the week—I had thanked her for her offer but needed to stay across town—but two days before my scheduled departure from Bangkok I wanted to return and say goodbye. But how?

Michelle, a backpacker from the Seattle area who I had first met three months earlier at the Thai-Cambodian border, helped me out. We met for dinner and I told her both Fon's story and my wish to say goodbye in a memorable way. "Take her a rose," Michelle suggested without much thought. It was a beautifully simple idea, and Michelle urged me to make the hour commute back across the city to follow through with it. "Trust me, she will remember a rose."

It was almost midnight when I arrived at Nana. A young girl—she couldn't have been more than twelve—was selling roses at the entrance to the complex. It almost seemed right that a child—someone who had an innocence about her, who might remind us of another way—was selling something as fragrant and tender as a rose. I walked up the steps, took a left on the second floor, passed several clubs, and was soon at Fon's. Someone else was sitting at the entrance though, and I asked her if Fon was around. The woman looked at the rose and smiled, then tore into the club to find her.

When Fon came out she looked surprised. Her face turned tender, and for a moment the tattoos looked like they didn't belong to her. Her eyes were vulnerable and her movement almost graceful. "I wanted to say goodbye before I leave Bangkok tomorrow," I said, "And I wanted to give you this rose."

All around us Nana roared. The music didn't stop, nor did the screams and giggles and whispered invitations to adjourn to a hotel for an hour. And it struck me that Hell and Paradise do not always have a large no-man's land between them, and that at times they may even share the same space. The vision of Paradise held by some Muslims—women available for sensual pleasure—suddenly looked as shallow as a muddy puddle. And the vision held by some Christians—personal salvation, just "me and God"—appeared emaciated and tragic.

At least this is what I thought when Fon took her rose. We stood together in the midst of noise and brokenness, but I also sensed that, at least for a moment, we stood together in the hope that right relationships are possible.

That is to say, we stood together at the door of paradise.

Joel Carillet is a freelance photographer and writer seeking to document life around the world in all its breadth, from political upheaval in Egypt, to the refugee crisis in Greece, to a tender moment between a mother and child in Estonia. "Red Lights and a Rose" was excerpted from his unpublished memoir, Sixty-One Weeks: A Journey Across Asia *and won the Grand Prize Gold in the Second Annual Solas Awards. His website is www.reflections ontheroad.com.*

We Wait for Spring, Moldova and Me

There are many lessons to be learned
teaching in the former Soviet Union.

It was a mistake, finishing that bottle of Kagor. But with no heat and no lights, no TNT all-night movies, there wasn't much to do, except wait for spring. But that was last night. This morning, outside my apartment block, the bare trees clump with snow, and the potholes in the road are filling. It's the end of March.

The country is Moldova, a wishbone of a land scrunched between Romania and Ukraine. The year is 2000, and Moldova has surpassed Albania as Europe's poorest nation. This is—will be—my third spring.

I ride the trolleybus, held upright by fur-coated people who squeeze from all sides. My wallet is in my front pocket. Stuffed in my shoulder bag are teaching tools and a towel. Down between my shoes, I watch the snow swish by through a hole in the floorboards.

The Didactic School of Language is on Armeneasca Street, four blocks off the main thoroughfare. It could be a village street. Its single-story houses with unstraight walls lean toward the sidewalk, and, as you walk by, you smell the steam of tea escaping beneath doors. The new snow muffles the noise of passing Ladas and makes the cars seem whispery and diffident.

I'm the first to arrive at the school, not from a sense of duty, but because there's no water in my apartment. First I make coffee. Then I remove my shirt. Then I take my towel and the hot electric tea kettle into the bathroom, add icy tap water, and pour the mix over my head, splashing my armpits and soaping my hair.

I will have six hours of English lessons, and then some placement testing, but it's Saturday, and in the evening—ah, the evening—we will have the yearly school-sponsored dinner at the restaurant Sanatate.

Most of my classes are downstairs in the windowless green room. It has the shape of an uneven triangle, wedged into a corner of the building. The classroom decor is post-communist modern, meaning that contents have been purchased through a Western philanthropic concern, and while desk chairs and whiteboards look new, they are falling apart because an administrator has cut corners. The furniture in the newly built home of said administrator is reported to be sturdier.

My twelve students, aged seventeen to forty, sit with their backs to the wall. Coats and fur hats overwhelm the rack in the corner, and occasionally topple it. The air is thick with body odor—no one likes cold-water showers in unheated apartments—but despite this, they look fresh, especially the girls, who are made-up and snug into outfits—dresses or skirts or jeans with boots—of which they own just one or two, but wear them bright-eyed, again and again.

Today this Level 4 class is subdued. Perhaps it's the snow. The students steer clear of English, whispering in Russian and Romanian, "R&R" as it is known in our class. The game

I have just made up, "Spill the Glove"—using one of my mittens and some torn up shreds of paper with questions on them—is not very good. But still they should try in English.

Eventually I start into a guilt-producing speech. How many hours are you in class with a chance to speak English? Five. How many hours in the rest of the week? One hundred sixty-three? And blah blah blah.

The speech sounds passionate and improvised, but after two years of teaching in the Republic, it is fairly well scripted.

"So you think about that . . ." I say, then exit the room without another word, ostensibly to quell my anger, but really to brew some more coffee.

In the teachers' office Carolina and Alyona prepare for their lessons. They are like all our Didactic teachers: mid-twenties, pretty, and serious. Because they have lives outside of the school, they take the office to be a place of work.

"I gave my students the speech," I say.

Carolina is shaking her head. "Kevin, *ty zaraza*." Literally, You're an infection. It means pain in the ass.

Alyona is cutting up strips of paper and doesn't bother to look up. She is divorced, dating a big jolly bear of a drunk, an ex-military man who brings his alcoholism to office hours. (Years later, he will, astonishingly, become a bigwig in TV production; then, at a family picnic, showing how Russian roulette is played, he will shoot his head off.)

"Hey, Alyona, did I ever tell you about Carolina's wedding night?"

"Everybody told me," she says.

For our first school-financed trip, in the spring of '97, we crossed the border to Romania. That first evening, Carolina revealed that she was married; in fact, the ceremony had taken place that very day. She did not invite her husband on the trip.

"Carolina wouldn't let me stay in her hotel room with her," I tell Alyona. "I wasn't going to make any moves. But it might've been my only chance at a wedding night."

"Stop, *tupeetsa*," Carolina says. Imbecile.

I get my coffee. "Remember, girls, tonight's Sanatate!" Back in the classroom, the students put on sheepish faces. One girl, with bright lipsticky lips and awful teeth, acts as spokesperson: "Kevin, we promise not speak R&R."

I accept this apology. Why not? I've got coffee now, and the Sanatate party tonight. The class deserves some fun, so we listen to Petula Clark's "Downtown," too loud, and one of the front desk girls arrives to scold me.

The day is long. Four eighty-minute classes, then testing. During the next lessons, I dash out for coffee, my guitar, some dice, a ball or a stuffed animal—anything that will get me through.

Halfway through the late afternoon class, the last one, just as the caffeine in me is no longer pulling its weight, I catch a break. Olga, who is eighteen, and bundled in a red dress, with a whisper of mustache, announces it is her birthday, and, in this part of the world, she is duty-bound to provide merriment. She brings forth a fluffy Moldavian cake dabbed with ashy-tasting prunes; then, from behind the coat rack, digs out a bag clinking with bottles of wine.

The whole class drinks. A big Romanian business guy, always in a suit, tells a joke in English. The punch line is, "A hat on his head drinking a rose." Everyone laughs. I pretend to. Why not? I've almost made it through the day.

"Kevin, you understand our specific humor?" the joke-teller asks.

"Not at all."

"Play 'Cel Mai Mare,'" a student requests.

I feign reluctance a moment, then pick up my guitar.

"Cel Mai Mare" is the only song I have ever composed in (mostly) Romanian, and stretches my knowledge of that language to the brink:

> *Cel mai mare*
> *Cel mai bun*
> *Cel mai mare*
> *Cel mai bun*
> *Cel mai mare*
> *Cel mai bun*
> *Feed me mamaliga*
> *With a silver spoon*

The English translation would go like this:

> *The biggest*
> *The best*
> *The biggest*
> *The best*
> *The biggest*
> *The best*
> *The biggest*
> *The best*
> *Feed me your traditional national dish made from ground hominy*
> *With a silver spoon*

One of the Vicas pushes in—the front desk girls are all named Vica—and she says, "You know that placement testing started five minutes ago. You are in the red room."

I carry a plastic cup of wine up the steep staircase and into a second-story classroom. There are windows, and the view from here astonishes me. Sunlight everywhere. In the last four hours, the temperature outside has risen twenty degrees. There is no snow in the trees, not a flake. The roofs of the one-story houses glint with light. There is not a trace of slush in the roads now, only brown puddles.

Prospective students come into the room, one by one, and face me. I question them for three minutes, five if they are girls, more if they are attractive girls. So what? The sun is warm. Wine lifts my insides. Spring comes running. And in several hours I will be off to Sanatate restaurant for the once-in-a-year night of cheer paid for by the school.

It is 5:00 P.M., still light, and there is lots of time, so I walk through the spring-the-pretender weather with Michael. He is the only other American currently at the Didactic School. He has a Ph.D. in literature, and a beard and glasses to prove it.

Stumpy the Dog is on the corner of Armeneasca and Scuisev, hobbling next to a plump woman with felt boots who sells cigarettes, candy, and detergent packs. Stumpy is homeless, but spends his daylight hours here, with the cigarette lady. He is dirty, wire-furred, and his right forepaw is gone. The stump is worn smooth, red and white like a neatly cut bone at the butchers.

"Two and a half years ago," I say, "when I came to Moldova, Stumpy's leg was longer. He used to actually walk on it. And I have honestly seen, I mean visibly, how it sort of got filed down."

We are both wondering what the years in Moldova have done to us.

We reach Boulevard Stefan Cel Mare (Stefan the Great), Chisinau's main thoroughfare, where the streetlamps often work, where cars swarm, where the fashionable find Big Macs, and the legless roll themselves on wheeled boards.

Farther down, the boulevard widens. Here are the government buildings, cast back from the main street; they have the look of mausoleums. We cross a park here, passing the blue-and-white onion dome church of St. Nicholas—storage shed in Soviet times—down to a street called The Youths' Prospect, and one kilometer to the restaurant.

Sanatate restaurant is folk-style Romanian. The staff is Romanian, the clientele Romanian. Old-style, wooden tables and benches. Fast Moldavian music with its Turkish and Gypsy influences. The Russians of the city prefer white table-cloth places and lip-sync pop divas.

Michael and I drink beer at the bar until the rest of the Didactic School of Languages arrives.

This is the big spring dinner, and there are thirteen of us—teachers, staff, and the director. Carolina and Alyona, among others, are no-shows. We're squeezed at one long table in a semi-private room. Waiters in baggy white shirts and sashes jam the table surface with traditional Moldavian fare, everything on a separate plate: first bread, and thick salads soppy with sunflower oil, fresh cucumbers and piles of dill and parsley, tomatoes stuffed with whipped garlic, salty squares of sheep-milk *brinsa*; and later, more plates, overlapping now, chicken and cutlets. And there are ceramic pitchers of wine, as much as we like.

But it's clear that no one really wants a big night. Everyone is tired. Everyone has problems.

I have a problem too.

"This wine," I say to Michael, "I can't even drink it." It is the mustiest thing I've ever tasted. I try to explain to the Romanian waiter, who must listen to my Russian. I don't know how to say musty. So I describe it as old and dirty.

"It all comes from the barrel upstairs," the waiter says. And he insists that I accompany him upstairs to prove it.

Up through a dark stairwell we go, then a dim corridor with chipped aqua walls, into a small room, where a metal wine cask is locked behind bars. The waiter keys open a pad-lock, and clanks upon the barred door.

"Now you will see that I'm not deceiving you," he says.

The waiter turns the spigot and fills me a glass. I drink. "It's disgusting," I tell Michael in English.

"Is it the same?" asks the waiter.

"Yes, it's the same all right."

This is not really the point at all, but the waiter believes the case is solved. He pours himself a glass, and toasts to our health.

It is one of those Moldovan endings, like the punch line "a hat on his head drinking a rose." Or like, to take things further, the reason we often have no electricity. The power plants exist only in the east, in a pro-Russian enclave called Transdniester, which has declared itself an independent country. They have their own borders, police, stamps, and money. They get testy on occasion, being poorer than the rest of the poorest country in Europe, and they pull the switch—presto, no electricity. They often do this at night. A student provides the punch line: "If they turn off light in the day people will not use it."

Downstairs a non-electric Moldavian band has started up. A stand-up bass, accordion, *timbu* (like a piano-sized hammered dulcimer), guitar, and pan flute churn out fast riffs for a few dancers. Only after an hour do they slow things down, and I ask our audio-visual girl to dance. Mariana is a sweet *moldavanka* with light skin. Her husband is in business, a blanket term for Mafia employment. Mariana is in tight leather pants, her plump rump not quite buying into the look. We're alone on the dance floor, and I ask a question.

"Why are slow songs so rare in Moldavian music?"

She thinks for a moment as we turn a small-stepped circle. "What do you name people who steal from rich and give to poor?"

"Bandits. Or Robin Hoods."

"Well," she says, "In these songs Robin Hoods sit and drink the wine."

Another unintended puzzle, a Moldova punch line.

But I for one am done with the wine. After the dance, I order ten bottles of beer to our table, hoping to jump-start things.

Just then, the teachers and staff start rising to go. And it's only ten o'clock.

"All right," I say, "you have forced me to be silly." I put a crown of parsley on my head and dill sprigs behind my ear, but their minds are made up, and I only succeed in being an infection.

Michael and I are the last to leave. We take our bottles of Chisinau beer with us out to the sidewalk. The night is coolly pleasant now, the morning's snow like a memory from another season.

"I'm going to walk home," I announce.

Michael suggests that it's too far, and unsafe. There are holes in the sidewalks. Police ready for the shakedown. Wild dogs. Robin Hoods. Bandits. Most of us foreigners have been hassled, or bitten, beaten, or robbed. Michael has even been pistol-whipped. But unlike our local friends, he doesn't insist.

I walk a long way, a good hour, through the city center, then up towards Telecentre, my region at the edge of the city. Three quarters of the way home, something comes over me—an infection of sorts, I suppose—and I set off through streets I have never walked before, roads where the streetlamps haven't worked in years, an area that looks like a village—with its thick-tree darkness, streets of mud, and shadowy dogs melting into the blackness.

And then, when I am utterly lost, like a miracle, I break out onto familiar Dacia Street, so close to the group of block buildings where I live. I feel wonderful, fate having guided me homeward. The first building, the tallest, has never been beautiful at all, a ten-story tombstone. But now coming out from the trees, the night so sharp and clean, seeing those rounded balconies on the corners, unlit but visible under the starlight in a faint glow. . . . So many stars. And everything makes sense for these moments. I feel like I have moved through the universe.

Here I am, in a city—the capital city of a country!—and there are so many stars I can practically feel the Earth moving through them.

Out of one season and into the next.

Spring is definitely coming soon.

Even Moldova deserves spring.

Kevin McCaughey grew up in Saratoga, California. Now he is a traveling English teacher. He likes recording music, and is writing a novel about a junior high school dance. This story won the Grand Prize Silver Award in the Fourth Annual Solas Awards.

♫ ♫ ♫

The Empty Rocker

Lives of quiet desperation are
sometimes not what you think.

The empty rocking chair echoed slowly, its arc poised in mid air. The chair's body still held the motion of another's warmer body. The seat back and curved arms molded themselves around the memory of the weighted flesh by whom they had been hastily abandoned, A rhythmic motion of patient waiting hung in the air; the chair tipped in anticipation of its owner's return.

Next to it, a soft fringed lamp, still on. A passerby could see boldly into the window, for the feigned modesty of lace valences fringing the edges were primly tied back. A confrontational rocking chair, aggressively empty, its full face turned to the passerby and still moving; a yellow lamp flattering the whitened glare of the window: emptiness.

Somewhere within, the half Indonesian prostitute Jung Li was applying her ministrations, rocking and rocking in other, more desperate arms.

She flung back her head in mock abandon, then opened her eyes quickly to glance at the clock in the corner. She shut her eyes again, calculating the kroner. "Again," she moaned. "Again."

It was Christmas in Amsterdam. Everywhere, the naked windows revealed interiors elaborate as Russian Easter eggs: fine filigreed Christmas trees laden with delicate decorations, soft glowing light, round tables in warm-looking rooms. One expected to hear a *clavecin* playing; to see round-bellied women tightly posed, their bejeweled slender hands resting upon those of their fiancees, front vision.

I had traveled from Paris, where everyone shuttered their windows, to Holland where apparently nobody did. But it was too deceptive, all that bluff Dutch honesty and openness. "Nothing to hide." I wondered what lay beneath.

The canals were bright, iced over, and a happy drunken jollity hung in the breath-fogged air. Strong ruddy men gestured to me and my friend Candy as we walked together, passing the many bars that gleamed beside us, warmly wooden and gold in their interiors. "Come in, come in! Have a drink with us. Don't be afraid," they urged. "It's Christmas, after all, Happy Christmas!"

Candy waved back at them as she pressed my arm, hurrying me past. "You just won't believe the sex shops," she said. "I want you to see them."

Our breath was freezing in the freezing air and she urged me away from the wistful warmth of the pubs and toward the icy bridges spanning the canals. We were hurrying away from safe conviviality toward the seamier parts of town. "You've got to see them. You just won't believe it."

I must have looked back longingly—the Dutch men seemed so welcoming—or perhaps one in particular had caught my eye. Candy grabbed my elbow harder, impatiently hissing through her teeth. "Come on, come on. They make me sick!"

Earlier that day, after Candy had met me at the train station, we had taken a trolley toward her apartment on the outskirts

of Amsterdam. The trolley trundled slowly along its icy
tracks. As we sat crammed together in wet wool camaraderie, Candy suddenly insisted that I change seats with her. She
gestured urgently. There was a young, blond, hearty looking
Dutchman sitting next to her, trying to make conversation
with what he perceived as a vivacious American woman. He
overheard us talking. "Are you American?"

"Here," Candy grunted, getting up and shoving me into
her seat. "You like them; you talk to him."

The man fell silent as I moved over into her seat. Candy,
now standing in the aisle, proceeded to bounce from the strap,
exclaiming as she looked out the window at the snowy scene
the bus traversed. "Whoopee whoopee, look at that!" She
added a few words in Dutch to impress me. "Hey, we're in
Holland. Right, white girl?"

Since moving to Amsterdam from Paris Candy had been
studying Dutch. "I guess I plan to stay here," she said. She
chanted her new words nonstop, repetitively showing off for
me. And I was totally impressed. She seemed to relish that
comic-sounding glockenspiel language. In her hyperactive
way, Candy, bouncing and swaying and chanting Dutch words
for "toilet" and "sausage" and "thank you," while cheerfully
commenting in English on the passing snowy scene—"Colder
than a witch's teat," she caroled, top voice—kept the whole
trolley car entertained. The young man next to me, amused
and fascinated, couldn't keep his eyes of her.

"Don't look at me," she warned him. "Look at her, not me."

"Men, I can't stand 'em," she muttered to me in a loud stage
whisper. Impossible Candy.

Candy! How did anyone so sour get to be named something like "Candy?"

Most likely she had named herself, ironically, in defiance
against the sugar of the concept. For the woman herself was
vinegar-sharp, tarragon by nature, with a bite to the person,

an independent tough-guy butchness concealing her generosity and vulnerability. She was small, built like a little tank, and
sported denim bibbed overalls and Muslim embroidered caps.
Candy, antithesis to sweetness, was a woman who, it
seemed to her friends, had completely reinvented herself.
What did we know of her? She told us many stories, perhaps
lies. She was the last of twenty-three children. She had been
brought up by a grandmother. She had lived her whole life
in orphanages. She went to college and grad school, became
a psychologist, moved to Oakland, California. There, if we
were to believe her, she counseled AIDS patients. Though
Candy was such a nonstop talker, so agitated and energetic,
so filled with hyperactive advice, that it was hard to imagine her sitting still long enough to counsel anyone, let alone
someone who was dying. But perhaps someone dying would
be too sick to notice their therapist bouncing from a bus strap,
saying "How ya' doin'?" happily to everyone around her, and
in Dutch.

Although a black belt in karate—"No motherfucker's
going to get near me"—the 1992 earthquake in California
frightened her enough that Candy resolved to sell her house
in Oakland—"And it was beautiful honey, and I'm talkin'
millions!"—and break with her lover of twenty years. "Girl,
that's one thing I ain't talkin' about." She took her life savings
and moved to Paris. "The U.S. is dead. Europe is where it's
happening."

Candy's older brother was the famous trumpeter Charles
Stone. He'd moved to Paris too, twenty years earlier. Now he was
there permanently, buried in the cemetery Pere Lachaise. "A
heart attack," Candy said. The other musicians who had known
him mourned his departure, but said little. Charles was an idol,
an icon, second only to Jim Morrison in the drawing power of
his tombstone in this crowded City of the Dead. His grave was
more famous than that of Frederic Chopin. On Sundays, groups

of young black men could be seen lolling about his tombstone, passing weed from hand to hand, while the punk white American kids with shaved heads, boys and girls, with their pierced nostrils, all wearing black leather and high tops, their surprising shafts of green and red mohawks like plumage, smoked herb on Morrison's gravestone by the opposite cemetery gate. Oh Charlie! Oh Jimmy! The visiting Americans made their pilgrimages to their heroes.

So Candy came to Paris because "Charlie liked it here." Soon taken up by the musicians who revered her brother, she found a little room on the Isle St. Louis and started to study French. That's when I met her. "I'm takin' a rest from the States, honey. How 'bout yourself?"

It was a winter of driving rain. Candy turned up everywhere, making cheerful trouble wherever she went. She attended an erudite lecture on "racism" at the Sorbonne and told me afterward, "I was the only woman, the only black woman, the only American, the only lesbian, and the only one stoned." She was indignant. "They wouldn't even let me talk, those men." But of course she had talked plenty.

The next fall a friend offered her an apartment in Amsterdam and, disillusioned with Paris, Candy moved. "They've got plenty of racism there," she said optimistically as I took her to the train. "Holland is definitely where I need to be. Yup. I'm goin' to organize those motherfuckers good." She looked small, vulnerable, lonely, despite her bravado, a person who drifted from one catastrophe to another. "Come visit me, girl." I hugged her, trying to give her energy and warmth, and promised I would.

Now here it was, Christmas break, and relieved to have a place to go, and a friend to visit, relieved that I did not have to spend Christmas alone, I kept my promise.

"These sex shops have got to be seen." Candy was tugging my arm, hurrying me impatiently against the freezing wind, a round squat figure in her overalls and down jacket. We passed furtive bands of men who, prowling wolves, looked over their shoulders at us, the only women out on the cold street so late. "Candy," I said nervously, trying to stall.

"Honey, these people ain't interested in you." Candy hissed cheerily, dragging me deeper and deeper into the seaminess of the town. "Here, get a look at these."

She clutched my elbow in a karate warrior's grip, hauling me to a stop in front of a store window. Embarrassed, I tried not to look, averting my eyes, which were stinging and tearing in the cold. "Hey," she cried enthusiastically, "will you look at that! Look at the size of that dildo!" Candy was ecstatic.

"How'd you like to try that out, girl?" Candy regarded the window with a fascination reserved for Lourdes. "And lookie here, right next door!" She dragged me a few feet down the street.

Oh Lord, why don't the Dutch have the decency to shutter their windows? The street was festooned in yards of pink extruded plastic, enormous fleshy penises, vibrators, and huge inflated dolls with unmistakable cunts. Everything was larger than life, including the leather objects draped over the plastic models, the underwear, the corsets and chastity belts, whips, and clever instruments of sexual titillation.

I turned away, unwilling to look. But Candy, talking volubly, kept trying to draw my attention to one large pink object after another. "Will you look at that! This size of it! Girl, isn't that just about one of the most beautiful things you've ever seen?"

As I waited for her on the deserted freezing Amsterdam street I wondered why I was here. It was Christmas; bloody Christmas, I was reminded through Candy's eyes that I was hopelessly white, heterosexual, and an utter prude. As Candy enthused about dildos and vibrators I would have given anything to be anywhere else, even back in Paris, alone in a small dark room, far from home and family and friends, drawing the covers over my head while every French person relaxed inside closed doors, embraced by familial warmth and delicious food and drink. I would have preferred to be walking self-consciously alone beside the freezing Seine in front of monstrous Notre Dame, looking out at innocent bridges and thinking vaguely melancholy thoughts. Candy might be American, she might seem familiar, but standing with her on Christmas Eve while she went on and on about sex shop windows was the most painfully foreign experience I could imagine. A few stray men passed us, then re-crossed the cold span of bridge to pass us again, staring, challenging, all the while.

"Candy, come on," I managed to say, tugging at her padded sleeve. But she didn't seem to care. "Let's go inside," she said. "I want to get me some of those things."

"Not me," I answered quickly. "You go ahead if you want. I'll wait here."

Chortling to herself, Candy disappeared inside. I could imagine her hyperactive glee.

The moments I waited for her in the icy wind were the longest imaginable. I stood, back resolutely turned to the window display, dropping my eyes at the aggressive looks of the men who passed and avoiding the occasional lone man who dared to accost me. What to do? I was trapped between the warmth and vulgarity of the sex shop interior, and the wait beside a frozen canal, my feet blocks of ice, at a prostitute pick-up stop that no prostitute would ever choose on a cold Christmas night like this one. I faced outward, feeling my face freeze disapprovingly, a prudish intellectual bluestocking from Boston, Massachusetts, and told myself that this was an interesting travel experience, one that I would never have had to endure had I comfortably stayed home. I wish: my adventurousness had once again gotten me into trouble.

Candy emerged, stuffing a package into her pack. "Come along," she said,

"I got someone I want you to meet." She was humming as she walked, our footsteps squeaking on the thin layer of ice crystals that lay sparkling under the street lamps. On the canals, tethered barges strained against their ropes and groaned in the frosty air. "I'm dreamin' of a White Christmas," Candy hummed. She was pleased with herself. It was almost two in the morning and from various parts of the city church bells started to peal. "A White Christmas. . . ."

"You know, girl," she interrupted herself, "if you hadn't come up here to visit I'd never be walking around like this." I was surprised. "Well, I had this breakdown in Paris after Suzy threw me over. Too much, after the earthquake back home and all. A real breakdown, honey. I knew it was coming. All those sick people, my friends, dying of AIDS. Yes siree, dying like flies in old Candy's arms. I just couldn't take it anymore." By now she was humming, whistling through her teeth, and talking, all at the same time. "White Christmas. . . ." She poked me for emphasis. "Bet you didn't know that did you? About my nervous breakdown, I mean. Why honey, by the time I came up here to Amsterdam I was so bad I couldn't leave the apartment by myself. Just couldn't get out, couldn't see anyone, didn't want them looking at me, see. Not enough black people up here. Everybody stares." Her isolation had lasted over three months, she told me.

Three months. I calculated quickly; from her arrival just up to my visit. "Come on, Candy," I protested, "it can't have been that bad."

But by now Candy was humming again and whistling and saying "Hey sport," and "Merry Christmas" in Dutch to whatever lonely guy we passed, also looking for a bit of Christmas cheer.

Now we stood side by side in front of a window on the street of prostitutes. An empty room, a rocker still moving. "They're the lucky ones. Jung Li works here. Some of the other girls, I got to know them too. Many little houses, many softly lit bared windows like the inside of a chocolate box." What lay behind the visible part of this town? I wondered.

"AIDS," said Candy. "This town is full of AIDS." She was surprisingly silent, watching and waiting. "Lousy with it. They bring these girls out here and then they just dump them," she said. "These men. They come here as workers and then they bring their women and then they can't support them. What can they do?"

The fragile figure that was Jung Li came to the window. She looked severe and pretended to ignore Candy and myself as we stood outside.

"Watch her," Candy breathed excitedly. "She'll pretend not to notice us. They lose their jobs if they move."

The woman placed herself carefully in the rocking chair whose embrace surrounded her as if she were home. A quick furtive rearrangement of a strand of hair, one ankle crossing the other: now the woman, the tableau, was stilled. Jung Li folded her hands upon each other and stared into the dark, somewhere far beyond us.

"It's supposed to be legal here," Candy said. "They pay off the police. They get medical inspections every week."

Not wanting to offend the prostitute by my too-direct stare, I allowed the whole street to enter my vision. The street was full of naked windows, with women waiting motionless in Flemish interiors. Fat women, thin women, women in all shades of color and costume. Women who looked at us with hard aggressive eyes. Women who did not even twitch. I could see their weariness, their bad skin, malnourished collarbones, could smell the perspiration from all their stale toil.

"Well, what else can they do? They're stuck here, working on their backs. And these are the lucky ones. The others, the one whose johns don't pay enough, they have to work outside." She took my arm, walking me away from this section of town, then waved a passing taxi to a standstill.

The women were motionless, holding themselves as much like embroidered dolls as possible, receding as we pulled away from them.

"They had a conference about AIDS and sex workers," Candy told me. By now we were back in her apartment, warming our hands around mugs of steaming tea, our frozen garments unstiffening themselves on the backs of chairs.

"You want to sleep in my bed?" she asked abruptly. "Or do you want your own mattress on the floor?"

I was thawing out, looking out the window, admiring her view of frozen trees that loomed darkly beyond the kitchen. The dark had a purplish light to it: not really early morning, but instead that headachy three A.M. glaze when one is too nervous and cold to get to sleep.

"O.K., the mattress," said Candy, not waiting for my answer.

I lay down on the mattress, fully clothed, not even taking off my boots, and pulled her down sleeping bag over me. Would I ever get warm?

"Want some music?" Candy turned on the radio full volume. "Want some hashish?"

"No, just to sleep now."

Candy took out a corncob pipe from the drawer, tamped it down, and stuffed it with weed. "I got my suppliers," she winked. "You can get anything you want here. Anything. We'll go get some more tomorrow."

"Candy, I really need to sleep. It's been a long day." Apologetically.

"Well, honey, don't mind me. I never sleep." Candy settled herself into her rocking chair and sucked contentedly
on her pipe. The radio blared full volume and I lay at her
feet, pulling the sleeping bag over my ears.

"Listen," she said, turning the radio up further. "Christmas
carols!" The song "Silent Night" in Dutch paradoxically shattered the air. "Ain't that somethin'?" Candy said, smoking.
She shook her head. "Holland!"

"You know," she continued dreamily. The hash was slowing her down. "They aren't allowed to use condoms, those
whores. Well, they're supposed to, but if they do, the men beat
them. Won't have anything to do with them. And if the girls
insist, the hotels and bars won't let them work there either."

"But don't they know they might get sick?" I was sleepily
trying to carry on my side of the conversation now that Candy
seemed to be slowing down enough to actually have one.

"Of course. But what can they do? Those whores need
work as much as anyone else. They know to use those safes,
but the johns will just go to somebody else."

I drifted to sleep as Candy was telling that in her opinion a
man and woman together was the most disgusting and sexu-
ally exploitative arrangement known to the human race. The
creeping warmth of the sleeping bag, the inevitability of her
words, and the *creak creak* of the rocker as she sat there smoking and talking somehow soothed me.

It was a restless sleep. I'd never in my life slept through a
radio so loud and I woke from time to time in the cold dark,
thinking of the women forced to screw without condoms,
knowing all along they were bound to get sick, the police
"protection," the medical exams not picking disease up until it
was too late; a whole refugee nation of women brought to and
abandoned in Western Europe with no skills and no future.
The rocking chair tipped and muttered in the dark and when
I briefly opened my eyes and shut them I could still see the

glowing bowl of Candy's corncob pipe as she inhaled, could hear her humming, could make out her stocky overalled figure and her little embroidered cap.

I woke finally with a splitting headache and the sense of not having had enough sleep, to a gray sodden northern European light that managed to leak through the windows from the park outside, insinuating dirt and grime in its wake. That light, even thinking about European light in winter, gave me a migraine. It was late morning and I remembered that it was indeed Christmas, the darkest most depressing day of a winter calendar full of despondent moments. Christmas!

In their smug well-lit homes the Dutch were no doubt being jolly in a red-cheeked Santa sort of way. I thought of my family back home in the Untied States and then was quickly, piercingly grateful that I had escaped the burden of creating enforced jollity by choosing to be miserable and lonely in Europe instead. But I hadn't escaped the headache.

Stirring a bit, pressing my exploding temple, I noticed Candy. Now in a long white nightgown, her feet tucked under her, the corncob pipe still in her mouth, she was sitting and smoking reflectively on the edge of my mattress, watching me wake up.

I closed my eyes again. "What time is it?" I asked. I wanted to ask, "How long have you been sitting there watching me?" But I didn't.

Instead of answering, Candy puffed on her pipe, looking exactly like Mammy Yocum in "Little Abner." She took the pipe out of her mouth. "Want some?"

I shook my head.

"You know, girl," she said, "you are the first white woman and the first straight woman I have ever let stay at my apartment." This in the tone of conferring a great honor.

Although I am white, I may be more bent than Candy was aware of, but I was not about to shatter her moment of magnanimous tolerance. "Awful white of you to let me stay here," I murmured, and took her hand. She cackled.

"Merry Christmas, honey," she said, and thumped her backpack onto my feet, drawing from it a large suspicious package. "Have I got a Christmas present for you."

"Oh no!" I remembered the sex shop of the night before. Candy smiled wickedly. I drew the stiff pink thing out of its tissue paper wrappings. "No, Candy!" I had brought her a pair of delicate filigreed pearl earrings as my Christmas present to her.

"Girl, girl, don't knock it till you've tried it." She handed me the pipe full of glowing hash, its odor sickly sweet in the room.

A huge Christmas mother longing overcame me, and I wanted to put my throbbing head down onto her wide lap and have her rub my temples.

"You know," she said, pensively, "I went to a meeting of those whores we saw last night. They were trying to organize themselves. How do you get a john to use a condom? One of them demonstrated how to put it on so the man doesn't even know that's what you're doing. You practice maybe three months with your teeth, putting safes on cucumbers, till you can do it in your sleep. Imagine that."

Her voice trailed off. We spent a quiet Christmas. We were careful around each other, gentle with differences.

How was anyone to know that six months later, Candy would be dead. Heart attack, some said, or drugs, or high blood pressure. Whatever the reason, she lay three days in her Amsterdam flat before anyone found her. Did she call for help in English? In Dutch? Smoking her weed alone, so far from home?

Kathleen Spivack is the author of ten books of prose and poetry. Her most recent are Unspeakable Things, *a novel, and* With Robert

Lowell and His Circle: Plath, Sexton, Bishop, Kunitz, Others. *She has awards from the Fulbright Commission, National Endowment for the Arts, Mass Arts Council, Discovery/92st., the Radcliffe Institute, Yaddo, MacDowell, Ragdale, American Academy in Rome, and others. Her work has received major prizes. Kathleen teaches in the Boston area and in France. Follow her at kathleenspivack.com. "The Empty Rocker" won the Grand Prize Bronze in the Third Annual Solas Awards and was published in* The Best Travel Writing 2009.

ॐ ॐ ॐ

From the Ashes

The life of Pan.

The smoke of wood fires dulls the sunrise, silhouetting the spires of Angkor Wat as hazy apparitions.

The incomparable beauty of these temples, the soul of the Khmer nation, are a surreal backdrop for the tale of horror I have come to record.

I see Pan approaching, fingering his prayer beads, his saffron robes seemingly ablaze in the yellow mist. He walks as though he is not really there, feet barely touching the ground, a saint incarnate to the world at large but in his own eyes, a simple, humble, monk. He carries a quality I cannot assign to words, but people sense this as I notice heads turn with slight bows as he glides past.

He is bent from time and suffering, having lived through and seen more than anyone should, and I know through mutual friends he wishes nothing more than to spend his remaining time in secluded meditation, but upon hearing of my book project he readily agreed to speak with me in the hopes that no one should have to relive it.

Pan is a Theravada monk, one of about 350,000 throughout Cambodia prior to the Khmer Rouge, and now one of but thirty to have outlived their regime. Besides surviving personal atrocities, he bears the weight of trying to re-establish a religious order dragged to the brink of extinction under a barbaric reign. Theravada means, "Teaching of the Elders." It is one of three main branches of Buddhism that originated in northern India and Nepal in the sixth century B.C. and rapidly spread throughout Southeast Asia until it was introduced to Cambodia in the thirteenth century via monks from Sri Lanka. It is a personal religion that worships no deity but rather teaches self-control in order to release all attachment to the material world and achieve personal enlightenment. Most Khmer men spend time as a novice before deciding to take the saffron robes or return to a secular life. For many it is the only escape from an existence of dire poverty and only hope for at least a minimal education. For Pan, it was a calling that almost killed hm.

It is hard to understand how university educated people could evolve into the senseless butchers that were the cadre of the Khmer Rouge, and yet their reign has become just one more footnote in a long litany of genocide that is the history of man. Whatever the base reasons for a government slaughtering a quarter of its own population for a political agenda, it was the Buddhist monks who bore the brunt of the assault here in Cambodia.

Their modest education made them a threat to the powers that wanted to return the nation to a Stone-Age agrarian commune of illiterate peasants, and since they do not work in the traditional sense of the word, they were easily made into the national whipping boy, publicly declared useless and a drain on society to be removed. Under the Khmer Rouge, the saffron robes were turned red.

Pan sits next to me on the stone railing of the Angkor moat bridge, lightly as a butterfly, radiating peace. From under his robes he produces an old oilcloth to reveal a small, shiny bowl; his rice bowl as he calls it.

In a matter-of-fact voice he tells me it is the top of his brother's skull, killed by the Khmer Rouge, and in true Buddhist fashion, he has kept it as a daily reminder of his own frailty and impermanence. After my initial shock, I decide it is a fitting prop to begin telling his tale. He stares at his dangling, sandaled feet, too short to reach the ground, as he speaks.

His story begins with the first night, when he was still a novice and lighting candles around the monastery when the door burst in and everyone was herded outdoors at gunpoint. Outside, in a huddled mass, the Abbott and all elders were singled out and summarily shot with a single bullet to the back of the head. By now, the attendant nuns were being stripped by the soldiers, intent on a long night of debauchery.

Next he tells me several monks were hung in the trees by their thumbs with small fires built underneath them, not enough to kill but just large enough to singe the skin. One of the nuns, now hysterical, was stripped, held down, and a monk was made to kneel between her knees. A pistol was put to his head, and he was ordered to copulate with her in front of all present. When he refused, a single shot rang out to the applause and cheers of the "soldiers" and another monk was brought forward. According to Pan, this went on for quite a while, until several monks had done the deed while several more had died in refusal. The fate of the nun was left unspoken

I search his face at this point for some sign, some emotional reaction, but see only tranquility. He has removed himself from this physical world and now occupies a separate reality. His road-map face is a spider web of creases but his eyes burn bright. I pray his religious advancement had brought him true peace and that he is not simply numb in relating such unspeakable events. He returns my stare with a slight smile and says, "Tell this story once so it might never be told a second time."

There is no self-pity or regret in his voice. To him it is karma, and all that surrounds him now is Maya, an illusion to wander through until he reaches true enlightenment. The realization of his unshakable faith hits me like a fist, and at that moment I yearn to find that level of peace.

We begin to walk into the main courtyard of Angkor, and though surrounded by thousands of tourists, I hear only Pan as he continues in his soft voice.

He was sent to the countryside and made to rip up railroad tracks, brutally physical work under a blazing sun while enduring non-stop blows from the fists and whips of his overseers. Soon, slowly starving, and with only putrid river water to drink, he was near death, the final plan for him from the beginning. In the end, his will to live overcame his belief in karma as he crawled away one night, into the jungle, and there, lost all track of time.

He recalled his first morning of this illusionistic freedom, waking in the crook of a tree, sucking the dew from leaves to ease his parched tongue, covered with ant bites. Dropping to the ground, his weakened legs would barely support him as he made his way into the bush, surrendering to the most basic human instinct, survival.

He was not sure how long he stayed in the jungle, but once there he soon found others like himself, survivors, all with an unspeakable story, all wishing to live. Everyone had a talent, some could fish, others snared small animals; Pan knew a lot about medicinal plants and soon became a gypsy doctor, moving every few days, avoiding roads and villages, helping the more needy for a handful of rice, defying the odds at the bottom of the food chain.

One day, while foraging near a village he spotted a saffron robe and, not believing his eyes, knew he had to talk with this brother. The Khmer Rouge were gone, but the damage had been done. Pan listened to the monk's litany of atrocities all day, but told me he fell asleep while doing so and the next morning, he woke up under a roof, on a cot, for the first time in months if not years.

When he revealed his identity, he was called to the capitol of Phnom Penh, where he was received as a revered elder and met a delegation of Theravada monks from Vietnam who had come to help re-establish the religion. Only then did he realize the extent of the genocide, the monasteries destroyed, the sacred texts burned, countless brother monks slaughtered, and for the only time in our conversations, I saw a single tear roll down his cheek.

Two subsequent visits with Pan were deliberately kept light-hearted and fun, and I learned that he loved shave ice and to laugh, but it is more of a sustained giggle than a laugh that spares no part of his face. His joy in all that surrounds him reminds me of a small child, and though I could not see it, I often felt his aura.

When I left, Pan was in great demand, traveling around to various monasteries, imparting the old ways—"The Teaching of the Elders"—to a new generation of monks who now use the internet, have cell phones and iPods, and ride motorbikes, but this does not seem to bother him in the least; how could it? Karma.

His goal has always been to spend his life in meditation, and I am sure that since our time together he has merged with the cosmos. I allow myself the fantasy to think he has been looking over my shoulder as I write this and knows that his story has been told, one more time, for the last time.

Today there are close to sixty thousand Theravada monks throughout the country and almost five thousand monasteries, all because men like Pan refused to give up their faith, and though he would laugh and shake his head at the thought, he is one who made a difference.

✿   ✿   ✿

James Michael Dorsey is an award-winning author, explorer, and public speaker who has traveled through forty-eight countries. For almost two decades he has visited the most remote tribal cultures on Earth to document them before they vanish forever. His book, Vanishing Tales from Ancient Trails *is a collection of personal narratives about these travels. He has written for* Colliers, Geo Ex Blog, Christian Science Monitor, Los Angeles Times, BBC Wildlife, United Airlines, Lonely Planet, *and for several African magazines as a correspondent for* CameraPix *of Nairobi. He is also a travel consultant to Brown & Hudson of London. "From the Ashes" shared the Grand Prize Bronze in the Eighth Annual Solas Awards and his stories have appeared in eighteen literary anthologies including* The Best Travel Writing *(Volumes 10 & 11), and the* Lonely Planet Literary Travel Anthology. *He is a fellow of the Explorers Club, and a former director of the Adventurers Club.*

TOM JOSEPH

❧ ❧ ❧

Fishing with Larry

They got together for one last adventure.

*D*on Juan says the Río Grande de Quetena holds trout. To make the point, he extends a muscled arm as if signaling a left turn: long as this and thick, too. He'll meet us four days from now at his hotel, Mallku Cueva. *"Voy a llevarlos."* I'll take you there. I'm skeptical about the trout, but that's not important. I only hope the guy shows up. We've just booked a five-day trip across a remote region in southern Bolivia where there are barely any roads, much less gas stations. Don Juan will be carrying our extra gas.

A nagging voice whispers caution. The Bolivian tour operator talks and smiles big. Like just that, an operator.

"What do you think, Larry?" I ask, and immediately the answer shoots across my synapses. Go for it.

What the hey, we're here for the adventure. So we pack our gear into Larry's '84 Toyota Land Cruiser and set off for the Salar de Uyuni, the world's largest salt lake. With my sister-in-law Babette and her friend Christophe, my wife Jeanne and me, plus our Bolivian guide Dieter, the car is stuffed to the max.

My brother Larry makes six, but he doesn't take up much room. He's in a Ziploc inside my fishing fanny pack. Larry died a year ago. I'm carrying his ashes.

Larry was a man of grand schemes that had an uncanny way of coming to fruition. His last was the grandest. Driving the Land Cruiser from New Mexico to Tierra del Fuego was only half the plan. The other half had Babette's Peugeot maneuvering from Corsica to parts east. He'd ship the Toyota from Chile to New Zealand, then north eventually to Southeast Asia. They'd crash the vehicles head-on in China. Larry would collect the insurance.

Traveling six weeks at a crack, over the course of several years the Land Cruiser had gotten as far as Bolivia, weathering a Colombian earthquake that created pandemonium in that already chaos-riddled country, and a Peruvian mudslide that left Larry with a concussion and he and Babette trapped in the car neck deep in a raging river. My brother always kept his head above water. But he didn't survive pancreatic cancer.

One of his last requests was that his ashes be divvied amongst his loved ones to do with as we chose. Jeanne and I brought our cupful on our hundred-day South American sojourn organized around learning Spanish, visiting our Peace Corps volunteer daughter in Paraguay, and meeting Babette in Bolivia. We began our trip at the tip of the continent in Punta Arenas. On the ferry ride across the Strait of Magellan, halfway between the mainland and Tierra del Fuego, I flung a scoop over the railing. It felt right. Larry was a nautical guy—a boater, diver, fisherman. On the return ride, in the afterglow of a blazing midnight sunset, a Patagonian dolphin surfaced at the same spot and paralleled the boat for a forever moment, eyeing me and nodding his head as if agreeing: good decision.

I'd only scattered half my Larry, though. I guess I still needed to keep him near.

Now, a month later with Babette and Christophe in Sucre, we've resuscitated the car, dormant four years. Three days of a whole family of mechanics' time cost fifty bucks, but we also had to pay an $800 ransom to liberate it from their brawny and resolute mother, who owned the garage and swore the deal was five Bolivianos a day.

We made our way through the massively wrinkled 14,000-foot desert landscape that is the Bolivian Altiplano, south to Potosí, where, booking a tour of Cerro Rico, once the world's richest silver mine, we met this thickly built, charismatic fortyish guy Juan Quesada, whose employees call him Don Juan. A chef by training, he's a born entrepreneur.

We leave his office about a thousand dollars lighter with an itinerary to some of the most isolated reaches of Bolivia.

After rendezvousing with Dieter—his only explanation for his German name is "my father was crazy"—he directs us onto the somewhat slushy Salar de Uyuni. "*No hay problema*," he says, the salt is ten meters thick. We dodge piles of drying salt destined for shakers as we drive to the Salt Palace Hotel, built entirely of blocks of the white crystals. The rooms are little igloos, complete with salt stalactites and comfy, if a bit dazzling, salt furniture. It was Don Juan who built this curiosity that actually works. I gain a little confidence.

Traversing the open Salar at our pedal-to-the-floor sixty miles per hour, the white is so intense, the lack of reference so complete that we have no feeling of movement. Babette says she feels as if she's in a boat on a perfectly calm day. Larry would have loved this. She scatters half her Larry out the window.

At the foot of Volcán Thunupa, its flanks streaked with the red of iron, the yellow of sulfur and the green of copper, sits a small village, tiny yellow and red flowers pushing through the salt soil of its church courtyard. Larry, an artist, would have loved this, too.

Dieter guides us unerringly off the Salar and through a landscape soaked in salt, borax, and a periodic table's worth of other minerals that is at once stark and intensely vivid. We summit barren mountain passes and ford unmarked streams up to our floorboards. Sometimes there's a road, sometimes just wheel tracks that flare off in random directions.

Our stops—other than the ones to blow rust particles out of a frequently clogged fuel filter—are as compelling as the environs. We stroll through an Inca necropolis in a field of coral boulders, the tombs containing the misshapen skulls—from being bound—that gave Inca noble kids that fashionable oblong look. We're voyeurs to male llamas draped lazily over lounging females: llaid-back llama llove. We view through a haze of heat all three species of Bolivian flamingoes, the black-winged Andean, the all-pink Chilean, and the James with its brilliant red-orange wings. An equal number of the magnificent birds stand upside down in the reflection of the unnamed salt lake. My overstimulated eyes find elephants, vultures, a throne, and two lovers in the bizarrely sculpted lava formations of the Rock Valley. Maybe the coca leaves I'm chewing are working better than I thought.

Exhausted and encrusted in salt, dust and sweat, two days later we reach Mallku Cueva, another of Don Juan's hotels. This one is built into the side of a cliff; its rock face forms the rear wall of our bedroom. The shower even has hot water. Better yet, as we follow our noses to fresh baked bread from the hotel's wood oven, Don Juan shows up with our blessed petrol and a bottle of Sangini, Bolivian cognac. He's brought his fishing rod, too, a decrepit-looking spinning outfit.

So we're a bit furry-mouthed and anvil-headed when our trout expedition sets out the next morning. I ride with Don Juan down a dirt track that keeps getting worse, finally narrowing to a footpath that plunges down a steep hillside, barely squeezing between two boulders. The blue Toyota bravely follows, Jeanne at the wheel. Don Juan's impressed.

After maybe an hour, we reach the Río Grande de Quetena. Grand it's not, so choked with weeds that you can hardly see water. Here and there are open spots through which a gentle current trickles. No way is this a trout stream. We climb a rocky hill to an overlook and peer down. Trout. Huge ones! A few spook and swim beneath the blanket of weeds, but several, including one monster matching the size and bulk of Don Juan's arm, just lie there. "*Ahora. ¿Me crees?*" Don Juan asks.

Yeah, I believe. Lordy.

That's when the pressure hits me. With so little water to work a fly through, how am I going to hook a fish, much less land it? And Babette has built me up as some kind of fishing maestro, whereas the truth is I'm not much of a trout fisherman. We have streams in northern Wisconsin, but a lot more lakes. I grew up with a spinning rod in my hand and a minnow bucket at my feet.

So I try to conduct myself in the manner of every trout fanatic I've ever met. I prepare fanatically slowly. I return to the car. Ease into my waders. Rub each section of my five-piece *caña de mosca* on the oily spot on the side of my nose before putting it together. Check each guide as I string it. Unwind, stretch, and restretch my fifteen-pound leader. Snug the loop-to-loop connection.

I open the large compartment of my fanny pack to pull out my fly box, and instead encounter the baggie of Larry. Whoa. Could this be the place?

"What do you think, bro?" I whisper it aloud.

One thing about my brother. Type-A though he was, he believed in letting people make their own decisions. That's why he left a dozen of us with ashes and no instructions.

Oh, the magical fishing days we shared. Northern Manitoba on the solstice, hammering the pike and walleyes as the sun dipped down and came up an hour later. Loreto, in Baja,

Mexico on my fortieth birthday, one of those cosmic jokes with me as the butt when I couldn't catch a fish to save my life, but it didn't matter, not even when the skies opened up and cancelled our last two days, because the sight of the orange, swollen river dumping into the aqua of the Sea of Cortez was unforgettable. Or another time camping in Baja when his outboard conked out and our next landfall, by Larry's reckoning, would be Australia. Or that final time in Captiva, Florida, a week before he died, when, under a double rainbow, Larry outfished us all.

But most treasured of all were evenings on the lakes of northern Wisconsin, in the cold or the rain, that ended with grins on our faces and a stringer of walleyes, basket of slab crappies, or memory of wide-shouldered bass caught and released.

We worked together twenty years. He was eight years my elder, ever my sounding board, but eventually our talk about relationships or kids or our current passions, his painting and my writing, had been as peers. We shared blood, genes, a somewhat obsessive commitment to family and a lot of wine. Yet of all the bonds between us, fishing was as important as any. When we fished together, the world was always right.

How Larry would have loved the utter improbability of this trout stream in southern Bolivia. I make up my mind: this is the place. Whether the fish are catchable is immaterial.

When I ask Don Juan permission to put Larry's ashes in the river, he says he'd be honored. We return to the rock overlook. Babette decides to scatter hers as well. The wind carries them to the edge of the weeds, where the double dose of Larry gently settles and sinks.

Don Juan takes out his spinning rod, gives it a quizzical look. He admits he's never fished with anything other than a seine net. I show him how to hold it, flip the bail, make a cast. He flips his one spoon from the overlook and whoops when one of the monsters turns to it, but the fish flashes off. I try to get him to come down to the river with me, but Don Juan is gaga over being able to see the trout below. I scramble down alone.

With the help of a wood pole, I slog through the weedy gook to where I can cast. I have no idea what to throw. I've seen a few dragonflies, so I try one. The wind behind me, I make a perfect cast. Phew, at least I didn't embarrass myself right off the bat. The fly floats back toward me. Nothing doing. I try several more times, then switch to a green tongue depressor, a Wisconsin smallmouth fly similar to a wooly bugger that Jeanne ties. *Whammo.* Don Juan sees the hit and is screaming like a kid. Fish on.

I'm glad for the heavy leader. The fish is strong, but, pulling horizontally, my six-weight affords good leverage, and I'm able to keep the trout from the weeds. Dieter has followed me with a landing net, large enough though the frame is way flimsy. I tire the fish out and instruct Dieter: hands on the frame, not handle. *La cabeza primero.* Head first. Fish in. Twenty-one inches, four and a half pounds, a fat, beautiful rainbow. In Bolivia. Thank you, Larry.

"*¿Quieres comerlo?*" I shout up the outcropping. Don Juan gives me the thumbs up. Hell yes, he wants to eat it.

I climb up with the fish. Time to help my host, who's still after the big one. Time after time the fish refuses the spoon, though it never spooks. So I thread the spinning line through a bobber I fashioned last night by boring a hole in a wine cork, then pinch on a split shot and attach a wooly bugger. A trout snaps at it immediately, but Don Juan misses the hit. He's chattering nonstop, having the time of his life.

I still can't get him to come down to the river. So I return. Wham. Twenty-three incher, another shimmering rainbow of a rainbow.

So the day goes. We eat lunch. Jeanne, Babette, and Christophe tire and leave. Don Juan, Dieter, and I, to say the least, don't tire. The boss is determined to tease that monster trout from on high. I don't have the heart to tell him that even if he hooks the fish, there's not a trout's shadow of a chance he'll raise it up a twenty-five-foot cliff.

Moving upstream to another hole in the weeds with a large boulder in the middle, in no more than six casts I land a twenty-three and two twenty-fours, all six to eight pounds. We have plenty for dinner for us and the staff; I'm ready to catch and release. But Don Juan wants me to keep every fish. He's having a party for his brother, who's turning fifty in a few days. The brother has cancer. This will be a birthday to remember. I feel Larry smiling.

By now, it's mid-afternoon and hot. I finally convince Don Juan to move to the stream. I want to take him to my boulder, but he insists on fishing downstream. Oh well, it's his river. I try to place him where he can get some action with his spoon, but he's not much of a listener. We see no fish for a good half mile.

So we return to the overlook rock. Yep, the behemoth is still there. Don Juan stands above to direct me. The wind has shifted and is now blowing down the river; it's tough casting. Staying in the shelter of the rock overhang, I can just manage to put a fly into position. A fish hits. Twenty-four inches. Beautiful. But Don Juan wants me to fell the giant. I keep casting and break lines on two fish I never see. So I tie on a piece of twenty-pound shock tippet and return one more time. My fly sinks, drifts, stops. Yeah. Fish on. "*Un caballo*," I yell.

I can't stop it from swimming under the weeds. I'm patient, though, applying constant pressure, and finally out comes the trout, running downstream. Not good. But it stays on and begins tiring. The landing net has long since broken, so I keep working, tiring the fish, which always seems to have strength for one more run. Finally, the oversized trout lies quiet on the surface, allowing me to cradle it. Twenty-nine inches, eleven pounds. A horse, for sure.

Don Juan is all grins as we pose for a photo, holding the fish between us, as long as our outstretched arms. He thinks there's still a bigger one down there. *"Bastante,"* I say. Enough. I try to impress upon him the importance of leaving some fish in the river. We return to the car and share a *trago.* Another universality, that post-fishing drink.

I pour a bit of Sangini on the ground both as offering to the earth goddess Pachamama and farewell to my brother. It's not easy to get into Don Juan's jeep and close the door. But it's necessary. Thanks for one more great day, bro.

The next day we walk through a field of geothermal pools with roaring steam vents and burbling pots of brown, pink, and gray goo. Then we cross an expanse of soft blond sand dotted with large dark brown boulders, bleak yet ordered, and appropriately named Salvador Dalí Desert.

Larry would have loved this.

Tom Joseph has published essays, short stories, humor, outdoor writing, travel pieces, and his novel Song of the Tides. *This essay won the Grand Prize Gold in the First Annual Solas Awards 2007 Solas Awards and was included in Travelers' Tales* The Best Travel Writing 2007. *Tom and his wife Jeanne live in Northern Wisconsin, where he serves on a non-profit board dedicated to connecting people with the natural world. Their travel to hard-to-reach places—most recently scuba diving in Raja Ampat, Indonesia—renews their spirits and belief that the world's natural places inspire, heal and connect us . . . and that it's our solemn duty to protect them.*

MICHAEL SHAPIRO

ℐℬ ℐℬ ℐℬ

Beneath the Rim

A journey down the Colorado River
with Captain John Wesley Powell.

> Our boats are four in number. Three are built of
> oak, stanch and firm (with) water-tight cabins. . . .
> These will buoy the boats should the waves roll them
> over in rough water. The fourth is made of pine . . .
> built for fast rowing. . . . We take with us rations
> deemed sufficient to last for ten months.
> — *John Wesley Powell*, The Exploration
> of the Colorado River and Its Canyons

What a difference 140 years makes, I think, as we pump
up our inflatable Hypalon boats and fill our coolers
at Lee's Ferry on the eve of a 297-mile journey down the Colorado River through the Grand Canyon. John Wesley Powell's
rations on his 1869 expedition included flour for unleavened
bread, bacon, dried apples, coffee and whiskey. The basics.
For our twenty-four-day trip, we pack pasta and pesto, fresh

organic broccoli and carrots, homemade apple and pumpkin pies, and a whole turkey, frozen in a block of ice, for Thanksgiving two and a half weeks after our launch.

Powell, a geologist, explorer, and Civil War captain who lost most of one arm during the Battle of Shiloh, set out in 1869 with nine other men to attempt the first descent of the Colorado. Among Powell's fleet were boats called *Maid of the Canyon* and *No Name*; the boat I'll help steer down the river is the *Black Pearl*. We learn from Johnny Beers, of Canyon REO, the company renting us the boats, that the *Black Pearl* was recently washed out of a Canyon camp by a flash flood and floated forty miles downstream. When found, it was upright, a map book still atop its cooler, Johnny said. An auspicious story, the kind of tale that whether true or embellished is calming on the eve of a river trip down one of the most ferocious whitewater rivers in the world. Much more reassuring than the blown-up photos on Canyon REO's wall showing a 1983 fatal flip in Crystal rapids.

Unlike most trips down the Canyon, we're guiding ourselves rather than relying on a commercial outfitter. We have sixteen people in five boats; rowing is shared but each boat has a captain responsible for rigging (strapping the gear down) and getting the raft safely through the most fearsome rapids. But no one in our group, other than me, has been down the Colorado through the Canyon before, and I've only done it once, twelve years ago at a different water level. It's a river whose hydraulics are unlike any other, with pounding waves higher than our sixteen-foot boats, and sucking holes that can flip a raft and hold on to its passengers, recirculating boats and humans like a washing machine. It's called getting Maytagged.

As the sunset turns the Canyon walls golden red, we finish packing our provisions. I wrap duct tape and cardboard around our bottles of tequila, gin, and Jack Daniels to protect our good soldiers from the rollicking rapids ahead. After sleeping fitfully through a frosty November night, our group leader Kristin, a twenty-six-year-old Outward Bound guide from Moab, Utah, calls us together and we meet with a Grand Canyon ranger. He makes sure we have all the necessary equipment: maps, ropes and other safety gear, and a "groover" for human waste.

Why is it called a groover? Back in the early days of whitewater rafting, the groover was nothing more than a large metal ammo box lined with a Hefty bag, so after sitting on it rafters would have a long groove on each cheek and thigh. Modern groovers have toilet seats but the name has, well, stuck.

After months of planning, preparing and provisioning, we're off. The Canyon is wide at Lee's Ferry, and the early afternoon sun illuminates the sculpted rust-colored walls. I share a boat with Owen, an Englishman in his early forties with a dry sense of humor who came to the western U.S. to teach snowboarding and do some tech work. Owen, our boat captain, takes the first pulls on the oars.

The euphoria of the journey's first moments, especially on a naturally flowing waterway, is palpable. We hear hoots and cheers from our companions upstream as we hit our first rapids. Powell had similar feelings of exultation when he navigated the first whitewater of his trip: "We thread the narrow passage with exhilarating velocity," he wrote, "mounting the high waves, whose foaming crests dash over us, and plunging into the troughs, until we reach the quiet water below."

We wake before the sun tops the rim on Day Two to see our fully laden boats on the beach, high and dry. The river has dropped precipitously, a result of timed releases followed by curtailed flows from the Glen Canyon Dam upstream. Without the dam we probably wouldn't have enough water to be boating in November. But I'd trade that in a second to get rid of the blockage that inundated a canyon many believe was as beautiful as the Grand, but in a gentler, more seductive way. Former Sierra Club president David Brower called the 710-foot-high, 1,560-foot-wide dam "America's most regretted environmental mistake." The reservoir the dam created is called Lake Powell, which I'm certain would make old Captain Powell, who reveled in the beauty of this place, wince. We know that eventually the water will rise and allow us to get our boats back in the river, so we wait. "That's what I like about there not being other groups around," says Lynsey, an easygoing outdoor leader and flute player. "There's no one to laugh at us," she says. "We can laugh at ourselves."

The sun is going down and the shadows are settling in the canyon. The vermilion gleams and roseate hues, blending with the green and gray tints, are slowly changing to somber brown above, and black shadows are creeping over them below; and now it is a dark portal to a region of gloom—the gateway through which we are to enter on our voyage of exploration to-morrow. What shall we find?

Powell's description shows not just apprehension about the monstrous rapids he expected downriver, but his reverence for the natural beauty of the Southwest. Unlike the dour explorers of his time, Powell appreciated the glory of the landscape.

Consider what his contemporary, Lt. Joseph Christmas Ives, who attempted to navigate the Colorado in 1857, said about the Grand Canyon and the river that runs through it: "The region . . . is altogether valueless. It can be approached only from the south, and after entering it there is nothing to do but leave. Ours has been the first, and will doubtless be the last, party of whites to visit this profitless locality. It seems intended by nature that the Colorado River . . . shall forever be unvisited and undisturbed."

Today several million people visit the Canyon each year and about a million of those hike into it, according to the

National Park Service. About twenty thousand people raft the Colorado River each year, mostly on guided commercial trips. The figure would be far higher if the park didn't restrict the number of boaters with a lottery permit system. Until a few years ago, there was a waiting list to get permits for non-commercial trips, like ours, down the Colorado. When the list stretched to more than twenty years it was phased out and replaced with the lottery system. If boaters can't use a permit, they can cancel, which happens with some frequency for cold-season trips—that's how we got our winning lottery ticket.

On Day Two we catch an eddy and pull over to scout House Rock Rapid, our first real test, seventeen miles down from the put-in (starting point) at Lee's Ferry. To scout we hike above the rapid to see it. Unlike Powell, we have a detailed map that suggests routes through the rapids. But the river is ever changing. Boulders tumble into it and can make formerly safe routes hazardous; the powerful current can rearrange rocks, and a rapid can be easy at low water but frightening at higher flows—or vice versa. So we scout and understand the name of this rapid: the current plunges against a rock the size of a house, creating fearsome hydraulics.

In the rapids a fast funnel of waves coerces our boat to the left, toward the Canyon's south wall. Lateral waves push the boat sideways. Owen pulls at the oars with all his strength—we get just right of two mammoth waves and a hole that could flip a boat. I peer into the churning maw of the rapid's recirculating hole as we clear it, the dark waves crashing in upon themselves.

We celebrate that evening at House Rock camp, just below the rapid, with gin-and-tonics and feast on fish tacos and fresh organic salad with goddess dressing. That evening I read of Powell's reliance on "flour that has been wet and dried so many times that it is all musty and full of hard lumps." Hanging off the side of each of our boats is a mesh bag filled with beer, staying cool and ready in the fifty-degree river water.

The next morning we scramble up eggs with spinach and cheddar. I overhear Kevin, the youngest member of our group at twenty-two, say "I don't need the hot cock this morning." Startled, I see Victoria, a nurturing soul who's become our camp mom, reach across the table, grab a bottle, and say, "I'll take the hot cock anytime of day." They're talking about the Sriracha chili sauce, with its proud and upright rooster on the label.

In the evenings Powell's party dispelled "the gloom of these great depths" by sharing Civil War stories around a campfire; many of his crew had fought in the conflict. Though we cook on propane stoves, we too build fires and share our "war stories" of prior river adventures, love gone awry and the misguided exploits of our youth. We brighten the cold, dark evenings with tiki torches and strands of battery-powered twinkly colored lights that we drape around our chairs, adding a note of festivity to our home for this one night.

And we sing songs like The Band's "The Night They Drove Old Dixie Down" and "Crow Medicine Show" and Bob Dylan's "Wagon Wheel" (a collaboration that spans decades as Old Crow added verses to a forgotten Dylan song), tunes that would have been as timely and at home in the nineteenth century as they are in the twenty-first. Our voices are leavened by Lynsey's plaintive flute and Kevin's acoustic guitar, toted on the river in watertight cases. Kevin, who just completed college, is considering a career in outdoor education, like his older brother Steve, a trip leader for Outward Bound and one of our five boat captains.

Powell wrote that his men would occasionally "shout or discharge a pistol, to listen to the reverberations among the cliffs." We blow off steam with pyrotechnics, setting an open can of collected bacon grease on a grill atop our campfire. "Is everyone at least ten feet from the fire?" Steve shouts as he fetches water from the river. Neil, a mellow river ranger and one of our boat captains, says "No, they're about two feet away." Steve: "Then get the first aid kit!" Steve has attached a pail of water to ten-foot-long oar and moves toward the fire. Some in our group start chanting: "Ba-con bomb! Baaa-con bomb! BAAAAA-CON BOMB!" Steve yells at us to back away and pours the water into the can of bubbling bacon grease. It explodes, sending a plume of flame fifteen feet into the air, as we leap away and howl.

In November, only one group is allowed to start a trip down the Colorado each day, compared to five or six in midsummer. We have the glorious feeling of having the entire Canyon to ourselves. And while our coolers and bar are extravagantly stocked, we've made a point to leave behind most of modern society's distractions. We don't bring a boom box—our music is homegrown—and cell towers are beyond our reach. One concession is a satellite phone in case of emergency.

Powell's party had its share of technical equipment too, most notably barometers for measuring altitude. Early in his exploration, before reaching the Grand Canyon, Powell's boat *No Name* was dashed to pieces, its hull caught in a turbulent rapid. The crew survived, but Powell's treasured barometers were in the stranded *No Name*. The captain sent two men into the river to rescue his instruments. "The boys set up a shout, and I join them," Powell wrote, "pleased that they should be as glad as myself to save the instruments." When the men returned, he saw they also salvaged a three-gallon keg of whiskey. "The last is what they were shouting about," Powell noted dryly.

Drink is what we shout about when we reach camp the next afternoon. As the sun disappears it gets cool, so we attach a propane tank to a camp stove and make some hot buttered rum. Over a dinner of pesto pasta with spicy sausage, I consider how decadent our trip is compared to Powell's expedition, whose members ate the same drab food every day and often huddled under cold, wet blankets. Until they lost some blankets after one of their boats capsized, leaving some men shivering in the frigid night with nothing more than a canvas tarp to cover them.

We flick a Bic and have a cook fire, our waterproof sacks keep our compressible zero-degree sleeping bags dry, and our inflatable boats can navigate even the Canyon's most ominous rapids, sparing us the torture of carrying boats over crumbly canyon walls around the biggest drops, as Powell's party did.

Yet we share Powell's appreciation of the Canyon. We see the "cathedral-shaped" buttes, towering monuments, and "grandly arched" half-mile-high walls reflected in calm stretches of the river, and the polished ochre spires that tower above it all. Our spirits soar as we float through Marble Canyon, with its pink and purple hues and "saffron" tints.

At a bend in the river, we find a deep oval opening scoured into the rock by millions of years of the river surging into it. Powell estimated that if it were a theater it could seat 50,000 people. Now called Redwall Cavern, it's a perfect spot for an impromptu game of soccer, and we exhaust ourselves chasing a ball over the sandy beach. A Frisbee gets pulled out and flung towards the water. We dive off the boats attempting to catch it, plunging into the chilly eddy like eager dogs.

Just downstream we pull over to explore a delicate waterfall spraying from peach-colored rocks. Lush green vegetation surrounds the cascade; the sunshine lights up the misty veil with all the colors of the rainbow. Powell named this place Vasey's Paradise for a botanist who had previously traveled

with him through the Southwest. Downriver we hike into
Nautiloid Canyon—I expect to see fossils of chambered nau-
tiluses preserved in stone but we find evidence of yard-long
creatures with tail fins for propulsion that I learn were ancestors of squid.

Every day my sense of wonder grows, I write in my journal, as the walls around me start to glow deep red in the dawn
light. I appreciate the perfect balance of water, desert, cliff
and sky, and find myself agreeing with desert gnostic Edward
Abbey who wrote: "There is no shortage of water in the desert but exactly the right amount, a perfect ratio of water to
rock, of water to sand, insuring that wide, free, open, generous spacing among plants and animals, homes and towns and
cities, which makes the arid west so different from any other
part of the nation. There is no lack of water here, unless you
try to establish a city were no city should be."

We take a day off from paddling and spend a layover day
at Nankoweap, the first place we'll camp for two nights. High
above us native peoples built granaries to store their grain.
I hike a few hundred feet above the river to explore what
appear to be windows in the Canyon walls. I sit alone among
the ancient spirits and feel gratitude for this trip, the bounty
in my life, and the now famous vista of the Canyon as it bends
to the right and the river disappears from view.

With limited rations, "an unknown distance yet to run"
and "an unknown river yet to explore" the mood of Powell's party turned serious at the Little Colorado. For us, the
Little Colorado River is another gorgeous Canyon feature to
explore. The sky-blue river is brightened by chalky mineral
deposits which have ever so slowly created tiny (a foot or two
high) travertine falls, little steps in the river over which the
shiny water fans. I sit mesmerized by the sounds of dozens of
these falls and their gentle music accompanied by the song of
canyon wrens overhead.

Back on the water, upstream gales hit us full force. The strength we've built during a week of rowing helps, but still we make only one mile per hour, compared to our average speed of four or five mph. At camp we play bocce among the stones, thickets and sand, the terrain adding new elements to the old Italian game. That night we make s'mores from graham crackers, chocolate bars and toasted marshmallows. River guides say most accidents happen on land. On that night is the closest I've come so far to injury. As Jason, who is Kristin's boyfriend and so pretty I call him "Boy Band," tells a story he excitedly gestures and a flaming marshmallow vaults off his stick and leaps across the fire, landing on my leg. But the burn is mild and easily remedied with cool water.

As we break camp on a rainy cool morning, I put on my Neoprene hood for the first time—it's a wetsuit for the head and makes me look like a dorky aviator from the 1930s. I can't picture Powell or his rugged men in one of these, but I'll gladly put vanity aside and don the hood, my fleece top, nylon splash jacket and Neoprene booties to stay warm.

After ten days I feel in tune with the cadences of the Canyon, but our isolation is interrupted by a stop at Phantom Ranch near the bottom of the Bright Angel Trail. This is a popular lodge and campsite for those hiking deep into the Canyon, and it's where we bid farewell to three members of our party, who hike out to return to commitments above the rim.

Though I'm tempted to eschew Phantom Ranch's conveniences, I go to its pay phone for two reasons: to tell my girlfriend and mother that I'm having the time of my life, and because it's my birthday and I want to hear the voices of my loved ones. It feels strange to touch a credit card and money. When an operator asks for my zip code to authorize the card, I can barely remember it. I reach my mother and she recounts the story she tells me every year: how at my first Thanksgiving, when I was a week old, I was placed on the table as the centerpiece and the turkey was bigger than me.

On the way back to the boats I catch the eye of a mule deer, a young buck that lets me get within a few feet of him. The deer doesn't seem to fear people, perhaps because in this park deer can't be hunted. I meet a couple of tourists from South Korea, who are astounded that we're in the midst of a twenty-four-day voyage. The young woman touches my shoulder in farewell; it seems that a part of them wants to connect to our journey. We refill our big plastic water jugs and get back on the river.

There is a descent of perhaps seventy-five or eighty feet in a third of a mile, and the rushing waters break into great waves on the rocks and lash themselves into a mad, white foam. We step into our boats, push off, and away we go, first on smooth but swift water, then we strike a glassy wave and ride to its top, down again into the trough, up again on a high wave, and down and up on waves higher and still higher until we strike one just as it curls back, and a breaker rolls over our little boat. Still on we speed . . . until the little boat is caught in a whirlpool and spun around several times.
                                                                    —*J.W. Powell*

The Colorado welcomes us back with some of the most technical and scary rapids on the river. Most rivers have a rating scale of Class I (flat water) to Class VI (virtually unrunnable), but the Colorado is graded from 1 to 10. Today we have several Class 8 to 9 rapids, the first being Horn, a mess of towering waves, rocks, chutes and holes. While Owen scouts, I put on my dry top with rubber neck and wrist gaskets to keep the water out. In the rapids we get knocked sideways, then slide backwards for a minute before Owen pulls the boat away from a gaping hole and into the calm water below.

Next is Granite. We spend more than half an hour scouting, searching for a route through it. As arduous as carrying the boats around the rapids would be, gazing at Granite almost makes me consider portaging. But that's not an option. Steve, only twenty-four years old, has volunteered to be lead boat. A true outdoorsman, Steve has been nonchalant leading us through all the rapids during the past few days.

But Granite is different than what we've seen so far: it has more hazards than we can count. The only possible run is a thread-the-needle along the right wall: if you get too far left an angry set of waves will probably flip you, too far right and you'll be slammed into the north wall. Steve's eyes blaze with fierce determination as he enters the river. He eludes the biggest waves, pulls back hard on the oars to stay off the wall and he's through. Up close, as we run it, Granite is faster and harder to read than from the river bank, and we get bounced around near the bottom, but with some strong, well-timed tugs on the oars, Owen pulls us to safety.

Hermit has a twenty-foot curling haystack wave in the center, is even bigger that Granite. But it's a straight shot down the center. Just hit it hard and straight, and enjoy the ride. We keep the boat straight and have a clean roller-coaster run. We float to camp to the celebratory sounds of cheers and beers being popped. My birthday celebration has begun.

On a sandy beach that evening I'm offered the camp throne, a reclining nylon chaise lounge. My other chair, battered by the river, is missing an arm—we name it the John Wesley Powell because he'd lost his arm before his Canyon journey. I dig out the bottle of Herradura tequila I've brought for this night, passing it around the campfire circle for all to swig. The group presents me with a blueberry muffin cake baked in a Dutch oven, a large, covered cast-iron pot that's set on coals for baking.

When I first considered a twenty-four-day Canyon trip, it seemed like a long time. At the halfway point, I feel time slipping away. There's so much to see every day in the side canyons: the fern-shrouded waterfall at Elves Chasm where Kristin others leap naked into the pool below, Blacktail Canyon with its magical concert-hall acoustics, and Deer Creek Falls, a thundering 100-foot-high cascade next to the river. I'm in no hurry to return home, but I am ready for some rest.

We take a layover day at Galloway Camp where we enjoy a warm solar shower (the water heated in a dark bag attached to a hose and shower head). A drove of about eight bighorn sheep stroll right through camp, scampering up an impossibly steep hillside as we approach. We wash our clothes in buckets of river water and drape them over the spindly desert trees.

I sink deeper into the Canyon's natural rhythms. I put away my watch and tell time by the progression of Pleiades, the Big Dipper and Orion across the night sky. We've become a resourceful group—we fix broken chairs with extra straps, we patch boats if they spring a leak, and erect shelters with tarps and oars when it rains. I appreciate this sense of self-containment and the group's confidence that we have the ability to handle almost anything that comes our way.

As we travel deeper into the crucible, past rock walls more than a billion years old, the Canyon gets steeper and narrower. Our sense of isolation intensifies. "It seems a long way up to the world of sunshine and open sky," Powell wrote. And it is: in the heart of the Canyon the walls are 6,000 feet—more than a mile—high. The sun shines through the sharp, narrow slot for an hour or less each day this time of year; we warm up when the river bends to the south and catches the late autumn sun in the southern sky.

By late August of 1869, Powell's crew had traveled for three months since beginning their journey at Green River City. By the time they reached the deepest part of the Grand Canyon, Powell wrote, their canvas tent was "useless," their rubber ponchos lost, "more than half the party are without hats, not one of us has an entire suit of clothes, and we have not a blanket apiece." When the rain pours down, "we sit up all night on the rocks shivering, and are more exhausted by the night's discomfort than the day's toil."

At Ledges Camp we sleep comfortably atop Thermarest pads on shelves of shiny black gneiss. I fall asleep to a column of stars visible through the Canyon's slot, the occasional meteor shining brilliantly for a flash before being consumed by Earth's atmosphere. I dream of a tiger in a cage; so lonely it's going crazy. It needs to roam. Then I dream of traveling across the U.S. entirely by water with my brother. Perhaps the inescapable Canyon is taking an emotional toll after all.

"Are we running Lava tomorrow?" Nathan, a wiry and strong former collegiate soccer player, shouts to our campfire circle. "Because if we are," he announces as he puts down his beer, "I need to stop drinking right now!" A few miles downstream, Lava is the most intimidating rapid on the river, with a precipitous fifteen-foot drop that tumbles into a recirculating ledge hole and ferocious lateral waves that seem to upend boats for kicks.

The mood the next morning is serious, quiet. We tighten lines on the boats so if we flip we won't lose our gear. Without a word we start stretching, we want to be limber, ready, in case we swim in the frothy madness. As we row downriver, the steep red Canyon widens slightly. Layers of basalt give way to black volcanic rock, the river's descent gets steeper. The water picks up speed. We hear the rapids' roar before we see Lava and pull over at the scout point just as two boats from the trip ahead of us are about to run the gauntlet.

At this water level the forgiving left chute is too shallow to run. The center hole must be avoided at all costs. So we'll run right. The first of the other trip's two rafts, a solo boater on a catamaran, drops in. The boat is buried by a crashing wave;

when it emerges, its pilot is gone, swept out by the rushing waters. The next boat gets slapped sideways by the first couple of grinding curlers, by the third its downstream side starts to rise and we watch helplessly as the boat flips, dumping everyone on board into the hammering current. We exhale when we see everyone flush out safely below.

At each of the life-threatening rapids we've run, Owen has rallied us by sounding his kazoo-like horn, a sort of Cavalry rallying cry. Each boat captain taps the top of his or her head, river sign language for "O.K." and "Ready." Owen blows on the kazoo but there's no sound—it's waterlogged—an ominous sign. He blows the water out and tries again—nothing. Then he shakes it out; the third attempt yields a warbled call, enough sound to give us superstitious guides inspiration for the run ahead.

Our map-guide says running through Lava takes twenty seconds. But we all know how long twenty seconds can be if things don't go well. And if they don't, it will take much more than twenty seconds to pick up the pieces and put everything back together again.

Steve, in our lead boat, drops in—we can't see his run from above—but Boy Band stands atop his boat and shouts: "One boat through!" Nathan follows and gets slapped around—he looks a bit sideways and one side of his boat starts to rise, but then it comes down and he's through. Kristin and Neil roll into it; we drop in just after them. It's hard to see exactly where we planned to enter—the frothy green-and-white maelstrom makes it almost impossible to chart a course.

But Owen is on target and hits the first wave hard and straight, just like you're supposed to. We break through the first hurdle, hit the V of the second wave right where we want to and punch through. Several fifteen-foot curlers break over our boat then we hit a wall of whitewater. *The Black Pearl* seems to stop, suspended above the mighty Colorado in slow motion. Then the river grabs us and drags us through the final drops. We're through the worst of Lava Falls. From here it's a rollercoaster of waves to the bottom of the rapid. We pull over at Tequila Beach, named for post-Lava celebrations, break out the Sauza and Hornitos, and pass the bottles around. The group that had the flip and swimmers is there too. We compare notes, borrow their Hula hoops and whirl as ecstatically as dervishes.

We've made it through the big rapids; all we need to do now is find a beach to sleep on. Kristin pulls us over about a mile below Lava, but the beach is tiny and covered with prickly shrubs. The group revokes her status as trip leader for the rest of the day. Owen, the only sober one among us, is given command. He locates a fine camp, and we play bocce on a spit of beach so close to the river that we sink up to our ankles in the watery sand.

Powell's journal suggests his party portaged the boats around Lava Falls and had a clear sense that they were near the end of the journey. They too celebrated after Lava, stumbling upon an Indian garden with ripe green squashes. Powell excuses his "robbery" by "pleading our great want." After so many meager meals, the captain is exultant: "What a kettle of squash sauce we make! True, we have no salt with which to season it, but it makes a fine addition to our unleavened bread and coffee." Powell estimates his team covered thirty-five river miles that day. "A few days like this," he writes, "and we are out of our prison."

Canyon veterans warn that trips can fall apart during the final few days. Once Lava has been run, the theory goes, all the pent-up and buried resentments surface, and group cohesion suffers. But we're a companionable, easygoing group. We know we won't fall prey to petty disputes.

After a festive spaghetti dinner we gather round the campfire to chart the rest of the trip. Because we're a bit behind

schedule and have a set take-out date, Kristin suggests floating over the flatwater at night. Steve is dead set against a night
float, his emotions amplified by alcohol. He conjures visions
of bodies in sleeping bags rolling off the boats, never to be seen
again. "I'd rather run Lava ten times than do a night float,"
he exclaims. Kristin gives him a nonplussed look that says
"Whatever," and suggests we talk about it in the morning.

With the return of daylight and sobriety, all is forgiven. At
Granite Park Canyon (Mile 209) we find an expansive beach,
set up a badminton net and prepare our Thanksgiving feast.
A solo boater floats by. His name is Jake and he's hungry for
company, so we invite him to join us. We put the turkey in a
metal drum and cover it with charcoal. Hours later it's burnt to
a crisp, but we scrape off the black crust and savor the feast of
tender poultry, mashed potatoes, warm stuffing and unheated
green beans—we didn't have any more pots—straight from
the can. For dessert we tuck into Martha's home-baked apple
and pumpkin pies, perfectly fresh after three weeks on ice,
and toast one another with wine and beer.

Thirty miles downstream, a wide side canyon opens to the
north, seeming to offer a way out of the Grand Canyon. At
this juncture, O.G. Howland asked Powell to abandon the
river and end the journey. Howland said that he, his brother
Seneca, and William Dunn were determined to leave. Powell
took out his sextant and found the party was about forty-five
miles from the mouth of the Rio Virgen, their destination, the
end of the Colorado's course through the Grand Canyon.

"All night long I pace up and down a little path," Powell
wrote. "Is it wise to go on?" he wondered. "At one time I almost
conclude to leave the river. But for years I have been contem-
plating this trip. To leave the exploration unfinished . . . is more
than I am willing to acknowledge, and I determine to go on."

In the morning Powell asked Howland, Howland and
Dunn if they still want to leave. The elder Howland said they

did. Powell sadly accepted their decision and left them his boat, the *Emma Dean*, in case they reconsidered and wanted to meet the party downstream. The men were never seen again. They may have died at the hands of Indians or Mormons; they could have perished from lack of food or water; no one knows. This place, at Mile 239, is named Separation Canyon, and we hike up to see a plaque in memory of the three lost explorers. We make camp here with deepening awareness that our journey is nearing its end. From Separation to the take out, the water is virtually flat, save for one nasty rapid caused by human intrusion into the river. It sounds strange to say it, but the river has been drowned, submerged by Lake Mead. The rapids are gone, buried by the tepid backwash from the dam downstream. The water here is stagnant and fetid. "Bathtub rings" from the rise and fall of the reservoir blanche the Canyon's walls. Helicopters with sightseers from Vegas buzz overhead; motorboats storm upstream past our rafts, their passengers pointing cameras at us and gaping.

Just two days after leaving Separation's beach, Powell's party triumphantly concluded their journey. They had navigated and documented the entire run of the Colorado River through the Grand Canyon, and Powell could not contain his glee.

How beautiful the sky, how bright the sunshine, what 'floods of delirious music' pour from the throats of birds, how sweet the fragrance of earth and tree and blossom. . . . Now the danger is over, now the toil has ceased, now the gloom has disappeared, now the firmament is bounded only by the horizon, and what a vast expanse of constellations can be seen! The river rolls by us in silent majesty; the quiet of the camp is sweet; our joy is almost ecstasy.
—J.W. Powell

As we paddle against the wind on Lake Mead, the Canyon widens. It's more open here, and I feel we've been released from its magnetic grip. By late afternoon, the incessant hum of the planes and motorboats ceases, vestiges of the Canyon's magic reappear. Lynsey plays her flute, the sweet music conjuring native visions At night a gibbous moon rises over our Hypalon boats, which make soothing whale-like sounds as the rub against one another. As tired and eager for comfort as I am, I savor this final night in the Canyon, caressed by the muted lullaby of the submerged river.

Michael Shapiro rafted the Grand Canyon again in 2016, this time as a boat captain, and rowed through all the major rapids without incident, surprising himself as well as his compatriots. Shapiro's book, A Sense of Place, *published by* Travelers' Tales, *is a collection of interviews with the world's top travel authors. His cover story for* National Geographic Traveler, *about Jan Morris' corner of Wales, won the Bedford Pace grand award. Shapiro's feature about sustainable seafood in Vancouver earned the 2016 Explore Canada Award of Excellence. He's bicycled through Mongolia for the* Washington Post, *tasted tequila in Jalisco for* American Way, *interviewed Studs Terkel for* The Sun, *and tracked pumas in Patagnia for a custom publication. Last year Shapiro co-authored a travel guidebook, the* Louis Vuitton City Guide: San Francisco. *And he writes a weekly gambling column for the* San Francisco Chronicle. *This story won the Grand Prize Bronze in the Fifth Annual Solas Awards.*

TOM MILLER

❧ ❧ ❧

Moving West, Writing East

The evolution of a journalist.

I moved west to escape the East. I stayed west to inform
the East.

This took place in the late 1960s, when the anti-war movement and its cultural twin were both flowering. There's that
window of opportunity we all have in our early twenties when
there's nothing—love, family, job, mortgage, school—to bat-
ten us down.

"Arizona," someone suggested with a nod and a wink.
"Arizona." I knew nothing about the youngest of the lower
forty-eight, except that Barry Goldwater and marijuana
both came from there, and I thought that any place where
those two elements are both at play is worth investigating.
I jumped through that window of opportunity and landed
in Tucson.

A squat two-bedroom adobe in a working-class neighborhood full of similar houses rented for $150 monthly. A friend
and I took the place. My bedroom window looked out on
a couple of lonely saguaro, and every morning, I awoke to a
Western B-movie set. An active anti-war movement was in
place, and I found a freelancer oasis—a fertile town with
no one else writing for the underground press or sea-level

magazines such as *Crawdaddy!, Fusion* or two-year-old *Rolling Stone.* I could take part in affairs that mattered and write about Southwestern mythology at the same time. For *Crawdaddy!* I wrote about the real Rosa's Cantina in El Paso and the copper-smelter workers who sipped away their afternoons at its bar. For *Fusion*, about the acid cowboys of northern New Mexico. And the bi-weekly *Rolling Stone?* They put me on retainer, sending me $50 an issue simply to be on call and give them first dibs on story ideas. I arranged for a hipster country band to play for imprisoned draft resisters at a minimum-security federal prison, then wrote it up for the *Stone.* Like that.

The people, the issues, the land, the air, the music and, yes, the language. All these ingredients constructed my new West. I grabbed a picket sign to march for farm workers in front of Safeway. I joined another demonstration against a university's Mormon beliefs of racial inequality. (That was at a college basketball game. Boy, were we popular.) Late one night, I ran with a secretive group called the Eco-Raiders and wrote up their efforts to combat urban sprawl. The war against Vietnam was a constant reminder of global issues, while the desert Southwest taught me the fragility and permanence of the land.

I had not just moved to the American West. I had moved to a region with an odd-angled line running through it—the international boundary. The north of Sonora and Chihuahua had much in common with New Mexico and "dry-faced Arizona," as Jack Kerouac called it. Mexico, too, became part of my faculty, and I, one of its pupils. I spent time in Bisbee, Silver City, Cananea, Walsenburg (Colorado, but who's counting), El Paso-Juárez, Morenci, Cd. Chihuahua, Douglas-Agua Prieta—many of these towns with huge mining and smelting operations. They were more than just colorful destinations on the map.

I cannot explain why I am attracted to mining camps and their stories. Traveling through the towns where copper, zinc, and coal rise to the surface and get processed, I've found a genuine kinship with miners and their families. Certainly it cannot be envy: I have no desire to descend hundreds of feet underground and extract ore or calibrate explosives in a shaft, nor do I want to drive mammoth yellow equipment pitched on tires three times the size of a pickup truck. It cannot be common background, either—the mining communities and I have no shared past. Still, time and again, I have been invited into miners' homes and felt privileged to listen to family histories and collective memories, to hear cherished songs explained and to read unpublished letters. It's been an honor—one-sided, as far as I can determine—and I've benefited by it enormously.

Back in the late 1970s, the 2,000-mile U.S.-Mexico border was a warm and inviting place (and still is, to a certain extent, though no one believes me anymore). I traveled that Third Country sandwiched between two large powers, listening to *fronterizos* and writing down my impressions. Only one other writer was traveling the frontier at the time, a fellow from *The New York Times* who invited me to contribute to his newspaper. And so I wrote about the American West for people back East—very part-time, nothing more than a stringer, but in a region full of life and rough edges.

They asked me to report conventional stories such as court cases, regional angles on national trends, and curious university research, but what assignment editors valued most was stories pitched from the field—all the more so, I discovered, if they evoked the Old West with dirt roads, dusty boots and barbed wire. Their notion of the Southwest was matched by my compulsive attempts to fulfill it, and soon, in deference to my editors, I put a sign over my typewriter: REMEMBER: COWBOYS AMBLE, BUSINESSMEN STRIDE, MARIACHIS STROLL.

One day, I learned about a Yaqui judge who helped a Jewish retirees' club unearth the old Hebrew graveyard at Tombstone's Boothill Graveyard. The rededication ceremony was to take place later that week. This Old West story linked Jews, cowboys and Indians—a threefer! I breathlessly called the National Desk. Instead of the usual follow-up questions, I was immediately green-lighted with an open-ended word count and a photographer.

Interpreting the Southwest for the East, I tried to give an accurate picture, though my credibility only went so far. To file a story, we'd type or handwrite our copy, then read it over long distance to the recording room in the bowels of the old *Times* building on West 43rd Street. A battery of transcribers would monitor our calls as we dictated our stories into their machines. We e-nun-ci-a-ted each word, especially names, which we'd spell out, and always spoke dis-tinc-t-ly, even giving punctuation commands. The transcribers would call back if they had any questions, period, paragraph.

In one story from the frontier's smallest border town, Antelope Wells, N.M. (population: 2), I wrote about the annual cattle crossing that attracted cowboys, livestock brokers, Department of Agriculture inspectors, ranchers, and customs officials from both countries. On my way to file from the nearest pay phone five miles away, I colored the story, describing the strong chuckwagon coffee served to gathering *vaqueros* at daybreak by "a few Mexican cooks." The next day, I was chagrined to read in the *Times* that the event attracted "a few Mexican crooks."

I liked interpreting the West for the East, and in chitchat with an editor one warm day, he asked about the racket in the background. "Oh, that's the swamp cooler," I replied, as matter-of-factly as if I had said it was my dog barking. "The *what?*" I explained that a swamp cooler worked on the principle of a cool damp towel tossed over the metal grill of an electric fan. This led to a major conference among editors, all of whom were intrigued with this exotic contraption—should they assign a piece on the poor man's air conditioner? (They did, but not until much later, and then to another contributor.)

One story I wrote included the word *campesinos*. A copy editor called back, insisting that I blend a translation into the article. I blanketed my exasperation and asked if he would agree that *campesino* is one of those foreign words that has been absorbed into contemporary English. The line went silent for a moment. "I'll tell you what," he finally said. "I'll learn Spanish if they'll learn Yiddish."

Touché.

One morning, the phone rang at seven o'clock, usually a warning that someone on the East Coast didn't understand time zones. It was an editor at *Esquire* who, after describing a story he wanted pursued in Texas, asked if I would, and I believe these were his exact words, "mosey on over to Houston." I informed him that if we both started moseying at the same time, he'd likely mosey into Houston before me.

The rhythm of the Southwest, its natural continuity and occasional brute force—I suppose that's what keeps me here. I tried to move away. Twice. Once to the San Francisco Bay Area, and another time to Austin, Texas. Neither venture lasted more than six months. Both times, I maintained my post office box in Tucson. I knew.

Thornton Wilder lived in Southern Arizona at various stages of his life, once in Tucson in the mid-1930s, just weeks after *Our Town* had opened on Broadway. One early summer day, he was asked how he liked his temporary home. "I like it very much," he answered, then tempered his reply. "There are three disadvantages, two of which would be curable. I miss a great library to browse in. I miss great music. And I came at the wrong time of year."

The library problem and lack of great music have both been cured, but not Wilder's third disadvantage. In more than four decades of living here, from my first arrival one August, I've never grown accustomed to the unrelenting heat of the summer, never liked it, and annually grumble that this summer will be the last one I spend here. The sun bores a hole through your skull until it singes the synapses in your brain and renders you powerless and stupid. Like Thornton Wilder, I came at the wrong time of the year. The rest of the year, I need the desert. Not all the time, please, but inhaling a good whiff of it now and then keeps the lungs satisfied and reminds me that I'm not too far from the dread unknown. I need the border for its anarchic sense of reality. I need Bisbee, population 6,800, for the stumbling satisfaction it conveys. I'd like a good river and more green, but then it wouldn't be the desert Southwest.

Tom Miller's eleven books focus on the American Southwest and Latin America. His books include Trading with the Enemy, The Panama Hat Trail, *and* On the Border. *He has appeared in* Rolling Stone, The New York Times, *and* Smithsonian, *among other magazines. He is also the editor of* Traveler's Tales: Cuba. *This story shared the Grand Prize Bronze in the Seventh Annual Solas Awards.*

KEITH SKINNER

Inside the Tower

A pilgrimage to Robinson Jeffers's Tor House.

As we walked into the room, I first noticed the bed—broad, slightly concave, uncomfortable-looking—covered with a thin, antique quilt. But it was the west-facing windows, unusually close to the floor, that caught my attention and brought back the words.

I chose the bed downstairs by the sea-window for a good death-bed
When we built the house; it is ready waiting,
Unused unless by some guest in a twelvemonth, who hardly suspects
Its latter purpose. . . .

A chill rippled across my skin as I realized that we were standing in that very room and the bed before me was the subject of the poem—the deathbed in "The Bed by the Window." Robinson Jeffers had written the poem as a young man shortly after building the house. Many years later, he had indeed died in the room, thereby fulfilling its destiny.

I had first read the poem while browsing a Jeffers anthology in a bookstore, a volume entitled *The Wild God of the World*. I knew little about the man but kept bumping into him in other writers' work. Noted authors and bohemian celebrities were always dropping in on Jeffers when passing through Carmel. There was often some degree of awe or reverence ascribed to these occasions, but very little mentioned about the man himself.

I picked up the book and, by chance, opened it to "The Bed by the Window." It was an eerie poem. More than eerie—it was downright creepy. It wasn't as though Jeffers had used death in a gratuitous manner; it wasn't a cheap, dramatic device. The bed seemed to be a fetish of sorts for him as he worked through his feelings about his own mortality.

I often regard it,
with neither dislike or desire; rather with both, . . .

Still, meditating on death in a poem was one thing; anticipating a lingering death in the distant future while still a young man, and building a room in which to die, was quite another.

As I read through several more poems, the voice, at times, seemed almost feral. The ruggedness of the language, the starkness of the imagery—Jeffers prowled like a lone wolf or, more accurately, a rangy coyote skirting the edge of civilization: hungry, suspicious, and angry. He seemed dark and self-absorbed. If Whitman was a Telemann concerto, full of trumpets and bright brass celebrating the world, it seemed to me that Jeffers was a melancholy cello solo played mournfully in a dim, candlelit room. For some unexplained reason, I felt compelled to buy the book, though it wasn't long before it was abandoned on a bookshelf and I had put Jeffers out of my mind.

Several days before I found myself standing in Jeffers' bedroom, and nearly a year after I had bought the anthology, I was staying in Big Sur and came across an article in a local magazine about the building of Tor House, Jeffers' home. I knew the house was in Carmel but knew little of its history. The article recounted how Jeffers had purchased an uninhabited plot of land on Carmel Point and had hired a stonemason to build a house for him. He apprenticed himself to the builder so he could learn how to set stone himself. Once the house was finished, Jeffers spent nearly four years building a forty-foot-high tower on the property, hauling boulders from a nearby beach and hoisting them into place by himself using only a block and tackle.

The story about the tower was as provocative and unsettling as the deathbed poem. Who was this guy? He had rolled boulders, some weighing as much as 400 pounds, several hundred yards uphill, through coastal scrub, and then had set each one by hand—alone. This only confirmed my suspicions that the man was obsessive and unpredictable, if not outright stubborn. But he had somehow gotten under my skin. I decided to stop in Carmel on my way home to visit Tor House, to see his mad man's tower, and to try to unravel the Jeffers riddle that kept resurfacing.

Our small tour group was still huddled around Jeffers' bed as if gathered to say our final goodbyes while the docent recited the deathbed poem. It was a sober moment for everyone. I looked out through the sea window with its simple curtains and wooden window seat, across the gray-green mat of garden sprinkled with drifts of May flowers, to the gunmetal surf churning in the distance. It was a stormy day and dark clouds were furrowed along the horizon. I wondered what had gone through Jeffers' mind as he lay dying, his head turned toward the window, gazing at a similar scene. Was there a sense of resignation? Regret? Fear? Or was the sight of hawks circling and pelicans diving for fish in the white foam a comfort to him, an affirmation that the natural rhythms of life overlap each other like the waves of the incoming tide? Rather than a morbid fixation, perhaps the deathbed was Jeffers' attempt to take some control over his own, inevitable fate.

What I had expected to be an ordinary tour had become something more profound. As we filed into the living room, a latent energy seemed to linger in the house, as if the family had gone out for a walk together and, at any minute, the two boys would come bursting in through the door with a dog at their heels. This sensation was due, in part, to the way our docent had made the home come alive for us. He told stories about each room that portrayed the fierce love affair between Jeffers and his wife Una, and of a family life that was often insular but very closely knit. The docent had recited Jeffers' poems in such a heartfelt manner at different places around the property that it was almost as if the poet himself was speaking and pointing out his favorite places—the cornerstone of the house, keepsakes from travels embedded in the walls of the house and the garden, and stones that had been carved with words or quotes, then placed along the garden path.

If the house seemed infused with the warmth of family life, the world outside, at least on this day, was more typical of Jeffers' flinty demeanor. I zipped up my jacket and cinched the hood tightly around my face as we crossed the small yard. It was perfect weather, I thought, to visit the tower that loomed in front of us.

Hawk Tower was an odd structure, simultaneously squat and gangly. Una had long admired the medieval towers found throughout Ireland and Jeffers had tried to replicate the style. But the structure in front of me looked nothing like those I had seen in Ireland, other than ruins where the ramparts had either been breached or severely ravaged by time.

There were two ways to move about within the structure—the wider, external staircase, or the interior, "secret" passageway that Jeffers had built for his sons. We were warned that the

passageway was dark and extremely narrow in places and the
steps, unusually steep. I chose the passageway because Jeffers
often used it himself and I had a hunch the other members of
my group would take the stairs. I would be alone with Jeffers
and the dark, cold stone.

> *Old but still strong I climb the stone*
> *Climb the steep rough steps alone*

I climbed past the first landing that served as a play area for
the two boys and up to Una's stronghold. Over a small fire-
place in the corner, Jeffers had carved a wooden mantle with
a line of Latin from Virgil that roughly translated to "Lovers
fashion their own dreams." It seemed to describe Tor House
so precisely. The stone buildings, the keepsakes everywhere,
the wildness of their surroundings—the Jeffers had carefully
created a world, a dream, solely for themselves. If the outside world chose to drop in for dinner or otherwise share that
dream momentarily, so be it. Robin and Una required only each
other's company and the promontory overlooking the ocean;
the rest of the world could be damned.

I continued up to the outside parapet at the top of the
tower, carefully navigating the steep, wet steps and pulling
myself up by the hefty anchor chain that served as a handrail.
The wind had picked up and gusts of rain stung my face the
higher I climbed. I turned southward and scanned the jagged
coast, the tree-lined shore that stretched into the distance and
wrapped around the bay to join Point Lobos.

> *White-maned, wide-throated, the heavy-shouldered children of*
> *the wind leap at the sea-cliff.*

I imagined Jeffers standing in this very spot in a squall,
pensive and content as he took in the surrounding natural
world that, at the time, laid claim to Carmel Point. Up on

this perch, he would become hawklike—calm, watchful, and uncomplicated, comforted by the elements and the power of wind and ocean.

Jeffers may have built the tower for Una but it was more than a simple material gift he had given her. It was himself—his blustery spirit, his wild-god heart embodied in granite, each stone placed as carefully as the words he arranged upon a page. As I gazed into the horizon and considered this thought, my hands atop the coarse, damp stone Jeffers had placed there with his own two hands, he no longer seemed a mystery to me. He was neither dark nor self-absorbed as I had first judged him to be. He was this tower, strong and resolute, incorporating all that surrounded him into its surface and protecting all that was dear to him within. I needed to hear his words within these walls, feel the wind and rain against my skin as he had, and view the world from his tower before I could grasp the essence of the man.

Keith Skinner is a writer and photographer from Berkeley, California, focusing on history and culture. His nonfiction has appeared in Travelers' Tales *anthologies,* The San Francisco Chronicle, Wile Musette, *and others. His travel stories have won Solas Awards in four consecutive years. He is currently working on a historical novel set in nineteenth-century California.*

JENNIFER BALJKO

❧ ❧ ❧

Castles in the Sky

Performance art, acrobatic prowess, and political
defiance merge in the streets of Barcelona.

I close my eyes, hoping not to witness imminent destruc-
tion. A young child, about five years old, hovers two stories above the ground, barely balancing on top of a shaky pillar
of flesh. I can't resist. Despite the pounding in my chest, I peek
through my fingers and watch another boy scamper toward
the sky. Pressing his hands and bare feet into the backs and
shoulders of men and women with wobbly knees, the lanky
ten-year-old tow-head passes the balcony where the mayor
and other dignitaries stand open-mouthed. The boy climbs
higher. The human obelisk sways.

In a few seconds, I'm certain, bodies will collapse upon
one another and screams will pierce the crowded Barcelona
square, now blanketed in silence.

"What the heck are these people doing?" I whisper to no one
in particular. Back home, this would be banned. The insurance
liability alone would send shivers down any actuary's spine.

This, though, isn't the United States. This is Catalonia, and
here, in a province fiercely protective of its customs, language,
and independence from Spain's stronghold, human castle-
building is as much a sport as an art form.

"This is not just a hobby," Cisco, a *casteller* (castlemaker) for about fifty years, tells me later. "I don't think there is anything I have spent more time doing, besides spending time with my wife."

The tradition dates back to the eighteenth century, and is loosely tied to a religious dance from Valencia, a city south of Barcelona. Over the years, the custom has morphed into an endurance event requiring a yogi's balance and Cirque du Soleil dexterity. Teams throughout Catalonia, which rests on the shores of the Mediterranean and in the shadow of the Pyrenees, train during the chilly winter months to perfect the technical aspects of *castell* (castle) construction and deconstruction. And, then in the summer and fall, wide-eyed locals pack open-air plazas to see if the spires—much like the Gaudí-inspired ones adorning La Sagrada Familia cathedral—will reach heaven.

An American ex-pat tipped me off about the *castellers*, and with a child's enthusiasm, he urged me to stick around for the weeklong La Mercè party in late September. The *castells* were one of the festival's highlights, and would be worth skipping a beach day to witness, he assured me. I pictured the U.S. equivalent of stuffing twenty frat guys into a phone booth. It sounded quirky. I was intrigued.

Now, instead of sprawling out on white sand, I'm watching children dangle in mid-air. I think I may end up in the hospital with a heart attack, along with the mother of the kid who is hovering a couple stories off the ground.

A few minutes ago, things weren't this stressful. I huddled among the masses in Plaça de Sant Jaume and waited for something to happen. Those in nearby apartment buildings hung out of windows, taking long drags on their cigarettes and Voll-Damm beer. Politicos in suits whooped it up on city hall's second-floor balcony. A father perched his daughter, ice cream cone in hand, on his shoulders. Tourists readied their cameras. Vendors hawked bottled water and balloons. The smell of *bocadillos* (sandwiches) and *pa amb tomaquet* (tomato toast) wafted through the narrow alleyways of the old town.

Four middle-aged men, with bullish physiques and attitudes to match, had elbowed their way through the noisy horde. They interlocked arms and formed a tight circle. A dozen other men and women of varying shapes and sizes, in mint-green shirts and white pants, slid into the middle of the ring. They crooked themselves under armpits, squeezed against the chests of the burly men and braced for what would be a painful ten minutes.

Along the perimeter, more green-shirted men leaned against the inner circle, and behind them, even more men and women pushed in for support, resting their arms on the arms of the person in front of them. Male spectators, stupefied, were yanked into the mix and crammed into a tightly knit circle that stretched at least fifteen people wide from the epicenter to perimeter.

A stocky man, taller than the rest, shouted commands. With the *pinya* (the base of the tower), firmly planted, it was time to climb.

Four men with sturdy, athletic frames, crawled on top of the lower level. They tight-roped their way to the inner circle and steadied themselves on the shoulders of the men below. They interlocked arms and shouted down to the captain. Hands from the base wrapped around tier two's legs and cupped their butts. I chuckled. I suspected this type of groping wouldn't go over well at summer fairs back home.

On cue, the next round of climbers—men and women with slighter builds—ascended. The four monkeyed up, and, with the precision of ninjas, placed hands and feet on tier two's calves, hamstrings, and shoulders. Together, the four climbers hoisted themselves up and closed their ring.

A hush fell over the restless spectators. Red-and-yellow striped Catalan flags, draped defiantly down building façades, snapped in the breeze. More *castellers* climbed. A drum beat droned. *Throoom. Throoom. Throoom.* Then the *gralles*, a cross between a clarinet and what looked like my sixth-grade recorder, filled in the beat, slow at first. My jaw dropped. This was looking more serious than a frat-boy stunt.

The green-shirted team, or *colla*, hailed from Vilafranca del Penedès, a Barcelona suburb bordered by vineyards. Though not the hometown favorite, the team had reputation for assembling towers that defied gravity. In the crowd, those in the know knew a 4-of-9 tower—a tower nine-people high with a circumference four-people wide—was a tower that demanded attention, and respect.

The next tier of *castellers*—teenagers, this time—was on the move. Gracefully, effortlessly, hands and feet synchronized in alternating pulley patterns. Right feet bent into the small of the backs of those already standing, just above black cummerbunds. Left knees found standing team members' shoulders. Hands tugged at the pants. The teens grabbed each other's arms, simultaneously getting their bearings.

There was no time to breathe. More climbers were right behind them. Boys and girls, barely past puberty, sprinted to the top.

I can't watch. I can't help but watch. I fidget. My heart races as the *timbal*, a small drum, thumps louder, faster. The *gralles* quicken to a Bolero-like crescendo.

The crowd stands still. The little girl on her dad's shoulders stops licking her ice cream cone. Behind me, a camera clicks.

Children, no more than ten, scurry like mice. A tug at the pants above. A clasp of a shirt collar. A mighty heave up the next person's back. Higher into the clouds. Level six. Legs quiver. Weary arms try not to sag. I'm afraid to exhale. Afraid that my breath may cause the human tower of Pisa to lean too far in one direction.

Two kids dash upward. They hurriedly create a two-person circle. The clock, a few feet above their heads, chimes the hour. City officials on balconies tilt back their heads. A five-year-old, sporting a floppy page-boy haircut, makes his way upward and squats into fetal position on top of the two kids' shoulders. The *aixecador* is suspended over a twenty-foot high shaft of bodies. I gasp. I wonder if his mother has already fainted.

All eyes lock on another child—the *anxaneta*, the only person for the ninth tier. The last to climb.

The captain bellows from the perimeter, encouraging the team, in those final moments, to find even more strength. Those in the inner circle grunt. I can't see their faces. I know, though, they are flushed and beaded with sweat, made worse by the eighty-degree temperature warming the square. I calculate the base must be holding nearly a ton on their shoulders. Probably more.

The ten-year-old *anxaneta* shimmies up the tower. An air of confidence replaces a brief trace of uneasiness in his soft features.

"I'm not afraid of climbing. I'm afraid of falling," the *anxaneta*, whose name is Marc, says afterward through a translator. He's been climbing for five years, and has had his share of falls. They're not fun.

"But, when the captain says it's O.K. to go, I go."

A cautious, but quick, combination of tugs and pulls propels him past each level. He gently shifts his weight to compensate for the trembling below. He's so high he becomes a blur.

The *gralles* and the drum escalate to a feverish pitch. I cover my eyes. I peek through my fingers.

The success of the tower—the hope of a people reaching for greatness—rests in this fifth-grader.

The *anxaneta* straddles the five-year-old at the apex. He places one hand on the back of the child. He throws up the other. Victory! He touches the sky.

At that moment, Catalonia shakes off Madrid's economic and political weight. At that moment, Catalonia stands firm, unwavering in a cultural test of persistence, tenacity and courage. At that moment, Catalonia is free.

Applause fills the urban canyons. Marc descends like a fireman sliding down a pole. Each layer peels off in the same way. The captain wipes his brow and grins a toothy smile. Men hug like brothers. Bystanders cheer in disbelief.

Without thinking, I raise my hands, too, and try to touch the Catalan sky.

Jennifer Baljko is a Barcelona-based writer who is currently walking home from Bangkok. (Follow her travels at bangkok barcelonaonfoot.com) This story won the Grand Prize Bronze in the First Annual Solas Awards.

❧ ❧ ❧

Philomen and Baucis

A modern tale of metamorphosis.

*I*was at one of life's crossroads, you know, the kind that either can or cannot divert you to a journey down an untraveled road. To move from L.A. to a tiny farming village in France was not an option, it was not even an idea. It often happens, however, that the things we don't plan are more likely than those we do, and the smallest, most insignificant event, can open up a path where there was none before. In this case, it was a detour on the way back from the supermarket. I was in France at the time visiting an American-friend-turned-Parisian at her house in the country. Our shopping out of the way, we drove through a village she thought I'd like to see—an ordinary sort of meander on a lazy summer afternoon. It was indeed a pretty village, but it was so small we were in and out of it in less than two minutes. As we made a sharp right turn at the end of the Grande Rue and rolled out onto the narrow country road, I looked back over my shoulder and saw a For Sale sign.

Once back home, I found myself talking to my friends about the house. I hadn't even liked it when I went to see it, a quick cursory look and I was off, but somehow it had entered the back of my mind and stuck there. One day I called the real estate agent—let's just see where this goes, I said to myself without much conviction. It would be a miracle of biblical proportions if the French gave me a mortgage and only divine intervention would persuade my employer to let me work in France. I had no experience with miracles, divine intervention, or, for that matter, even exceptional luck.

It's the surprises that change our lives. The mortgage got itself arranged by fax, as did arrangements with the seller with respect to certain pieces of furniture that were too big and too heavy to be moved. Eda, my friend who'd shown me the village in the first place, signed the closing papers as my proxy, and I moved to St. Aubin in time to put up a Christmas tree. The stay would be short. I was due back in L.A. after the holidays—the deal with my employer was that I would show up regularly to meet deadlines and see to it that everything was actually printed and out the door before leaving again.

Instead of using the Santa Monica Freeway to get to work, I would be using international airlines. Mortgage payments and consolidator flights, I figured, added up to about the same cost as an L.A. apartment. I'm not absolutely sure of that calculation, but that's the way it looked in rough on a yellow pad. In any case, it was close enough. I'd lived in France before, and its call to me was always there, like an undertow. I could make it work, I reassured myself, and, as I would be pinching pennies most anywhere, better to do it in a country where even the most modest of restaurants serve three courses and the wine is cheap.

On New Year's Eve a neighbor appeared. It was dark as the edge of space outside and raining. My house—an old farmhouse of fieldstone—sat behind a high wall, just like all the others on the Grande Rue. That somebody was inside the wall and outside my house was signaled by a shrill, off-pitch sound that sent currents of ice water through my arms and legs. I stopped what I was doing and stood still, not daring to move.

It came again, and again. Then with a flash the lights went on outside in the courtyard, my front door flew open with the force of storm wind, and a man walked in.

"*Bonsoir*," he called at the top of his voice.

I had moved into the hall at the top of the stairs, my hands holding tightly to the railing as I looked down at him. "*Bonsoir*," I replied tentatively, not sure whether he should be welcomed or not.

"You didn't answer your doorbell."

I decided to go downstairs and have a better look at him. Offering my hand, I spoke the truth, "I didn't know I had a doorbell."

Raymond introduced himself as my neighbor and thrust a bottle of excellent champagne at me. He began to say something about a woman alone on New Year's Eve, but broke off in mid-sentence to bend over and sneeze explosively, twice, into a pressed white handkerchief. "I'm sorry I can't stay longer," he wheezed, "I have a very bad cold." With that he was gone, and I didn't see him, or anybody else, until I returned in the spring.

It was the first day of May when I next landed in Paris, picked up a rental car and headed south—direction Joigny-Auxerre. My mood was very much different this time. I'd had time to get used to what I'd done. This was now *home*. The car windows were down, the air smelled like *France*, and I was exhilarated by *life*. When I turned off the auto-route and picked up the country road that led to St. Aubin, I was greeted by an amazing expanse of yellow. All the way to my tiny perched village, the gently rolling hills were patched with geometrically shaped fields of bright yellow flowers, their borders separated by rows of tall dark evergreens and lush shrubs. It was the most stunning thing I'd ever seen in my life.

It wasn't very long before I met Philomen and Baucis. In fact, it was probably longer than you would expect, as they could not be missed, but I was discovering there was a lot more to the house and the land I'd bought than I had realized. The house was huge, and I had thought it small. Around the corner from one of the stables, I found a small garden, and one morning while chatting with a neighbor, whose name I learned was Marie-Thérèse, I mentioned that I might put in some tomato plants. After lunch a tall man showed up with a basket of plants and a hand plow. He introduced himself as Jean, the husband of Marie-Thérèse, and said he was there to turn the soil of my garden. When he was finished he asked me if I liked the view from the orchard. We opened the little garden gate and walked out on the slope. From there we could see the entire valley and its geometric shapes of color, crops that had already rotated to another hue and grain since my arrival through fields of startling spring yellow. In the orchard, Jean pointed out which trees were cherries, which were pears, apples, and walnuts. He then spoke of how I should care for them. I looked around the orchard and then at him, "Is this part of my property?"

A single-lane road ran along the side of my house and my orchard, and dead-ended at an old cemetery. In front of the cemetery wall were two enormous trees. One was a linden and the other an oak. They were very old, even ancient, and as they had grown over the years they had begun to lean toward each other, tangling their branches in such an intimate way that I thought of Philomen and Baucis the first minute I saw them.

Philomen and Baucis are the devoted couple from Ovid's *Metamorphoses*, generous farmers who offered hospitality to strangers, two men who happened to be gods in disguise. The gods rewarded them by granting their wish to be together for

eternity, thus morphing them into oak and linden that would
forever live side by side.

Two travelers once, it is said, appeared in modest disguises
that hid their glory, for Jove and Mercury were the two.
They knocked on door after door seeking a bed for the night,
but over and over again were turned away. In the end, in
one they found a welcome—

The villagers welcomed me in thoroughly surprising ways.
To use a French term, they embraced me. I met them all
at once (we were 480 at peak season, which is to say when
the Parisians were in residence) at the Feu de Saint Jean, an
annual big deal, which, near as I could tell, was a community
outdoor cookout to celebrate the first day of summer. Raymond, Marie-Thérèse, Jean, and I would walk down to the
plain below where the commune had bought an old mill and
its grounds for occasions such as this.

It began more or less as I expected, but after we'd eaten the
grilled this and that (sometimes it is better not to be specific),
drunk quite a few bottles of local burgundy, and it had grown
quite dark, some men fired a haystack which was big as a
barn. Lighting a fire outdoors, of any sort, can be a terrifying
sight to someone from Southern California, but these people
seemed to know what they were doing. As the flames roared to
the sky we all—men, women, children, and the American—got
up to hold hands and dance in a circle around the fire. This was
a pagan ceremony old as the time man first stood up straight and
recognized the summer solstice. And in St. Aubin, generation
after generation had passed down the secret of staying upright
on treacherously slippery grass as the dance gained momen-
tum. It got faster and faster as the circle changed direction,
and then again, and again. The villagers held securely to my
hands, then my wrists, then my arms, and I to theirs.

By mid-summer my failed efforts at gardening had become evident. Maybe too much water, maybe too little. It turned out that it didn't matter at all because every time I went out someone thrust a bowl of strawberries at me, a bag of tomatoes and cucumbers, or a dozen ears of corn. Also, I was often invited to lunch, feasts that progressed through course after course, rituals that lasted for hours and were accompanied by bottles of wine that never seemed to be empty. Is it any wonder that I began to see Philomen and Baucis, known since antiquity for their generosity, as symbols of St. Aubin?

Baucis set out a plate of olives, green ones and black, and a saucer of cherry plums she had pickled, and an endive and radish salad. She had cheese and some roasted eggs . . .

Afterward,

Baucis served her cabbage and pork stew. For dessert there were nuts, figs, dates, and plums, and baskets of ripe apples and grapes . . .
When Philomen went to refill the wine bowl,
He picked it up but felt that it wasn't empty. Instead, as much as they drank, the wine had replenished itself, and the bowl was as full as before.

There was no way I could reciprocate such generosity. I couldn't even give my neighbors fruit because everybody else had orchards too. My orchard had turned out to be a big producer, and a big pain. I couldn't keep up with the picking, the eating, or the preserving, and overnight the grass had grown high as an elephant's eye. It was a village eyesore, but I was in no mood to go out there with a scythe, nor did I want to pay somebody to tackle it with a tractor—we're talking a couple of acres.

Nothing went unnoticed at St. Aubin, and anything that happened at my house spread like wildfire: by telephone, over the fence, and among the women who lined up every morning for their baguettes. The American, as I was known to most, was a source of intense curiosity. This I knew from Raymond. He was quite a well-known singer who traveled the world but had a solid foot in the country and understood the mind-set of the neighbors far better than I did. He also had a wacky sense of humor and delighted in telling me what others were saying about me. (Clearly he would only know if he had participated in the gossiping!) Just because they had embraced me didn't mean I was immune to criticism.

When I first moved in several households devoted their late afternoons to watching reruns of *2000 Malibu Road* on television, which went against me in some circles. Most people in the village had not seen foreigners since the German occupation of France during the Second World War, and as far as Americans were concerned, nobody could remember ever wanting to know one. Down below, a farmer's daughter, who was mute and heavily pregnant (the father, a young itinerant with curly red hair, spent his afternoons on a wooden bench in front of their farmhouse eating raw onions as if they were apples), went so far as to sign to the postmistress that The American was going to turn her house into a hotel. What's more, it would have a flashing neon sign in front. And one day when I was shopping at the open market in the next village over, a woman dressed in black and bent with age—widows of the war still dress in mourning—approached me with, "Ah, so you are The American." When I confirmed it, she said she hadn't seen me in church, and when I told her I was Protestant, she replied with, "*Alors, on est Chrétien ici.*" Well, we're Christian here. I simply let it pass. My ancestors were French

Huguenots—heretics to some, victims to others. I thought to bring that up would only make things worse. None of the gossiping, or even the confrontations, were mean-spirited, it was just the way it was. After all, I—a foreign woman living by herself—was the odd one.

It is hard to say how many people discussed the condition of my orchard before I had a visit from a couple I hadn't yet met. They came in a pickup with five young sons, who spread out in as many directions to explore everything hidden behind a closed door above ground and below. The couple asked if I would like to have a pair of donkeys in my orchard. They would eat the grass and keep me company.

No donkeys had appeared before I left for California. The snow had taken care of the grass problem. When I returned in May, a pair of donkeys was there, along with a foal. The baby donkey was only marginally younger than the yellow Lab I'd just let out of the car. My puppy was already known as Lincoln. He'd been given to me when he was barely nine weeks old. I could have refused him, but I didn't. I picked him up, held him near, he kissed me on the cheek, I kissed him on the top of his small head, and that was that. We boarded a plane together the day he turned three months and was entitled to travel papers. By bringing a dog to live at St. Aubin I knew I'd crossed a bridge that I hadn't yet come to. It was a bit like buying the house—I'd first do it and then figure out how to make it work.

The news that Philomen and Baucis might be cut down reached me on my first day home. It struck like a thunderbolt. These beautiful old trees had been planted as seedlings in front of the stone wall that enclosed the cemetery at about the same time the ground was consecrated. It was under their budding leaves that my neighbors paused to take in the breathtaking expanses of yellow colza in the fields below the village, announcing the arrival of spring. In deep summer, their shade cooled the footpath, and people sat there on the wooden bench to chat while watching tractors cut through the tall wheat. Even when autumn rains began the change and when snow fell, people took their dogs up there, to pause and to reflect on the meaning of life. It was the most hospitable place in the village to admire the changing seasons, and no one ever, ever went there without feeling the presence of its ancient sentinels. However, the roots of Philomen and Baucis had grown too long and spread too far. They were rattling the bones of the dead.

As the cutting-down process was not yet definite, I quickly became distracted by the imminent arrival of *my car*. I didn't yet know what kind it might be or even what color it was. Eda, my resourceful American friend-turned-Parisian, had found it for me. I'd sent a check, and *voilá*—instant car owner. No more expensive rentals. It was being driven down from Paris by Anne, Eda's daughter and my favorite young lady of all time. I'd known her since she was two, when I was a strug-gling (read: perpetual housesitter) artist and she kept me com-pany in the atelier that belonged to her parents. This night she would stay to meet Lincoln, and the donkeys.

Anne was the first of what would be a procession of house-guests. I'd acquired certain necessities like furniture, plates, knives and forks, wine glasses and picnic baskets—that sort of thing. Marie-Thérèse had given me bed linens—the kind that float over your body like a cloud—from her own trousseau and her grandmother's. They'd been packed away for years as too good to be used, only to be deemed as utterly useless by her daughters who wanted only polyester blends. I was thrilled.

My houseguests were varied and many. Several old boy-friends showed up, and one old husband. Some people I didn't know—an overflow from Eda's house. Then came a woman, the friend of a friend who was the clandestine friend of a female friend who would be horrified to know that I'd met

this woman (these things *do* happen), and just about everybody I knew in Los Angeles plus some from London, and
some new friends from Paris.

I love people, especially those I know, and they wouldn't
have come if I hadn't invited them, but I soon realized that a
lunch, drinks, or dinner relationship is much different from
a visit by a fish out of water. There were those who couldn't
sleep, wouldn't sleep, because it was too quiet. Others were
speechless to learn that there was no air conditioning in my
little second-hand French car and cranky the same evening when the house turned chilly and they had to go find
a sweater (cranky, because they wanted me to close the windows and turn on the heat), and others were outraged that
the part-time employee in the post office didn't speak English. Some never picked up the rhythm of the house or of the
place: they ate breakfast at nearly noon and wanted to go out
to eat in the late afternoon, even though there are virtually no
restaurants in the French countryside that serve lunch after
two, which meant that after emptying the refrigerator they
were not hungry again until after all the restaurants had long
since finished taking evening sitters. Grocery stores closed at
noon, didn't open again until four, and closed again at seven.
These hours absolutely flummoxed people who were used to
24/7. France has a lot of rules that have been embedded in
the culture for a very long time, and they have a lot of attitudes that do not graciously accommodate people who do not
think—and eat—like the French. Those travelers who don't
believe it, or think a smile will get them into a restaurant after
closing hours, are wrong. Those people grow to hate France,
and unfortunately some of them were my friends.

The year-of-the-houseguest resulted in an inevitable
thinning out of friends and acquaintances. It also marked a
change in me. All the griping had pushed me solidly into the
French camp. Between visits I'd often sit on the veranda in

the evening (wearing a sweater) and sip a glass of wine while trying to figure out what it was about this place that I liked so much. It was beautiful, but lots of places are beautiful. I'd left one of them to come live here. At first it had been the nineteenth-century character of the village. Virtually nothing had changed since then, and I found living in another century a riveting experience. Also, I loved the challenge of functioning in another language.

As I got used to the time warp and as my French got better, I became part of the weave. The small friendships of village life became numerous and more important. Most of the early frustrations—like the orchard—had been resolved. The family that came twice a day to feed the donkeys was also picking the fruit and delivering it to the mobile distiller who came every once in a while and set himself up in front of the church on the main square. There, aided by volunteer tasters, he produced barrels of liquid lightning. While the village was literally in the middle of nowhere, I was by no means isolated. Within an easy thirty-minute drive I could cast my eyes over a ridge of medieval fortified castles and their pastoral grounds where fat white sheep graze when the grass is at its greenest, listen to Gregorian chants in the Cistercian abbey at Pontigny or hear Bach in the basilica courtyard at Vézelay.

More towns than not were ancient works of art, and it was there in the midst of living museums that I bought lipstick and new shoes, shopped for food, and went to first-run American movies. At home, the braying of donkeys got me out of bed with the sunrise (they wanted carrots), and, after a stand-up breakfast of French roast and local croissant that heaped shame on Starbucks, I could step into a state-of-the-art office that instantly connected me with the outside world. Of course I couldn't use any of that modern technology at midday because everybody was cooking lunch and there was not enough electric power to go around. If that got to me, Paris was an hour and a half away.

When the ultimatum came—and I knew it would—to spend more time in the Los Angeles office, I bit the bullet. I'd felt it coming when I accepted Lincoln. I knew he would grow too big to travel back and forth, and I knew I would never leave him in a kennel for months at a time. The bullet was a tough one. Residence permits for foreigners are only for those who can prove that their income is earned outside of France. Work permits for non-Europeans are rarer than McDonald's. There was no way around it. I'd always said a writer could live anywhere in the world. It was time to test the theory.

I managed to stay there, in St. Aubin, for a little over ten years. I never got tired of it, and when I left it broke my heart.

In the end Philomen and Baucis were cut down. The villagers and farmers took it far better than I did—they, of course, were on more intimate terms with nature's life cycles than I could ever hope to be. Just as Philomen and Baucis bid a poignant final farewell to each other when the gods transformed them into trees, I began saying farewell to my friends and neighbors while preparing to transform myself back into an American.

Lincoln, at ninety-two pounds, would travel in an airline cage the size of a studio apartment and Gatsby in the cabin with me. Gatsby had appeared on a soft June morning in the rafters above the veranda. One of six tiny kittens, he was the issue of a cat that visited regularly to eat, but not for a caress. Shortly after the morning debut, the mother cat walked five of her litter across the roof, never to return, and left Gatsby behind. There was nothing wrong, no reason to abandon him—he was clearly a parting gift.

Returning to the States was a decision whose time had come; the problem was deciding where. I was exploring cities on the internet like a holiday traveler trawls airfares and

becoming more befuddled with each day. Again, it is the surprises that change our lives. One day when having lunch with
an American artist who lived close to Paris, and whom I had
not seen for a very long time, I learned she had a house for
rent in a small American town.

"Stonington?" I asked. "Where's that?"

*Pamela Cordell Avis was born in Colorado and has since lived in
many places. Once having finished her undergraduate work in art
history and studio art, she painted in Provence until she was hired
during a Cannes Film Festival to market feature films, which took
her to New York, then Los Angeles, and then all over the world.
Later, while living in St. Aubin, the subject of this story, she discovered a film in a neighbor's attic, which sent her back to school
to get a graduate degree in Holocaust Studies. She is currently
writing a book about the hero whose story was hidden in that attic.
"Philomen and Baucis" won the Grand Prize Bronze Award in
the Second Annual Solas Awards.*

☙ ☙ ☙

The Train at Night

An entire world is riding those rails.

According to Hasidic tradition, thirty-six "saints" (lamed vavnik) are hidden in the world at all times, holding it together through their secret good deeds. Disguised as socially marginal figures—peasants, porters, and homeless, nameless wanderers—they appear among strangers and, through their seemingly trivial actions—or even through nuisance they cause—bring about shifts in people's perception that create community and lighten human sorrow.

I wish I could sleep every night on a train. Not alone in a berth, but in the coach with everyone else, our seats tilted back, the long car dim. I love listening to the sound of the rails at night, that *da doom, da doom, da da doom* and sometimes *chuh chuh CHUNG,* and the way you sometimes get that little shuffling, wheezing noise, or maybe a sharp little bark like a small dog. Or a little piping noise, like somebody hiding between the coaches with a flute.

I enjoy most of the sounds the passengers make, too, when it gets dark and they turn on the little rectangular white and cobalt night lights in the ceiling—the blue end pointing in the direction of the train so nobody gets lost coming upstairs from brushing their teeth. People rustling and whispering as they get ready to sleep, dropping their pillows in the aisle, lifting up their footrests, reclining the backs of their seats.

"Put on your socks!" "Do you want some more?" People stealthily zipping and re-zipping their fanny packs, someone eating something out of a box, trying to be quiet. It's cozy and it makes the world seem not so lonely. It would be good to sleep every night on a train.

Some nights aren't as quiet. The Capitol Limited had pulled out of D.C.'s Union Station in the early evening. At eleven we were just beyond Martinsburg, Pennsylvania, the lights dimmed, the coach snug. I was sleepless as usual, trying to look out the window but mostly seeing us passengers reflected back, young sweethearts curled up tight under a thin pink blanket, friends stretched across a whole row with their feet in each other's faces, old couples asleep holding hands. And then me, alone, the only one awake, with my glass of merlot, looking out onto the dark river, maybe an occasional houseboat light or a lighted buoy bobbing alone on the dark water. The seat next to mine was empty: my son was sleeping in a vacant row he had found far down the aisle on the other side.

It was summer. My twelve-year-old son and I were riding the train home from Washington, D.C. via Chicago after settling my mother's estate. I was shaken by my mother's death, and on this trip, I'd hardly seen my son at all; from early morning to very late the kids joined up, all backgrounds, all ages, and roamed the train (under the kindly eyes of the coach attendants), teaching each other card games, sharing their Skittles, and laughing at *Coyote and Roadrunner* cartoons in the downstairs café.

You'd think I was the only mother whose boy ever grew up. Because that evening I kept remembering this same trip with him when he was six, how we'd leaned together against the window and pointed out the scrap metal barges, the horses galloping away from the train, the colorful tags spray-painted on warehouses. How we'd shared little pepperoni pizzas from the café. And when it got dark, after we'd brushed our teeth and put on our sweatshirts, how he'd put his head against my shoulder and needed a story. You'd think I was the only woman whose marriage ever faltered. . . .

I was feeling lonely, the kind of existential loneliness where you feel the wind blowing through your insides, and you're so desolate you've got to hug yourself and double over.

Suddenly I heard a loud snore two seats up. Then a gurgling sigh like a bad drain. Silence for a moment. Then a passionate bellow-snore, wet, vibratory, with a choking gasp of panic at the end. Now everyone was awake. Rasping, chain sawing, "I'm-going-to-die-now" snores. The train was slowing and I read "Three Rivers" on the station wall. The snores abruptly stopped.

A lanky man in a flannel shirt helped himself to water in a tiny paper cup at the stair-head water fountain. While he sipped, he turned with friendly eyes to inspect the snorer. "I thought I saw a sign that said Three Rivers, but I'm not sure. You going to Chicago?"

"No," responded the snorer, now awake, and he and the man exchanged a few more words. The train pulled on. I put away my wine glass, tucked my pillow into the corner between the seat and the window, and tried to sleep.

Suddenly I—we—were wrenched wide awake by an alarmed snortle from two seats up. Then another volley of raucous, wet snores. I looked at my watch—one A.M. We were passing the West View Authority Water Treatment Plant; a chimney pumped out orange flames.

"Give his seatback a good shove!" I whispered to the woman in front of me. Several seats around us suddenly emptied as people rethought their seating arrangements. I wandered, sleepless and dizzy, downstairs to the bathroom. There

I amused my haggard self by practicing mobster faces in the mirror. Should we loom over him and hiss, "Stop snoring, or we'll have to kill you"?

I came back up the stairs, paused near his seat to glare at him. Fast asleep, his mouth open, he looked pasty and unshaven, like somebody homeless or just out of jail. Vulnerable. His right arm was lying flat and white down his big belly. And now I noticed that it wasn't an arm at all, just a white fin that tapered at the end.

I stopped at my son's seat. "That man is making me crazy," I whispered.

"It's really kind of sad," he whispered back. "His arm is *mutated*." Then he re-wrapped his head with his ingenious noise-abatement device—two little train pillows tied together with a length of string—and shut his eyes.

I continued up the dim aisle to my own seat. The woman ahead of me had moved her son to a quieter row, but she stayed behind the snorer.

"Me, he don't bother at all. My husband snored for twenty years," she announced cheerfully to the coach. Again I felt the pang of deep loneliness.

Now the snoring had stopped. Up and down the aisle, seats were tilting back again. Meanwhile, the Monongahela River gleamed by. A gibbous moon rose on a long, silver, rippling stilt, and three lights on the flank of a dark houseboat threw on the water three rippling shafts of illuminated gold. I began to drift off. . . .

A raucous snort broke the silence. Then a tense quiet in which one passenger said, under his breath but distinctly, "Dickhead." Then abruptly the snorer was at it again with renewed vigor. The ones who hadn't noticed his hand were no doubt wishing him dead, and we, the elect who had, were exchanging gently pitying smiles with strangers. Elect or not, none of us slept.

Early the next morning, passengers from our coach began to wander into the lounge to get coffee and exchange amused or exasperated notes about the night's ordeal. We smiled and nodded or shook our heads at the wonder of having made it through the night at all, and then struck up conversations. We had been kept awake half of the night, and yet everybody seemed cheerful and refreshed. At an unusually early hour, the lounge car was alive with conversation.

When the snorer himself walked into the lounge with his white flipper hand tucked against his belt, everybody was really nice to him. We were nice because of his hand and because all of us shared a secret to keep from him: that at 2:00 A.M. he had innocently had every one of us wide awake, cussing in our seats. And we were grateful to him because his snores had brought us together. His snoring had transformed a coach full of strangers into a community—and had made me forget my lonesome sorrow.

Everybody was nice to his buddy, too—a jowly, seedy, middle-aged, outgoing man who looked like he'd done time—because he *was* his buddy, bringing him a soda from the downstairs café, striking up friendly conversations with other passengers and then drawing his disabled friend skillfully in. So with cornfields and crossroads passing outside the big windows, and the golden morning light streaming into the lounge, and Porky Pig cartoons playing cheerily on the tube, with cups of sweet hot coffee, we all felt tender towards the man with the flipper hand. There he was, salt-and-pepper stubble on his round blanched face and a stale white undershirt, like a vagabond, really, an ex-con, most likely—and all sorts of people from our car, simple or sophisticated, were chatting warmly with him and his buddy. Diffident at first, he gradually expanded in the warmth, smiling and nodding, and soon he was circulating shyly in the lounge as a sort of guest of honor.

His buddy turned to him affectionately. "You were sawing logs pretty good there last night, pal. So loud I got up and
went down to the café car."

I held my breath; I felt all our coach holding our breaths.
Our secret was out: his phenomenal snoring was exposed.
Would he and his buddy suddenly shrivel up—poof!—and
disappear, leaving us all strangers again? But their magic
was good; if anything, the camaraderie in the lounge car
increased—soon people were sharing their life stories and
ham and cheese sandwiches.

"Ah, got a book, eh?" the buddy said when I walked past
them. They were both drinking beer now and chuckling at
the cartoons. I suddenly felt that they had no destination; they
were just riding the rails.

"Yes," I said, showing them the cover. "*Nonfiction Prose*. It's
a collection of essays."

"Oh, yeah, I read this book once—I recognize it," said the
buddy, taking it gently in his hands and turning it over. "It
was white, like this. Yeah, I'm pretty sure it was the same
book. Had a white cover."

From then on, whenever they'd pass my seat, they'd stop.
The snorer would smile and the buddy would ask me kindly,
"Still reading that book, eh?" They asked me so many times, I
began to dread their passing. I put my book away. Then I felt
bad because they were so friendly and trying to be kind, so I
got it out again. Perhaps they thought I was lonely since I was
reading a book. Well, Chicago in a few hours was the end of
the line. My son and I would board the Southwest Chief, and
they'd be getting on another train or a Greyhound bus. And
I *was* lonely: now that the day was wearing on, my loneliness
was creeping back, so much that I was already dreading the
night, wondering whether I'd be able to sleep at all.

At Chicago, as the crowd gathered at the gate for the Southwest Chief, I was a little disconcerted to suddenly find them

just a few yards away. But it was a long train, dozens of cars, and no doubt they would be assigned seats in a faraway coach. They both looked pale under the fluorescent lights, different from the other travelers, as if gravity were somehow heavier for them. The snorer reminded me suddenly of a merman lost on human shores with liquid warm brown eyes and a desolate white flipper. Now I felt certain they had done time. When they saw me, they both nodded, smiling approvingly at my book.

We left Chicago. In a few hours I was sitting in the lounge car, looking out the picture windows. To our right, the sun was setting scarlet. Our train ran along the Mississippi River, flushed rose and silver from the almost full moon on our left. The river was a mile wide with low forested banks on the opposite shore. Huge black tree trunks floated on the silvery water; rusty, flat barges slid slowly and imperceptibly down the middle of the river, pushed by a white boat. Big lotus swaths lay wherever the shore curved in, their pale blossoms shut up for the night. Little black islands. White herons. One or two lights blinked on the distant wooded shore. Shreds of mist lifted off narrow inlets. The sky dimmer, the moon now radiant yellow. Slow, the quiet wide dusk river. So lonesome, wandering without a home. So peacefully flowing, so softly by.

"Five minutes to Fort Madison," the attendant announced. There was a stir in the car. According to the route guide, we were about to cross the Mississippi on the world's largest double-track, double-decker swing span bridge. I loved the phrase; I wrote it down—a talisman against grief. We crossed, and darkness fell.

The coach was dim and half empty when I went back to my seat. Everybody was asleep, my son down the aisle in an empty row he'd found for himself. For a long time I sat with my glass of merlot and my white book, watching for the dark river outside the window. Finally I closed my eyes, but as I had expected, sleep refused to come. I turned the little reading light back on and, hoping to catch glimpses of houseboats with their golden lights, pressed my face against the window. But of course the river was far away now. Loneliness swept over me again, seized me, and I hunched down in my seat, wide awake and desolate.

Suddenly our coach door slid open and two men came bumping down the aisle toward me. The buddy and the snorer. Dear God. I closed my eyes and pretended to be asleep, afraid they would stop at my side. "Still reading that book, eh?"

"Here's our stuff," said the snorer in a thick voice. "And our seat." They must have been drinking all evening in the café car. They stumbled into the row directly behind me, next to the stairwell.

The buddy said, "Hell, we're not going to sleep at all with that fucking stairwell light." They may have thought that they were whispering, but they weren't.

The snorer laughed and asked whether the bathroom was still locked downstairs. When the buddy said yes, the snorer yelped. "You mean I have to go all the way to the next car every time I wazoo? I'm not going to make it. I might just have to wazoo right here." *Oh, God,* I thought.

"Man," the buddy laughed, "I feel sick. I just might puke."

The snorer was struggling with his footrest. "I can't get it to stay up!" he laughed.

And the buddy said, "You can't keep it up? What do you want me to do? *Hold* it for you?" He giggled. "Can't keep it up, huh? Maybe *she*"—and I knew they meant me because I was pretending to be sound asleep—"maybe *she* can get it up for you." Alarming giggles from both of them.

And then the buddy belched and said, joking but not laughing now, "I hope some gang-bangers don't come up those stairs and sit on my lap." As they settled bumpily into their seats, it suddenly seemed to me that they were like men secretly carrying a terrible cargo, one they could discuss only between themselves, late at night, when everybody else was asleep and only, perhaps, when they were drunk.

Then I realized I was the only one in the whole car awake, and these men, so gentle and kindly during the day, were now staggering drunk and making lewd remarks. Men who'd probably done time. What if they made a pass at me? What if the buddy threw up on me (I pulled my sheet right up under my chin) or if the snorer snored all night, right behind my head? At the same time, I felt oddly braced and cheered by my position, like the heroine in a fairy tale facing the Three Dangers. What should I do, then, with ex-convicts at the back of my neck? Get out my Mace?

But I felt too cozy to move, and besides, if I moved, they'd ask me about my book.

Then I thought, what dangers? Why, these men are like the wandering Mississippi. For us secretly awake or peacefully sleeping passengers they are carrying the weight of innumerable dark and broken things, things we cannot guess: black uprooted trees, the world's debris, barge-loads of loss and loneliness and grief. Homeless, nameless, they carry our burden, keeping the darkness at bay, so that for us the darkness scarcely presses outside or inside the windows of our quiet coach.

And then I knew, both, that this was unfair beyond all human understanding—and that we—all of us in the coach—were blessed by these two drunk and seedy men. Blessed that of all the coaches in a long train, it was our coach they'd found. And my heart was suddenly comforted, light and free and protected. I let the sheet slip down, carelessly from my chin. "*Da da doom, da da doom, da da da doom*," went the train in the beautiful night.

Then the buddy whispered to the one with the white flipper, bitterly and passionately, like someone in a Shakespeare play: "Those fucking gang-bangers. They'll tear the heart right out of your chest."

And we all fell asleep.

For twenty-three years, Gina Briefs-Elgin was a professor of English, teaching composition and creative nonfiction at New Mexico Highlands University in Las Vegas, New Mexico. She died in 2011. This story won the Grand Prize Bronze in the Fourth Annual Solas Awards, and was published in The Best Travel Writing 2010.

۶۵ ۶۵ ۶۵

The Good Captain

"When the sea is calm,
every ship has a good captain."
– *Sailing proverb*

I watched the sleeping ocean from a corner of the cockpit.
In the deep darkness, blind waves broke and collapsed in
rhythmic, drawn-out hisses, luring me to sleep as they misted
me with spray. Even in sleep, the ocean swell rolled forward,
constant, like a shark that never stops swimming. I had felt
that I could go on forever too, sailing west without stopping
across the great expanse of the Pacific.

Then a few hours before sunset, a faint smudge had floated
into view amidst the clouds on the horizon. A Marquesan
island, hazy through the atmosphere, marked our entry into
Polynesian waters. Sighting land awakened in me dormant
memories: limitless freshwater, a bed that didn't move, the
quiet pleasure of a walk. Having sailed day and night for
three weeks, I'd already spent the time I'd wanted with the
open ocean. Having seen land, I was now starved for landfall.
But the distant island was not a port of entry, and we could
not lawfully stop there. We had to carry on; we still had one

more night till our destination. We were headed for Nuku Hiva, a dead volcano thousands of miles from any continent. I had three hours and twenty-seven minutes before Chet would relieve me from my watch. After dawn, we'd trade places and I'd flop into one of the bunks he and I and Cyrille—the other hitchhiking crew member—all shared, the cushions still warm from his body. In the meantime I stared down the sky.

On night watch, the very real (albeit unlikely) possibility of annihilation is balanced against total boredom. I watched for signs of changing weather or a ship's light on the horizon. A 900-foot container ship cruises at around thirty nautical miles an hour with minimal crew to keep costs down. On autopilot, the captain literally asleep at the wheel, a container ship could run us down without ever knowing it had hit us.

In the groping dark, inky cumulus clouds were assembling behind us along the eastern horizon. The clouds could have been nothing, an annoying obstacle between me and the sunrise, or they could have been a squall, a localized storm. Without a moon, I couldn't tell. I could barely see the clouds—gobs of black in an even blacker sky.

A squall could bring strong winds that might tear sails, break rigging. We couldn't afford breakages so far from help. I turned away from the horizon and closed my eyes to relieve the painful pressure behind them, exhaustion from straining into the night. I just wanted an easy final watch. I didn't want the hassle of deciding whether the clouds were going to coalesce into a squall. If, in fact, a localized storm was forming behind us on the eastern horizon, the trade winds would blow the squall onto us. Then, I'd need to determine if we could ride it out, or if I would need to wake the captain. And waking the captain was the last thing I wanted to do.

Chet didn't like to be called "captain." He'd told Cyrille and me, "I don't want to create a weird dynamic. We're all just part of the crew." Once, after he made some unusually pointed request, I said as a joke, "Alright, Cap." Cyrille winked at me, but Chet cringed and went below without saying anything.

Still, on night watch by myself, when I needed to decide whether or not to wake the one person who charted our course, who rebuilt and rewired every inch of this boat, *his* boat, the one person ultimately in charge, I thought of him as captain.

For the most part, Chet was right: we were all just part of the crew, though as the newest member, I felt I had to prove myself. I knew Chet trusted me, but he trusted Cyrille more. Cyrille had joined the boat three months and 300 miles before me. His time on the boat showed; while I milled about gearing up the gumption to ask Chet what needed doing, there was Cyrille coming down the dock with a chipper smile and a cart full of potable water jugs anticipating our need to top up the fresh water tanks before Chet had asked. Cyrille was Johnny-on-the-goddamn-spot, a valuable member of the three-person team we had fast become. Still, I wanted to be first among equals.

I had connected with Chet—and by extension Cyrille—through *Latitude 38*'s online crew list. Other boats had dismissed me, saying they wanted young, strapping (they didn't explicitly say *male*) crew to help with heavy lifting. Those boats that did welcome me aboard wanted a cook and a maid, often asking if I would be open to a relationship. One captain old enough to be my grandfather declared himself a balding sex machine. Chet, thankfully, just wanted me to sail the boat. He was impressed that a twenty-six-year-old had a decade of sailing experience. I had a lot more if you counted the years I captained my childhood home, a fifty-foot sailboat, from the safety of my father's lap. I liked that Chet and Cyrille were only ten years older than I and European; I was hoping to sidestep American "bro culture." Chet was a certified skipper, and *Sudden Stops Necessary* (*Stops*, for short) was a seaworthy boat—big enough for three people, with a galley, a navigation station, two cabins that were already taken, and a salon for me to sleep in when we weren't underway. Chet and I emailed, Skyped, and checked references, until there was nothing left for me to do but fly down to Mexico for a get-to-know-you sail. Since that first night passage along the coast of Jalisco, the guys had trusted me to stand watch while they rested below.

First light glowed indigo on a distant edge of the horizon, while the clouds bled into a continuous line. Every fifteen minutes it was time to look again. If I saw a ship on the horizon ten miles away, closing half a sea mile a minute, I would have twenty minutes to determine if we were on a convergent course, devise a plan of action, and alter our heading to avoid a possible collision.

I stood to scan the horizon, and the cloud line behind us, now a fully fortified rampart, startled me with its height and solidity. I leaned closer and looked without blinking, trying to let in as much light as possible. Beneath the cloud line loomed the darkest corner of the sky. Pushed by a following wind and fast approaching, the clouds would soon be on top of us.

I circled my ankles, flexed my calves and checked the self-steering wind vane keeping us on course. *Stops* was steering itself. All was in order. I took one last look and went below. At the nav station, I turned on the radar as the deck lurched out from under my feet, and I stumbled backward, disoriented. A large swell rolled under *Stops*'s hull. I grabbed at the edge of the chart table to keep from falling across the cabin, then leaned back hard in the opposite direction, as the counter-roll tried to throw me into the radar. *That was a big one. Pay attention.* If I let myself forget where I was, I could break a rib being flung across the cabin.

Embarrassed, despite the lack of observers, I shook off the large swell, assuming it to be the tallest wave in the set, and pulled myself toward the radar. I didn't consider, perhaps chose to ignore, a fact I knew: big waves are often pushed by big winds.

On the radar screen, large green blotches marred with red announced squall clouds with a lot of rain. Since a few degrees north of the equator, we had been skirting around and through the doldrums. The doldrums, or the intertropical convergence zone, are not a place marked on any chart. Between the reliable trade winds, they are a shifting region of low pressure known for days or weeks of windless calm punctuated by squalls. At first we had motor-sailed around the squalls, altering course a few degrees to dodge each pregnant, low-slung cloud. Then one afternoon we had come across a squall too big to avoid. Chet had taken the helm and driven straight through the gusty downpour. Since leaving the doldrums we'd been pounding through one squall after another.

North of the equator, I had known to expect a predictable burst of wind and rain. Squalls in the South Pacific, however, had taken on different personalities. Would this squall be calm, almost windless, absentmindedly dripping a wet, persistent drizzle? Or would it have no rain but a lot of wind, or both? A squall could push strong winds and a torrential deluge, a wall of enormous drops that rip into the water like gunfire, obscuring the horizon and shrinking the visible world around the boat. My favorite squalls started thick and close, then eased out, pulling back the curtain of rain to reveal undulating silver hills embossed with braille.

In the last few weeks, I'd sailed through more squalls than years I'd been alive, and still I didn't know what to make of this one. Sizable lakes of green and red pooled twenty miles wide on the radar screen, but size, as they say, doesn't tell you everything. We had double-reefed at dusk, significantly reducing our sail area to safely ride out the inevitable squalls. The only reason I would need to wake the captain was if the winds were going to be so strong that we needed to shorten sail even further. The radar, whose radio waves echoed off rain, but not wind, couldn't tell me either.

The captain lay a few feet from me in the salon and I let my eyes wander over his sleeping body. Chet was curled on his side in gray, checkered boxers, limp on top of his white sheet, unable to tell me what he wanted. The thought occurred to me, *Maybe he isn't really sleeping.* If he wasn't sleeping, I reasoned, I wouldn't technically be waking him. The steady rise and fall of his white t-shirt, however, confirmed he was asleep.

I sat there at the nav station in the captain's chair, watching him. A week before, we had sailed across the equator. Crossing the equator, a maritime rite of passage, transformed me forever from a *pollywog*, a rookie, into a *shellback*, an experienced sailor. I believed in tests of skill and willpower, and the possibility of arriving on the other side stronger, wiser, truer. Somebody different, somebody new. A person could cross a line that meant she had gained enough experience to know the answers in difficult situations. I believed that I'd already arrived at that other side, and I loathed myself for not knowing what to do now. The squall felt like a test whose sole purpose was to humiliate me. *If I were a better sailor*, I thought, *I would be able to reef single-handed, to handle this on my own.*

The waves were gathering force, and to keep from falling, I crawled on all fours back up the companionway ladder. The deck pitched at steep angles. All around me in the dim morning, more night than day, the gray surface of the ocean throbbed rhythmically, the pulse of waves visible only as movement. I couldn't see their height, but I could feel them growing. *Big winds*, I allowed myself to remember. If only the squall could wait till Chet's watch.

As the only girl on board *Stops*, I didn't want to sound the alarm unless I had a good reason. I had to divine the true nature of the squall as well as the moment when the captain wanted me to wake him, if it got bad. Too early and I was afraid he'd be angry, lose respect for me; too late and we'd be in trouble.

I could feel the squall's power even before it reached us. The steady wind speed hit thirty knots and gusts struck with surprising force. The sea around *Stops* heaped up as the wind tore the foaming tops off waves in white streaks. On land, this wind would throw whole trees into motion.

Adrenaline flaming through my veins screamed bigger winds were coming. I had to wake Chet. How could I have waited this long?

In the muffled quiet below deck, I crept toward Chet, trying not to disturb Cyrille, even as the stiff crinkle of my foul weather gear rustled to a roar. My shipmates' sleeping bodies appeared dead to the impending squall.

I shook Chet's shoulder. He pushed up his sleeping mask, "Have we reached Nuku Hiva?" Chet's instant lucidity made me wonder if he'd been sleeping at all. Maybe *Stops'*s increasingly agitated motion had woken him, or maybe he'd been awake anticipating landfall.

"I need your help." Chet leapt from his bunk

Back on deck the instrument panel showed wind speeds exceeding forty knots. The wind clawed down the backs of waves with a force that would tear limbs from trees. Though thick clouds blotted out the dawn, the squall was now clearly visible. Massive gray clouds stretched in a formidable front as far as I could see in either direction. Beneath this advancing army, winds beat the sea into a fury a few hundred yards behind us.

Chet's large eyes widened as he took in the mega-squall. The acid taste of imagined insults were on my tongue. *What's wrong with you? Why didn't you wake me sooner?* Chet's eyebrows pursed together, then fell back. He wasted no time squabbling. "Let's reef. You've got the wind vane?" For the captain, only our safety mattered.

With a hand on the wind vane's thin control lines, I steered *Stops* into the wind to take the burden off the sails. I braced my feet as the boat slammed headlong into oncoming waves. The mainsail swung close above my head, whipping itself in the wind, each crack of canvas cutting through me like a gunshot. No longer caught in the hand of the wind, the boat's machinery was a loose flung thing, predictable only up to a point.

Chet threw himself about the winch, grinding down the mainsail even further, then folded and secured the sail. On his mark, I turned us back downwind. The mainsail, now smaller, filled and steadied us in the following seas. We rolled in more of the headsail and *Stops*' jerking motion lost its frantic edge. Practice had made us good at this.

Without saying a word Chet took the helm from me, unhitching the wind vane to steer by hand. Then a long, high-pitched cry let loose from the sky, and the squall hit. Strong winds blew seawater skyward and forced rain sideways, slantways, anyways but down. A gust tried to push the boat over, but 6,000 pounds of ballast in *Stops*'s keel kept us upright. If we hadn't shortened sail, the gust could have knocked us down, slamming the boat on its side, the cockpit pitched vertical, the sails pushed all the way down against the waves.

Chet squinted into the wind and rain. He resembled a wet cat; his rain-drenched hair clumped into random hunks. But most of all it was his long, matted eyelashes, blinking away the water streaming into his partly closed eyes, that made me thankful not to be Captain. Instead, I was safe and relatively dry beneath the spray hood.

Though rousted from sleep minutes ago, Chet stood at the wheel without complaint. It was as if he'd been waiting for this opportunity to prove himself. *Chet Against the Squall.* There was an assuredness about him that spoke to his years of ocean racing. Here was the sailor who, when Royal Yachtmaster test officials turned off the GPS-enabled, electronic charts in the middle of the night, was able to find his location and pass his exam using only a depth sounder and paper charts to feel his way over the bottom.

I relaxed back into my corner of the cockpit, even as a coiled sense of unease pressed against my chest. Despite my best efforts, I'd woken him too late, though he didn't seem upset.

"Nice and wet," Cyrille said, spitting saltwater out of his mouth. Standing half out of the main hatch, he had caught the full brunt of a wave. The hollow clinking of winches would have amplified through the hull. That and *Stops's* catapulting motion must have woken him.

Cyrille stepped into the cockpit wearing what he'd been sleeping in: swim trunks and nothing else. "You should really have a tether," Chet said. I'd made that mistake before, coming on deck in weather without the tedious safety gear—life jacket, tether, foul-weather pants and jacket—that the conditions required. I was glad it wasn't me this time.

Cyrille opened his mouth as if to say something, but just nodded his chin into his chest and went below. I knew that feeling; it was hard to be told what to do first thing in the morning when you just wanted to see what the commotion that woke you looked like, and harder still that Chet was always right.

A few minutes later Cyrille reemerged in full regalia. He sat in the small, dry-ish space beneath the spray hood opposite me and flashed a good-humored smile, wrinkling the corners of his eyes—the only hint of age. Cyrille seemed to greet each day with ease. He'd shrugged off the recession that had reclaimed his house. And then slipped out of half-ownership in a restaurant to be an extra hand on a racing yacht. That was two boats and six months ago. Though he was from Brittany, France's sailing capital, he hadn't sailed there and was learning as he went. I never caught him looking back, not once. How was that possible? I wished I could live as effortlessly.

The wind fell away and the sky opened, releasing large drops that relinquished themselves to gravity. The rain clattered against the silver surface of the ocean, hollowing out 10 million tiny craters. Waves sloshed against *Stops*'s hull with idle energy left over from the wind. "This is like sailing in England," Chet said in mock complaint. "You don't need to go to the South Pacific, it's rainy, dark, cloudy. Jesus, it's like the English Channel. Right?" He was playing around; he knew that of the three of us, only he had sailed there. He continued, "Look at this thing. Is it getting bigger, or . . ." Waggling his head, he said in a ludicrous falsetto, "We're gonna die."

If Chet was joking around, maybe he really wasn't angry? We shortened sail in time. The boat was intact. No one was hurt. Then why was I queasy with the thought of what could have happened? Instead of feeling elation for having survived the squall, fear hollowed out a hole behind my solar plexus. I'd made the cut, but barely. Maybe all those other captains who'd dismissed me had been right.

It didn't occur to me that I'd used my knowledge and skill to make a call that was well-timed *enough*, considering my exhaustion, my newness to South Pacific weather patterns, the vagaries of the ocean.

From far above, the sun murmured through clouds, raising the ceiling and brightening our morning. Then the rain subsided and the world expanded all the way to the horizon. There, like a forgotten promise, the hazy shadow of our destination floated between sea and sky. "Nuku Hiva," I pointed straight ahead excitedly. This time there was no question; I identified our barely discernable island with certainty.

"You haven't seen it yet?" Chet said, that same surety slapping a grin across his face. Apparently, while looking forward steering the boat, he had seen the island ages ago. For him, Nuku Hiva had always been there, poised near the ninth parallel for 3 million years. With my attention directed back towards the squall behind us, the island had snuck up on me.

The sea has amnesia. An hour after the sky had opened up, the trade winds returned and the waves relaxed back into a manageable size. Our bodies and the boat were dry. The only reminders of the squall were a gray ceiling of clouds and a cool, misty morning veiling Nuku Hiva.

Nuku Hiva's mass and density solidified as we approached. A dark mist on the horizon grew into the sleeping body of a blue-gray whale lumbering on the sea. I had been expecting the startling mountains that Tania Aebi, the first American woman to sail around the world, described in her 1989 book, *Maiden Voyage*. To me, however, Nuku Hiva at a distance was flat as a tabletop, the island's gently sloping volcanic rock slouching into the sea.

As we got closer, the island multiplied into a quintuplet of headlands separated by deep bays. One of those headlands marked the entrance to Taiohae (pronounced Tie-ee-oh-hay) Bay, where we would finally anchor.

With Chet at the wheel, I tried to make sense of our satellite position on the digital chart below deck in relation to the actual rock, dirt, and leaves off our starboard side. I was anxious to be the one to find our headland. I wanted to prove—to him and to myself—that I could do something right.

Eventually, Chet lost patience and gave Cyrille the helm. I was crestfallen. After consulting the chartplotter, Chet turned us in the direction he thought Taiohae Bay. Sure enough, the trail on the plotter corresponded exactly with our new heading. We were now aiming for our destination.

Large ocean waves couldn't penetrate the deep bay. The incessant motion that had rattled my body for more than three weeks began to ease. Standing in the cockpit became easy. I could walk around deck without holding a handrail. It was like breathing deeply when I hadn't realized I'd been holding my breath.

"Wanna take the helm?" Chet asked me.

"Really?" I didn't move, unable to believe that Chet wanted me to steer us into our first South Pacific port, the port that marked the end of our long and successful journey, a port that neither of us had ever seen before.

"It's an easy entrance," he said. Chet knew the island was steep-to, sloping downward toward the seafloor 13,000 feet below.

"There aren't any reefs or rocks to worry about?"

"You'll be fine." Chet's eyes were kind, vacant, expectant. He really did want to give me this honor. Besides, he needed to consult the sailing guide to decide where we'd drop anchor.

In one synchronized movement, Chet stepped away from the wheel and I slid in. I assumed the captain's stance, back tall, legs wide, hands firm. Though the ocean had emptied me of more energy than I thought I had, my senses sparked to alertness as my hands grasped the wheel. At the helm, my fears receded. I was driving and being driven, captain and passenger.

My hands hold the memory of every boat I have ever steered, though none are held so tightly as the first. From my father's lap, I clasped the knobby handles of the ship's wheel on my family's boat. The open wood grain, weathered in the sun, was smooth and rough in my small hands. I was always oversteering, turning the wheel too far and worrying us off course, then over correcting in the opposite direction. My father told me again and again to look straight ahead, to keep the mast in line with our destination. The fifty-foot sailboat swaggered back and forth as I found and lost and found our heading.

The morning we sailed into Taiohae Bay, I navigated a straight course. Cyrille prepped the anchor, and Chet surveyed the bay for a good place to drop the hook. In a few hours, I would walk the crescent footpath around the bay, waves smashing against the beach, then draining back through large, smooth stones in a silvery clatter reminiscent of rain.

Glenda Reed is a writer, artist and adventurer. She was recently awarded the Minnesota Regional Arts Council Next Step Grant, as well as participation in the Loft Literary Center's Mentor Series. She is also a winner of The Moth StorySlam. Reed is currently working on a memoir about hitchhiking around the world on sailboats. This story was originally published in the Winter 2016 issue of Creative Nonfiction *and shared Grand Prize Bronze in the Tenth Annual Solas Awards.*

ACKNOWLEDGMENTS

About the Editors

James O'Reilly, publisher of Travelers' Tales, was born in Oxford, England, and raised in San Francisco. He's visited fifty countries and lived in four, along the way meditating with monks in Tibet, participating in West African voodoo rituals, rafting the Zambezi, and hanging out with nuns in Florence and penguins in Antarctica. He travels whenever he can with his wife and their three daughters. They live in Leavenworth, Washington and Palo Alto, California, where they also publish art games and books for children at Birdcage Press (birdcagepress.com).

Larry Habegger, executive editor of Travelers' Tales, has visited more than fifty countries and six of the seven continents, traveling from the Arctic to equatorial rainforests, the Himalayas to the Dead Sea. In the 1980s he co-authored mystery serials for the *San Francisco Examiner* with James O'Reilly, and for thirty-one years wrote a syndicated newspaper column, "World Travel Watch." Habegger regularly teaches travel writing at workshops and writers' conferences, is a principal of the Prose Doctors (prosedoctors.com), and editor-in-chief of Triporati.com, a destination discovery site. He lives with his family on Telegraph Hill in San Francisco.

Sean O'Reilly is editor-at-large for Travelers' Tales. He is a former seminarian, stockbroker, and prison instructor who lives in Virginia with his wife and three of their six children. He's had a lifelong interest in philosophy and theology, and is the author of *How to Manage Your Destructive Impulses with Cyber Kinetics and Authority*. He is also CEO and Founder of the Auriga Distribution Group, Johnny Upright, Fifth Access, and Redbrazil.com, a bookselling site.

CPSIA information can be obtained
at www.ICGtesting.com
Printed in the USA
LVHW01s2327170817
545453LV00002B/2/P